CAPITAL OF SPIES

CAPITAL OF SPIES

Intelligence Agencies in Berlin during the Cold War

SVEN FELIX KELLERHOFF

BERND VON KOSTKA

Translated by Linden Lyons

CASEMATE

Philadelphia & Oxford

Published in the United States of America and Great Britain in 2021 by
CASEMATE PUBLISHERS
1950 Lawrence Road, Havertown, PA 19083, USA
and
The Old Music Hall, 106–108 Cowley Road, Oxford OX4 1JE, UK

Previously published as Sven Felix Kellerhoff and Bernd von Kostka and *Hauptstadt der Spione*: *Geheimdienste in Berlin im Kalten Krieg* (Berlin Story Verlag, 2017)

Hardcover Edition: ISBN 978-1-63624-000-8
Digital Edition: ISBN 978-1-63624-001-5

A CIP record for this book is available from the British Library

Printed and bound in the United Kingdom by TJ Books

Typeset in India by Lapiz Digital Services, Chennai.

For a complete list of Casemate titles, please contact:

CASEMATE PUBLISHERS (US)
Telephone (610) 853-9131
Fax (610) 853-9146
Email: casemate@casematepublishers.com
www.casematepublishers.com

CASEMATE PUBLISHERS (UK)
Telephone (01865) 241249
Email: casemate-uk@casematepublishers.co.uk
www.casematepublishers.co.uk

Contents

Acknowledgements

Sven Felix Kellerhoff

Books owe their existence to more than just the authors named on the cover, and this is certainly the case for *Capital of Spies*. In my work for *Die Welt* over the past couple of decades, I have revisited on many occasions the espionage quagmire that was the four-sector city. It was Wieland Giebel's idea that a book could be made from this scattered preliminary work in cooperation with Bernd von Kostka. Just as important for the realisation of the project were Patricia Bohnstedt and Norman Bösch, both of whom designed and produced the German edition of the book, and Nadin Wildt, who was responsible for looking after the fourth edition. I would like to express my thanks to them, as well as to my friends Lars-Broder Keil, Dr Berthold Seewald, and Uwe Müller. Many others who have helped prefer to remain anonymous. What else is to be expected from a book on spies in Berlin?

Bernd von Kostka

I would like to thank Dr Helmut Trotnow for allowing me to access the archive of the Allied Museum for my research and to make use of pictures from the museum's holdings. A big 'thank you' to everyone who actively supported me in conducting research for this book, provided me with important information, and made my work much easier: Iain McGregor and William Boyd for being my points of contact in the UK, Ruth Sheppard for handling things on the Casemate side, and Linden Lyons for translating and carefully reviewing the translation. Finally, I would like to thank my wife Ingrid and my daughter Julia for their patience as I spent a large portion of my spare time with 'spies' rather than family.

Foreword to the English edition

As the world changes, some things stay the same. 'Berlin is the European capital of agents,' says Hans-Georg Maaßen, who was responsible for counterespionage as the head of Germany's domestic intelligence agency, the Federal Office for the Protection of the Constitution (BfV), from 2012 to 2018. 'In no other city are there more spies.'[1] In the new world 'disorder' between Islamist terror and Russian and Chinese neo-imperialism, as well as all other kinds of challenges, the German capital is a focal point of espionage. This is hardly any different to the period during which Germany was divided, when the hottest front of the Cold War ran through Berlin. And this is by no means a secret. The 29 episodes of the espionage series *Berlin Station* (2016–2019), broadcast by the pay television network Epix and later by Netflix, revolve around the CIA's branch in Berlin. In the first season of the series, CIA agent Daniel Miller is tasked with exposing a whistleblower while also fighting Islamist terror. The ruins of the former listening station on Teufelsberg served as a backdrop for several key scenes. What made this listening station so unique can be read about in our book.

Tourists in Berlin would easily be able to recognise the espionage centres in the government district, as bronze signs are displayed near their portals and national flags fly proudly on masts. It is highly likely there are at least six embassies in the city centre that serve as listening posts: the American, British, and French embassies on Pariser Platz, the Russian embassy in its late Stalinist palace on Unter den Linden, the North Korean embassy in its prefabricated building on Wilhelmplatz, and the Chinese embassy near Jannowitz Bridge. Unusual objects can be seen on the roofs of all these buildings, sometimes in the form of a white cylinder and sometimes built into penthouse-like structures. Presumably, their purpose is to monitor all sorts of communication. 'There are thousands of interesting conversations in central Berlin', says Marcel Dickow, an expert in cybersecurity at the German Institute for International and Security Affairs in Berlin. 'If you know the right numbers, you can accumulate a lot of information. However, nobody really knows what exactly is going on.'[2] It is almost impossible to prevent such eavesdropping. Helmut Kohl paid a great deal of attention to this matter during his chancellorship in the 1980s and 1990s. Car telephones at that time were far less secure than today's equipment, so Kohl's chauffeur always kept spare change should Kohl wish to stop and make a call at a phone booth. It is interesting to imagine the German chancellor standing in a lonely phone booth somewhere in the rain whenever he really wanted a confidential conversation. This method would not work nowadays, as computer programs can automatically search for certain keywords across thousands of telephone calls simultaneously. Berlin is thus still a centre of international espionage today. In the wake of Brexit, Great Britain, having withdrawn all combat troops from German soil at the beginning of 2020, seems much further away from Germany. Under President Trump, the United States also considered withdrawing troops from Germany, although these plans have been put on ice under President Biden. An understanding of these current developments requires a closer look at the Cold War era. American, British, and French soldiers on the one side and Soviet soldiers on the other were very much a part of the cityscape and therefore of great importance to the identity of Berlin. It was in the former capital of the Reich that spies and intelligence services discovered their favourite playing field. That is what this book is about.

Originally published in 2009, this book has since gone through four new editions and was translated into Hungarian in 2012 and Swedish in 2019. Now the English edition has arrived. Over 11 years, we have reviewed and updated the whole book. Even though the Cold War ended more than 30 years ago, our knowledge of the invisible contest between the intelligence services continues to grow. Files previously unavailable have been released, contemporary witnesses have broken their silence in old age, and sometimes it has been by pure chance that our knowledge of intelligence operations has been expanded. In addition, the literature on espionage in the Cold War has grown. While, in 2009, our book offered insight into the world of shadows, it has now become more of an introduction to the history of espionage in Berlin. Several chapters have been expanded over time. The West Berlin police officer Karl-Heinz Kurras, the man who killed Benno Ohnesorg, had only just been exposed in the spring of 2009 as a former Stasi spy. The result is that, since the publication of the first edition of this book, it has been possible to consult and incorporate the findings from more than 30 volumes of Stasi files pertaining to Kurras. Unfortunately, he died at the end of 2014 without having provided his account of events.

It is not only the release of intelligence documents that lead to new findings. As early as 1997, the Allied Museum in Berlin had arranged the excavation of the first original components of the Anglo-American spy tunnel. Two more segments unexpectedly emerged in a forest near Pasewalk, in Mecklenburg-Vorpommern, in 2012. It turned out that East German pioneer units had excavated them, transported them 140 kilometres to the north, and employed them there as shelters. Some of those segments from Pasewalk have been on display at the International Spy Museum in Washington, DC, since 2019. A 500-page work by American journalist Steve Vogel on the British spy George Blake and the spy tunnel in Berlin was published in the same year.[3] Sometimes, the confessions of a former spy can shed new light on the past. This is the case with Jeff Carney, an American soldier who had been a Stasi spy for years while working at the listening station in Marienfelde in West Berlin.

Scene from the series *Spy City* with Leonie Benesch and Dominic Cooper.

After hiding in East Berlin for a while and becoming naturalised as an East German citizen, he was tracked down by CIA agents and kidnapped on the street in 1991. Released after more than 12 years in prison in the United States, he published his memoirs in 2013. At the request of the American government, several passages of his book have been blacked out. These episodes and many other new insights have been incorporated into this first English edition of *Capital of Spies*.

The eternal secret contest of agents remains one of the favourite subjects of the entertainment industry. *Spy City* is the name of an international miniseries, about Berlin in 1961, created by bestselling author William Boyd. Against the backdrop of the divided city, shortly before the construction of the Berlin Wall, MI6 agent Fielding Scott must find a traitor in his own ranks. The city is teeming with spies, traitors, and double agents of the Soviet KGB, the French SDECE, the American CIA, and Britain's MI6. Also involved are the East German Stasi and West German BND, not to mention all sorts of shadowy characters.

In our research of historical events, it has often occurred to us that some of the operations that took place are so amazing and incredible that it is hard to imagine they could have been thought of in the first place. Based on a variety of sources, this book will immerse the reader in those operations in the capital of spies between 1945 and 1994 and will thereby confirm the statement made by Mark Twain that 'truth is stranger than fiction'.

Foreword to the first edition

The hottest front in the Cold War

Martin Ritt did not find the Berlin Wall particularly impressive. It consisted only of rough piles of bricks and stones joined together with cement in a makeshift fashion and reinforced to varying degrees with barbed wire. A set designer would have no difficulty in recreating it. The successful Hollywood director had made his way to West Berlin in the summer of 1964 to scout possible locations for his next project, an adaptation of John le Carré's *The Spy Who Came in from the Cold*. He wanted to get a taste of the atmosphere that would give his film a sense of authenticity. With his American passport, Ritt was even able to go through the border crossing, known as Checkpoint Charlie, from the American to the Soviet sector of the divided city. The circumstances on the other side of the Wall, however, were enough to convince him that he could spare the effort of requesting a shooting permit: 'I can only make such a film if I have complete freedom. There is no chance they would let me shoot over there, as they would of course not agree with the content'. He therefore abandoned his original plan of shooting at the site of the real Berlin Wall and instead had a new one built at Smithfield Market in the middle of the old town of Dublin in January 1965. It took 42 day and night shifts for around fifty Irish workers to erect a detailed reconstruction of the border crossing. The scene eerily resembled reality. Even though the Jameson Irish Whiskey Distillery lay around the corner on the 'East Berlin' side, with 'Soviet soldiers' rushing past it on their way to the 'border crossing' in order to prevent the escape of the British double or triple agent Alec Leamas and his girlfriend, and even though the extras told West German reporters at the press conference on the set that they felt a bit strange in their Red Army uniforms, the set in Dublin, when captured on film, could barely be distinguished from the real border in Berlin. Only Berliners might have been able to tell the difference. Ritt was satisfied: 'What is important to me is what the Wall represents. It is the key element of the dirty business known as espionage, defence, intelligence, or whatever'.[1]

The Spy Who Came in from the Cold is just one of many spy films set in Cold War Berlin. Others include, but are not limited to, *Torn Curtain* by Alfred Hitchcock, *Funeral in Berlin* by Guy Hamilton, *The Innocent* by John Schlesinger, and the James Bond thriller *Octopussy* by John Glen. Espionage and Berlin were synonymous

The German film poster for the spy thriller *The Spy Who Came in from the Cold* depicts Checkpoint Charlie, the set for which was built in Dublin.

for the decades between the end of World War II and the collapse of the Soviet Union. Nowhere did the Eastern and Western Blocs meet more directly than along the inner-city border. Before the construction of the Berlin Wall, an invisible front ran through the city of millions along which a dirty, secret, enormously expensive, dangerous, and often murderous confrontation took place. In the 1950s, the Cold War and espionage were a part of everyday life in East and West Berlin. The autobiography of British double agent George Blake provides a good picture of the nature of espionage at that time. He described the variety of activities of the various intelligence agencies as a large spiderweb that spanned all of Berlin: 'One had the impression that at least every second adult Berliner was working for some intelligence organisation or other and many for several at the same time'.[2] Something of the kind remained the case even after West Berlin was cordoned off on 13 August 1961. It is true the circumstances in the city changed and with them the general conditions under which agents tried to monitor, infiltrate, or harm the other side. The invisible front was now made of concrete and could not be missed. However, the overall situation was the same. Berlin was, and remained, the capital of spies. It was a trial of strength that lasted for decades until the reunification of Germany in 1990.

It is of some surprise that there have hardly been any books on the role of intelligence agencies in Berlin during the Cold War. Countless books have been written about the construction of the Wall in 1961 and the East German uprising in 1953, not to mention the Stasi and its octopean reach that, on behalf of the Socialist Unity Party (SED), stretched across East Germany in its entirety and, to an alarming extent, well into West Berlin and West Germany. Secret service veterans David E. Murphy and Sergei A. Kondrashov, and army officer George Bailey, published a remarkable book with the title *Die unsichtbare Front* (originally published in English in 1997 as *Battleground Berlin*), but its focus is largely limited to the confrontation between the intelligence agencies of the former members of the anti-Hitler coalition. The activities of German intelligence services receive little attention in it, yet they were just as important in Cold War Berlin as were the services of the four major powers. Furthermore, the book ends its story with the construction of the Wall, but the clandestine war in and around Berlin lasted at least until the Peaceful Revolution of 1989. Even German authors have paid little attention to intelligence operations in Berlin. Journalists Klaus Behling and Thomas Flemming have each written books with identical titles, *Berlin im Kalten Krieg* (Berlin in the Cold War), both of which are useful but nevertheless do very little in terms of what they claim. Behling merely lists various locations where espionage action took place, while Flemming, in his book of less than 80 pages, only scratches the surface.

The lack of literature on the topic is very much due to the shortage of available information. Many secret service files remain classified. When renowned British historian David Stafford was working on his book *Berlin Underground* (originally published in English in 2002 as *Spies Beneath Berlin*), he was unable to obtain any official information from British intelligence. The spy tunnel that ran from Rudow in West Berlin to Altglienicke in East Berlin, for example, is still a taboo subject as far as British authorities are concerned. The situation is not much better in the United States. Although hundreds of documents that deal with Cold War Berlin between 1946 and 1961 have been made available by the historical staff of the CIA, those that pertain to the spy tunnel have been restricted. Documents on the matter that had already been released and could be viewed on the CIA website in 2007 were subsequently removed in part or rendered illegible.[3] Research on the work carried out at the listening station on Teufelsberg is even more difficult. No scholarly study on it exists to this day, for the American sources that would provide any sort of insight are still top secret.

The situation is only slightly better with regard to sources on German intelligence. The Stasi Records Agency has made vast quantities of material available from what had been the archives of the state security service of the East German regime. On the activities of the West German Federal Intelligence Service, there is only one investigative study that has been carried out. Written by Armin Wagner and Matthias Uhl, it is a good study and filled with formerly classified information.[4] Aside from this, most documents produced by West German services remain classified or have been disposed of, but this does not mean there is not a wealth of information on the intelligence war in Berlin. Many details are available outside the archives. Intelligence agencies may have waged their war with as much secrecy as possible, but they often aimed to influence public opinion and therefore could not avoid being visible from time to time. The propaganda battles between East and West certainly produced a tremendous amount of material, and most of it is still awaiting proper evaluation.

It was a challenge to present the information in this book in a manner that is both logical and interesting. The authors have decided to describe the activities of the secret services in Berlin in accordance with the structures that existed at the time. The first part of the book deals with the intelligence agencies of the major powers who formally shared responsibility for Berlin until 1990, while the second part is devoted to the German services. If there was any aspect of the confrontation that affected the interests of the major powers, the German participants—be it the dictatorship in East Germany or the democracy in West Germany—had little say in the matter. In order to make the primacy of the major powers clear, the part of the book that deals with the activities of those powers, especially of the three Western powers, has been placed at the beginning. This part of the book is written by Bernd von Kostka. The lack of available sources, however, means a thorough account of the acts of espionage of the Western powers between 1945 and 1990 is impossible. Bernd has therefore decided to take a closer look at certain events and organisations that have largely been neglected until now. Starting with the emergence of Berlin as a hub of espionage after 1945, the first part of the book provides information about the Allied listening station on Teufelsberg and about the countermeasures of the KGB and the Stasi. This part demythologises what is perhaps the most spectacular operation of the secret war, the Anglo-American spy tunnel from Rudow to Altglienicke, and investigates the risks of the 'legal espionage' carried out by the Western military liaison missions in East Germany. The second part of the book, written by Sven Felix Kellerhoff, focuses on the German secret services and the role they played in the capital of spies. Even here, there are limitations imposed by a lack of available sources. After a description of the early days of the secret war from the German point of view, the focus shifts to the state security service of East Germany and on the institutions that supposedly infested West Berlin. There are then half a dozen cases that illustrate the execution of espionage operations in Cold War Berlin. Towards the end of the book, the exposure of West Berlin police officer Karl-Heinz Kurras as an enthusiastic Stasi spy and convinced communist is covered. This is an example of how it was not unusual for the world of espionage to cause a sensation.

Berlin, 17 June 2009

Sven Felix Kellerhoff
Bernd von Kostka

PART I: FOREIGN INTELLIGENCE SERVICES

BERND VON KOSTKA

CHAPTER ONE

Espionage hub of Berlin

Intelligence services in Berlin and Vienna

Ideal conditions for spies

Berlin emerged after the end of World War II as a geographically and politically ideal base of operations for secret service activities. As the point of intersection between East and West, Berlin exerted an almost magical attraction on intelligence agencies. Operations could be planned and carried out behind the Iron Curtain there. After the Wall was built, Berlin became recognised around the world as the symbol of the Cold War. It could almost be said conditions in Berlin were unique had it not also been for the capital of Austria.

For 10 years, from 1945 to 1955, the geopolitical situation in Vienna was similar to that in Berlin, as occupied Vienna was also divided between the three Western powers and the Soviet Union. This situation was even portrayed in the renowned film *The Third Man*, starring Orson Welles, in 1948. However, the distinguishing feature of Vienna, in comparison to Berlin, was a sector, known as the First District, administered by all four powers. Austria was fertile ground for recruitment by the intelligence agencies of the Western powers. Hundreds of Soviet occupation personnel in Austria and Hungary defected to the West in the years immediately after the war. So-called ratlines were set up to smuggle important defectors to South America and to give them new identities. This was also the case for many former figures of National Socialism. Even membership of the SS or active participation in war crimes did not disqualify a potential informant from intelligence activities.[1] In addition, the Americans paid their full-time informants in Austria between U.S. $130 and U.S. $200, a significant economic incentive in the immediate post-war period. The price for the sale of information in Berlin would have been similar.

After the end of the occupation of Austria in 1955, the respective powers placed their intelligence operatives in their embassies, usually in the economic or cultural departments. The late Helmut Zilk, mayor of Vienna from 1984 to 1994, said the staff numbers of the Russians and the Chinese in the city would have been enough for another 20 embassies.[2] Although Vienna remained an important centre of espionage in Europe until the withdrawal of occupation forces in 1955, various events towards the end of the 1940s meant Berlin would become the undisputed number one for

Poster of the U.S. military government in Berlin from the 1980s.

espionage in the years and decades that followed. The Berlin Blockade (the first confrontation of the Cold War) the founding of the two German states, and, finally, the 45-year presence of the four victorious powers in Berlin very much ensured the growing status of the city as the capital of spies.

The United States did not possess any noteworthy foreign intelligence at the outset of World War II.[3] The Office of Strategic Services (OSS), led by General William J. Donovan, was formed during the war and dissolved in October 1945. However, the Secret Intelligence and Counter-Espionage Branches of the OSS were taken over by the War Department and then transferred to the Central Intelligence Group (CIG) when it was created a few months later. The CIG was finally reconstituted as the Central Intelligence Agency (CIA) on 18 September 1947. Of course, the American air, sea, and land forces maintained their own intelligence departments, with several secret agencies being formed in the years and decades that followed, but the CIA was to remain the most well-known and arguably most influential American intelligence service during the Cold War. That the CIA became a synonym for American espionage, and that it continues to be so today is due to the fact the director of the CIA is responsible for the coordination of all U.S. intelligence services. Aside from this organisationally prominent position of the CIA within American intelligence, our image of the CIA has been shaped by novels and feature films. The CIA showed great interest in Germany and especially in Berlin for many decades. The departments of the CIA that were particularly interested in Berlin were the

Salute in front of the Brandenburg Gate during a parade in which all four victorious powers took part in the summer of 1945.

Office of Special Operations and the Office of Policy Coordination. The situation on the ground, however, was not particularly encouraging. Little was known about the Soviet Union, still an ally, in the first few years of the occupation. Richard Helms, who would one day become the director of the CIA, was an OSS lieutenant in Berlin in 1945. He would report later that there existed almost no knowledge of Soviet plans. 'If you came up with a telephone book or a map of an airfield, that was pretty hot stuff'.[4]

As in Vienna, the Americans paid for their information in Berlin, and usually very well. This business practice was to become a major problem for the CIA, although it was not apparent until many years later. Informants who had nothing to offer simply made-up information! The more money paid for intelligence, the more worthless it tended to be. Within a few years, a veritable network had come into being dedicated to spreading false information. It was not necessarily its goal to harm the CIA. It simply exploited the profitable state of the market for its own benefit. Richard Helms concluded after several years that at least half of the information contained in the CIA's files on the Soviet Union and Eastern Europe was fabricated and that the CIA stations in Berlin and Vienna had become factories of fake intelligence.[5] CIA analysts at that time were hardly able to tell fact from fiction. They knew too little about what was going on behind the Iron Curtain and the small pieces of information they obtained could not be cross-checked with other sources. Until 1947, there was not a single secret service officer in Berlin with knowledge of the Russian language, even though the city was supposed to play a central role in intelligence activities against the Soviet Union.[6] The U.S. intelligence service was based in a villa in the Zehlendorf district of Berlin (Föhrenweg 19–21) after World War II and moved to the headquarters of the U.S. armed forces on Clayallee, just a few hundred metres away, in the early 1950s.

From 1945 until the founding of the Soviet Committee for State Security (KGB) in 1954, the structure and organisation of Soviet intelligence services in Germany were so confusing that even Soviet reports were likely to mix up areas of responsibility.[7] The result was that the American side remained completely in the dark when it came to understanding Soviet zones of jurisdiction. Soviet intelligence activities were so well concealed that Western intelligence could get no clear picture of what work was being done or who was doing it.[8] Soviet agencies involved in intelligence work were the NKGB (People's Commissariat for State Security), MGB (Ministry for State Security), and KGB. Running parallel to these organisations for several years were the foreign intelligence service—the KI (Committee of Information)—and, of course, the intelligence department of the general staff of the Soviet armed forces—the GRU (Main Intelligence Directorate).[9]

American general George Patton and Soviet marshal Georgy Zhukov at a parade in Berlin on 7 September 1945.

Once the Soviet Union had assumed responsibility for its zone of occupation in post-war Germany, it was not long before an intelligence department was set up in East Berlin. In August 1945, the station of the Soviet foreign intelligence service in Karlshorst was composed of only six officers. This rose to 90 in only a few short years. The NKGB became a part of the MGB from the spring of 1946, although the latter would have to hand over the former to the newly founded KI in 1947. This put a considerable strain on the relationship between the KI and the MGB, especially in East Berlin. The lack of cooperation between these two intelligence agencies continued until the dissolution of the KI at the end of 1951, with the MGB once more being put in charge of foreign intelligence activities in 1952.[10] When the KGB was founded in 1954, it took over full control of international espionage. However, there was a problem with Soviet intelligence that became apparent at the beginning of the Berlin Blockade and would recur throughout the Cold War. The reports sent to Moscow did not necessarily correspond to reality; rather, they anticipated what those in the Soviet capital wanted to hear. This phenomenon was particularly pronounced under Josef Stalin. Nobody wanted to risk conveying bad news, and, as a result, there were a number of false and misleading reports.[11]

The Cold War becomes warmer

The first crisis in Berlin

The first significant event of the Cold War was the Soviet blockade of Berlin in June 1948 and the subsequent airlift organised by the Western powers. The second was the establishment of the two German states in 1949. Close cooperation between the United States and the Soviet Union was nearing its end by 1947 as a result of the Truman Doctrine, the development of the Marshall Plan, and, finally, the failure of the London Conference to resolve the German question. It was in that year that the American journalist Walter Lippmann coined the term 'Cold War' to describe the anticipated conflict between the two major powers. Berlin was where those powers directly clashed for the first time. On 22 December 1947, the CIA submitted a memorandum to President Harry S. Truman stating that the Soviet Union would attempt to force the Western powers to withdraw from Berlin.[12] The seriousness with which the situation in Berlin was regarded in the spring of 1948 is demonstrated not only by this CIA memorandum but also by the concerns of General Lucius D. Clay, the American military governor in Germany. Clay initially enjoyed good relations and friendly cooperation with the Soviet military governor, Marshal Georgy Zhukov, but, when Zhukov was replaced by Marshal Vasily Sokolovsky in March 1946, the relationship between the two sides deteriorated, thereby making the four-power administration of Germany more difficult. Clay only gradually perceived that a change in the nature of the relationship had taken place. A report from the CIA station in Berlin, known as Berlin Operations Base (BOB), described Clay's growing disillusionment with the relationship and his increasing interest in the work of American intelligence.[13]

The climax of this change in attitude towards the Soviet Union is evident in a telegram Clay sent to Washington on 5 March 1948. He wrote that he had originally thought no war would occur. However, he now had the feeling it could come about quite suddenly. Clay stressed that he possessed neither facts nor evidence. It was just a feeling.[14] Clay did not intend his telegram as some sort of warning war was imminent. Nevertheless, it was taken very seriously at the Pentagon. What was the likelihood of war breaking out in Europe? The opinions on this matter varied among the various analysts. The director of the CIA, Roscoe H. Hillenkoetter, was dissatisfied with having so many different assessments of the situation. He wanted clear statements if war was imminent so they could be presented to President Truman. The trauma of the surprise attack on Pearl Harbor cast a long shadow. It was one of the reasons why the CIA had been founded. On 16 March 1948, Hillenkoetter posed three very precise questions to be answered by a committee made up of the various intelligence services under the chairmanship of the CIA:

1. Will the Soviets deliberately provoke a war in the next 30 days?
2. In the next 60 days?
3. In 1948?

The first two questions were answered in the negative that very day. The committee requested more time to investigate the third question and finally provided an answer on 2 April. The likelihood the Soviet Union would start a war was assessed as being low.[15] Even so, there existed the danger of being drawn into an armed conflict due to the unusual situation in Berlin. Troop transfers and manoeuvres by the Soviet Union, as well as incidents at the sector borders, contributed to the concern of the American military in Berlin.

In April 1948, the Soviets introduced checkpoints on the railway line leading to Berlin, a situation the Western powers were unable to accept. The result was the suspension of all rail traffic for 12 days. It was during this time the Americans began to supply their garrison in Berlin by air.[16] Leading military leaders in the West recognised that the supply of Berlin and the presence of the Western powers in the city ultimately depended on the goodwill of the Soviet Union.

The course of events in April made it clear to Clay and his superiors in Washington that, even if the Soviet Union was not interested in a military confrontation, the American occupation forces in Berlin faced a political challenge.

A meeting of the Allied Health Committee in Berlin, around 1946 or 1947, in which the four victorious powers were represented.

Not giving up West Berlin

The Berlin Blockade and the Berlin Airlift

In the first few years after the war, the Western powers failed to negotiate an agreement on routes of access to Berlin with the Soviet Union. The Western powers took it for granted that they would be able to travel from their zone of occupation to their sector in Berlin. As a result, signing treaties for routes of access by land or sea was not given priority. It soon emerged that this was a disastrous misjudgement. Only one aviation agreement was concluded and ratified by all four occupying powers in 1946. This had been on the initiative of the Soviet Union, which wanted to avoid uncontrolled air traffic over its zone of occupation. It was thus that three air corridors to and from Berlin had been established. The width, length, and altitude of these corridors were clearly defined and would remain in force until the 1990s.

What prompted the Soviet Union to impose a blockade on West Berlin? Although no Soviet documents are known to exist that clearly reveal the origin of the idea for a blockade, or the motivation for putting it into effect, it is still possible for some conclusions to be drawn about it today. The blockade was probably an immediate reaction to the currency reform in the western zones of Germany in June 1948. This

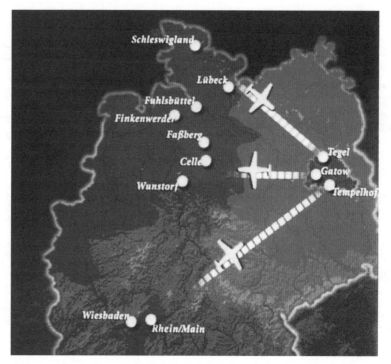

This map shows the three air corridors to and from Berlin as well as the airports used by the Americans and the British during the airlift.

reform extended to West Berlin. The basic idea behind the blockade was quite simple. The Soviet Union had control of the access routes to Berlin and, thus, the lifelines of the city. Cutting off these lifelines would demonstrate the weakness and incapability of the Western powers to the people of West Berlin. America, Great Britain, and France would ultimately have to withdraw from the city. The uncomfortable 'sting' that was West Berlin would thereby be removed from the middle of the Soviet zone of occupation. Various misjudgements by the Eastern Bloc, and certainly on the part of the Soviet secret service, eventually led to the failure of the blockade. First and foremost, it was believed that those in the West—including U.S. military governor Lucius D. Clay, U.S. president Harry S. Truman, and British foreign minister Ernest Bevin—were not fully committed to Berlin. Second, the logistical capabilities of the Anglo-American air fleet had been underestimated. Third, although less significant, the dependency of the economy in the eastern zone on the now absent imports from the western zone had not been properly recognised.

The logistical achievement of the airlift to West Berlin is legendary and, in the end, led to the lifting of the blockade. What is little known, however, is the fact that aerial espionage took place during the airlift. The Americans regularly sent reconnaissance aircraft through the air corridors to Berlin in order to take

British Dakotas land in Tegel on the occasion of the official opening of the new airport on 18 November 1948.

high-resolution photographs of the territory of the Soviet zone, which was later to become the German Democratic Republic.[17] These aircraft flew with the large numbers of transport planes, but they did not land in Berlin. They simply made use of the corridors. This aerial espionage continued until the fall of the Berlin Wall in 1989. Because of this, the area below the three air corridors became one of the most thoroughly documented territories in the world for more than 40 years.

Overcoming the blockade led to the realisation that it was possible for a serious political crisis to be resolved with logistical means and without military measures. Neither combat aircraft nor rockets had been necessary to deal with the first crisis of the Cold War. At the same time, the Berlin Airlift had shown how much effort would be required in future to prevent the Cold War from heating up whenever problems or crises arose. Another important event that was to make Berlin the capital of spies was the founding of the two German states in 1949. These were the Federal Republic of Germany in the West and the German Democratic Republic in the East. The Iron Curtain was slowly being drawn across the inner German border. West Berlin was the enclave behind this curtain, the outpost of the Western powers and, therefore, the ideal base of operations for the West in conducting espionage in the states of the Warsaw Pact.

On your marks, get set, go!

The activities of the French and British secret services

In France, before World War II, information procurement was the responsibility of the French Army. Its intelligence service was called the Service de Renseignement

(SR). During the German occupation of France, the employees of the SR were forced to go underground.[18] When the Service de Documentation Extérieur et de Contre-Espionage (SDECE) was founded in January 1946, it was directly subordinate to the prime minister of France, who accordingly had control over its objectives and activities. The general director of the SDECE was supported by two deputies in the first few years after the war. One was based in Saigon, Vietnam, and had to deal with military problems in the former colonies; the other was stationed in Baden-Baden, Germany, and had to define the role of France in the emerging Cold War in Europe.

An important goal of the French intelligence service during the first few years of the occupation of Germany was to obtain information that would help restore the strength of the French Army as quickly as possible. The knowledge of German officers and scientists was to be absorbed for this purpose.[19] Political issues came to the fore after the founding of the Federal Republic of Germany. The rearmament of Germany was closely monitored, as was the potential threat posed by Soviet forces in the country. Indeed, information on the Red Army was at the top of the list of the French intelligence service. Germany and Austria, in which France served as an occupying power, offered ideal conditions for obtaining such information. Operations could be conducted, and agents recruited, from there.

In Berlin, however, the French stood somewhat apart from the secret service activities of the United States and Great Britain, both of whom formed an intelligence community for carrying out certain projects. The best examples of this are the Berlin spy tunnel and the listening station on Teufelsberg. While the Americans and the British worked closely together in Berlin, the French were not included. Nevertheless, France later established a good working relationship with the German Federal Intelligence Service (BND).

The British secret service has the longest history. It was founded more than 400 years ago as a political espionage organisation. The British foreign intelligence service in its present form was created in 1909 as the Foreign Section of the Secret Service Bureau. It became a separate intelligence agency in 1922 and was called the Secret Intelligence Service (SIS). It is also referred to as Military Intelligence, Section 6 (MI6), although it has become better known as the Secret Service because of the popularity of the James Bond films. After World War II, the SIS conducted operations in West Berlin. Its aim was to exploit the knowledge of German scientists and to learn as much as possible about political and economic events in the Soviet Union. It was a perfectly legitimate goal of the victorious powers at that time to gain detailed knowledge of the potential of German military technology. They were not just interested in controlling German capacities; they wanted to be able to exploit military knowledge for their own purposes.[20] The leading German scientists had to be identified and won over. The best-known example is most certainly Wernher von Braun, who had been the technical director of the Army Research Centre at Peenemünde from 1937 to 1945. He fled to Bavaria shortly before the end of the war and turned himself in to the Americans. Together with some colleagues from Peenemünde, von Braun was taken to the United States in 1946 where he worked soon after as a consultant for an American missile programme. He became an American citizen in 1955 and was appointed deputy head of the National Aeronautics and Space Administration (NASA) in the early 1970s.

If the Western powers were still reluctant in 1945 to offer work in the armaments industry to qualified Germans from the former arms plants of the Nazi regime, they were no longer so the following year. The British launched their own programme, Operation *Matchbox*, to poach German specialists working in key military industries in the Soviet occupation zone and the later German Democratic Republic. Operation *Paperclip* was the name of a similar American programme.

For its part, the Soviet Union did not just rely on the voluntary cooperation of German specialists. Deportations of German scientists and their families to the Soviet Union started as early as 1945, with one great wave being organised on 21 and 22 October 1946. Approximately 2600 people were transported to the east by train so their knowledge and labour could be put to use in the Soviet Union. The Western intelligence agencies sprang into action when the deported scientists were brought back to East Germany between 1949 and 1958. The scientists were located, and contact was made with them. Many of the returnees were prepared to answer questions about their activities in the Soviet Union. Efforts were also made to persuade them to emigrate to the West.

The success of such Anglo-American persuasion was impressive. It was based completely on voluntary cooperation and involved no deportation whatsoever. By November 1949, the British had convinced at least 332 scientists to leave the Soviet zone. Many of them did not want to work in Great Britain, but they found work in the western zones of occupied Germany. In the same period, the Americans were able to convince around 1,000 people to work in the United States.[21] All four occupying powers sought to acquire German know-how in the field of military technology by enticing German scientists and engineers to work for them. The Americans and the Russians had the most success in this regard. Both countries particularly benefited from the transfer of knowledge in the area of rocket technology.

A blessing and a curse for the secret services

The wave of refugees from East Germany

Berlin had already seen a wave of refugees heading west in the years immediately following the war. Millions of people were on the move to return to their old homes or find new ones. The wave of refugees in the early 1950s, on the other hand, was more politically motivated and was a reaction to the establishment of the two German states. Even though the desire for better economic conditions certainly played a role, the two different social systems in East and West were decisive factors for leaving home.

This poster from around 1954 draws attention to the plight of refugee children and asks for donations.

The potential of the politically discontent—of those who had turned their backs on East Germany and who sought their fortune in West Germany—for intelligence work was recognised by the secret services in the West. The image of East Germans voting with their feet and demonstrating their dissatisfaction with the system by fleeing in droves is an accurate one. This fact could be put to good use by Western propaganda. In addition, the emigration of qualified workers weakened the East German economy. Given that East Germany was supposed to be the most important satellite state of the Soviet Union, any weakening of it indirectly meant the weakening of the Soviet Union itself. That the stream of refugees in the 1950s seriously and substantially weakened East Germany and, at the same time, brought West Berlin to the limit of its capacity is shown by the following figures. In 1950, around 60,000 East Germans fled to West Berlin and just under 140,000 to West Germany. The peak of the refugee wave was in 1953. In that year, 297,000 people fled to West Berlin, although there were only about 34,000 who escaped to West Germany due to the fact that restrictions on people crossing the inner German border had been tightened. Between 1950 and 1955, 759,000 registered refugees fled to West Berlin.[22]

This flow of refugees continued unabated until the construction of the Berlin Wall. Between the founding of the two German states in 1949 and the commencement of construction of the Wall in August 1961, more than 2.6 million East German citizens had emigrated to the West. These refugees played an important role in

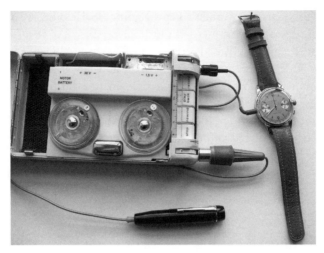

A Minifon P55 wire spool recording device with microphone wristwatch and microphone fountain pen were special espionage accessories.

the psychological warfare against East Germany and were able to provide valuable intelligence.[23] Many of them were questioned upon their arrival in West Berlin. The Americans and the British cooperated closely in this regard and shared their intelligence with one another. The following questions were of particular interest. What profession did the refugee practice? Did they live near a military facility and did they observe anything there? Furthermore, the informal and social connections in East Germany were of great interest to the intelligence services.

If a refugee proved to be cooperative when questioned, attempts were made to win them over as an agent. If they agreed, they were immediately sent back to East Germany before their escape had been noticed. In this way, the secret services were often successful in recruiting new agents.[24]

Most refugees were asked to write down the names of relatives and friends in East Germany who might, like them, disagree with the regime there. The intelligence services thereby built up a large pool of potential agents and informants. The wave of refugees from the East was undeniably hugely profitable for Western intelligence. Corresponding letters were posted to the potential recruits from within, rather than from outside, East Germany so as to attract as little attention as possible. Such letters provided a telephone number and the address of a meeting point in West Berlin. The real reason for the meeting was initially disguised and only stated at the meeting itself. The recipient was to be recruited as an agent in East Germany. One recruiter for the French intelligence service is said to have written to approximately 350 people between 1948 and 1955.[25]

The recruitment of Soviet soldiers stationed in East Germany was another goal of the Western secret services. The Americans named this Operation *Redcap*. Attempts were made to use German women for persuading Soviet officers to defect to the West. However, this operation met with little success.[26]

Yet the refugee wave also posed a threat to Western intelligence services. It was the gateway to West Germany for East German and Soviet agents. Well-educated scientists and students almost always found employment in business or administration not only in West Germany but sometimes also in Great Britain or the United States. With refugee numbers in the millions, the Eastern secret services could insert their people completely unnoticed among those fleeing to the West. However, when the Berlin Wall was built in August 1961, the gold-rush mood that was the recruitment and intelligence gathering associated with the refugee wave came to an end.

The end of an era

The construction of the Berlin Wall and the consequences for Western intelligence agencies

Western intelligence services were taken by surprise by the swift construction of the Berlin Wall on 13 August 1961. They had for several years been considering the question of how the East German regime might try to put a stop to the continuous flow of refugees. It was expected that barriers might be set up between the sectors, or that there might even be a renewed blockade of Berlin, but this was all just speculation.[27] While the construction of the Wall itself might not have been entirely unexpected, the secrecy and the speed with which it was done was astonishing. It demonstrated that East Germany had the ability to plan and carry out extensive projects without the knowledge of West Germany and the Western powers. The intelligence agencies of the West, to their dismay, had been kept in the dark.

A radical change in the working methods of the intelligence agencies in Berlin was required. They had previously relied on the human being as an agent and as a source of information. Now, the recruitment of the sort that had taken place amidst the refugee wave of the 1950s had become extremely difficult. Furthermore, communication with agents already in East Berlin and East Germany would become a problem. In September 1961, the CIA proposed that their approximately 100 agents in East Germany be equipped with radio receivers so contact could be maintained with them.[28] However, after the Wall was built, it turned out that the most reliable method of communication between the secret services in the West and their agents in East Germany was by using dead drops. A case officer would put new instructions, money, and any necessary equipment in a hiding place and would collect the information deposited by an agent. The disadvantage of this method was that communication was slow, as it could take several days, sometimes weeks, until items or information were collected. Maintaining this communication channel, however, became increasingly difficult due to the continued improvement of the

A U.S. Army patrol driving along the Berlin Wall in 1965. All three Western powers carried out such patrols on a daily basis.

surveillance methods of the East German Ministry for State Security, also known as the Stasi. This was also the case for communication by regular post, which risked the exposure of informants in East Germany.[29]

The CIA recognised the impact the Wall would have on their work in Berlin. The possibilities for obtaining information deteriorated significantly by September 1961 and the CIA feared morale would drop among its employees in the city. The staff of Berlin Operations Base (BOB) was to be reduced from around 95 to 75.[30] The importance of BOB as an outpost in hostile territory diminished after 1961. This was especially true of what the Americans and the British called HUMINT (human intelligence), namely the gathering of intelligence by agents. Reconnaissance flights by the American U-2 spy plane over the Soviet Union had been undertaken since the mid-1950s with great success. As will be seen, other indications of the changes taking place in the gathering of intelligence were the construction of the Berlin spy tunnel and the erection of large listening stations in the city. The focus on the human being as a source of information—as a secret agent—began to wane. Technological progress meant that telecommunications and electronic surveillance became the most important tools of espionage.

CHAPTER TWO

Rising from the ruins

The enemy is listening

The Anglo-American listening station on Teufelsberg

The Americans and the British used the highest point in the western part of Berlin to set up a listening station. This enabled them to hear the radio communications of some of the states of the Warsaw Pact. For more than 20 years, the station on Teufelsberg was a clearly visible symbol of the technological side of the Cold War. However, its history and development are closely linked with the Nazi era and World War II.

There was no hill in the area between Heerstraße and Teufelssee when development commenced there in the mid-1930s. It was the plan of Albert Speer, the general building inspector for the capital of the Reich, for the University City of Berlin to be built there. The first building was to be the Faculty of Defence Technology of the Technical University, and Adolf Hitler personally performed the first hammer blow when the foundation stone was laid on 27 November 1937.[1] The construction plans were revised several times over the course of the next two years, which meant that, by the outbreak of World War II, only the main building of the faculty was near completion.[2] With no more buildings being constructed there during the war, the incomplete main building, 50 metres in height, was one of many ruins that stood in Berlin in 1945. For the clearance work that was carried out in the years immediately after the war, locations were sought on the outskirts of the city where the rubble could be deposited and disposed of. The area around the former Faculty of Defence Technology and near Teufelssee was one of those locations. The rubble—12 million cubic metres of it—piled up so high that it completely covered the building. The new hill, Teufelsberg, was named after the nearby lake, Teufelssee. Alongside the likewise 115-metre high Müggelberg, Teufelsberg remains the highest point in Berlin to this day.[3] Two hundred thousand trees have been planted there since the 1950s so as to better integrate it into the surrounding nature. It soon became a popular recreational area, especially for winter sport enthusiasts. In addition to a large toboggan run, there was a ski slope on which a World Cup ski race was held in 1987.[4]

The secret services of the West became interested in the ever-growing artificial hill. As it lay in the British sector of Berlin, the British were the first to set up a

Aerial view of the listening station on Teufelsberg in Berlin at the end of the 1980s. There were no changes in its structure during the time it was in operation.

Aerial view of Teufelsberg, Berlin, on which trucks, trailers, and antennas can be seen in November 1962.

mobile listening station there. Between 1961 and 1963, the Americans negotiated with the British for the military exploitation of the hill. The American occupation forces were given control of Teufelsberg, while the British armed forces were allowed to make use of the site.[5]

Anglo-American units worked with mobile equipment on Teufelsberg in the 1960s, with the listening station there constantly being expanded. Between 1969 and 1971, the Americans built a permanent complex of buildings, and, from 1972, they started listening round the clock. In the same year, the British moved the 26th Signals Unit from Gatow to Teufelsberg in order to utilise a 120-metre-high antenna that had been built by the company Rhode & Schwarz.[6] For 20 years, the American and British secret services used this building complex for their telecommunications reconnaissance.

In addition to this well-known facility, there were a number of other spots in the western part of Berlin used for the same or similar purposes. This is because the unique geographical location of the city made it an ideal place for the radio-electronic reconnaissance efforts of the West.

Rather insignificant were the sites in Rudow and Grunewald; more important were those in Marienfelde and Tempelhof is the conclusion of a Stasi file.[7] Although the Western secret services remain tight-lipped about their listening activities in West Berlin, information about the espionage work on Teufelsberg and the technical capabilities of the Western powers can be obtained from the files of the Stasi. East Germany and the Soviet Union were in the position to be able to gain extensive knowledge of the radio-electronic reconnaissance work of the Western powers. The role of spies in this regard will be discussed later.

American forces in Berlin were based on Aschberg in the district of Marienfelde in the western part of the city. This location was only slightly less than 1,000 metres away from the East German border. The base had been established between 1962 and 1965. Of the 14 buildings there, six were used for monitoring communications.[8] Stationed there was the 6912th Electronic Security Group; its task was to record and evaluate all electromagnetic signals, referred to in Anglo-American terminology as SIGINT (signals intelligence).[9] Other methods of acquiring intelligence were COMINT (communication intelligence), which monitored data transmissions from satellites to teleprinters, as well as ELINT (electronic intelligence), which dealt with the interception, recording, and deciphering of various signals and codes. The station in Marienfelde was able to record and evaluate all emissions in the frequency range from 25 megahertz to around 20 gigahertz. According to the Stasi, this meant Marienfelde could 'ensure all-round monitoring of signal traffic in the territory of the German Democratic Republic, of most of the Polish People's Republic, and of most of the Czechoslovak Socialist Republic'.[10] Like Teufelsberg, Marienfelde was in direct contact and exchanged information with the headquarters of the National Security Agency (NSA) in Fort Meade, Maryland, in the United States. The results of the work at Marienfelde were forwarded to the NSA via computer-aided electronic data processing.[11]

The American listening station in Marienfelde, Berlin, in September 1967.

The listening station in Tempelhof stood on the grounds of the airport there. A modern radar installation was set up in the summer of 1984 which enabled the detection of other active radar installations within a radius of 360 kilometres, specifically those that belonged to the East German National People's Army (NVA), the Group of Soviet Forces in Germany (GSFG), the Polish People's Army, and the Czechoslovak People's Army. Radar transmissions could be analysed to determine the type and purpose of the enemy installations.[12] According to the assessment of the Stasi, the Marienfelde, Teufelsberg and Tempelhof stations constituted an effective early warning system for the Americans. Any aerial activity of the states of the Warsaw Pact within a range of 500 kilometres of those stations could be detected.

In addition to their premises on Teufelsberg, the British had a building at their airfield in Gatow where they carried out radio-electronic reconnaissance. In the 1950s, approximately 5,000 British conscripts were taught the Russian language so they could listen to Russian radio traffic, and Gatow was one of the locations where they might be posted. The most talented among them were even given the opportunity to study the language at the prestigious University of Cambridge.[13] In 1983, a new radar station was constructed in Gatow that enabled the detection of civil and military aircraft within a range of a few hundred kilometres.[14]

Little is known about the radio-electronic reconnaissance of the French occupation forces in Berlin. The Stasi was unable to obtain any useful information in this regard and probably did not even have any spies embedded in the French secret service. All that has been determined about the military area of the airfield in Tegel is that radio equipment was installed there for an unknown purpose and that the security restrictions for this area were very high. There is also little information about Camp Foch, where the intelligence service of the French armed forces in Berlin was located.

Monitoring everything

Espionage in three-shift operations

The possibilities of electronic reconnaissance have improved continuously in the age of satellite communication and computer technology. From the mid-1960s, telephone traffic between continents had become possible via satellite, so underground and underwater cables were no longer necessary. Today, countless communication satellites are buzzing around the earth. Calls are transmitted from continent A to a satellite and are directed from there to a receiving station on continent B. Secret services can intercept information that is transmitted in this manner. Any satellite-supported data transmission—whether a telephone call, an email, or a fax—can be intercepted. 'Echelon' is the code name for the network of listening stations in the United States, Great Britain, Canada, New Zealand, and Australia. It was created and is coordinated by the NSA.[15] The international telecommunications satellites (Intelsats) used by most telephone companies can be monitored worldwide. The flood of data is filtered by analysis programs equipped with search functions. Names, numbers, organisations, and even voting patterns can be searched for.[16]

Since monitoring stations usually require very large antennas, their locations have been known for some time. Until 2004, there was a station in Bad Aibling that was integrated into the Echelon project and was therefore also involved in signals intelligence. Another large SIGINT station in Germany was operated by the Americans in Lechfeld, near Gablingen, until the mid-1990s.[17] All American listening stations in Berlin were integrated into the global network until they were closed.

There are various sources of information on the work undertaken on Teufelsberg, the most well-known listening station in Berlin. Nevertheless, a large part of its story remains top secret. Details on the precise nature of the work there, and the specific pieces of information that were focused on, are classified. Given there are still American listening stations around the world today whose tasks and equipment are similar to those of Teufelsberg, it is hard to imagine that details on Teufelsberg will be made public within the next few years.

In July 1961, the Special Operations Unit of the American 78th Army Security Agency (ASA) set up the first mobile listening station on 'the Hill', as Teufelsberg was colloquially referred to by the Americans.[18] From 1962, this unit came directly under the command of the headquarters of the ASA in the United States. In 1967, the unit was renamed Field Station Berlin (FSB). As a result of restructuring in 1977,

FSB on Teufelsberg was integrated into the Intelligence and Security Command (INSCOM) of the U.S. Army. Also stationed on the Hill was the 6912th Electronic Security Group of the U.S. Air Force. It was the NSA, though, that determined the objectives to be achieved and the tasks to be carried out on Teufelsberg. The FSB also had to respond to requests made and tasks set by the headquarters of the U.S. Army in Europe, which was based in Heidelberg.

Up to 1,500 people worked in the buildings of the listening station. About 1,000 of them were members of the U.S. Armed Forces and another 300 to 500 of the British Army and Royal Air Force. This large number of employees was necessary due to the three-shift system. The soldiers selected for the work on Teufelsberg were highly qualified and well-trained, but there were also several ordinary roles like kitchenhands or technicians. The foundation that was the pile of rubble was somewhat unstable and this had an impact on the buildings there. Cracks often appeared that needed to be examined and repaired.[19] The entire supply of this small town on rubble had to be guaranteed 24 hours a day, 365 days a year.

The latest and most innovative technical equipment was used by FSB in order to fully exploit the mass of information being collected. Teufelsberg was where much of this equipment, intended for everyday use, was tested for the first time. The equipment was financed by the American taxpayer and not, like the general equipment of the three Western powers in Berlin, by the German taxpayer. This was because of the need for secrecy. In the event Berlin should be seized by the enemy in its entirety, the technical equipment in the listening stations was not allowed to fall into the hands of the enemy under any circumstances. There was, therefore, an exercise conducted several times each year which dealt with the destruction of electronic devices. Although such exercises were routine in the military, a serious accident occurred in the listening station in Marienfelde in 1986. A document shredder exploded and injured 34 Americans.[20]

There were many translators on Teufelsberg. Their work was of the utmost importance to the intelligence activities of FSB.[21] Knowledge of German, Russian, and Polish was required. Some of the special training for FSB personnel was completed at the headquarters of the NSA in Fort Meade, where translators were informed of the type of information NSA analysts were interested in.[22] Analysis was not the task of the personnel of Teufelsberg. Their role was to receive, gather, and pass on information. It was to the headquarters of the NSA that the information had to be sent, where it would then be determined what was important and what was not. A small group of NSA employees was also stationed at Teufelsberg and they worked closely with the commander of the field station.

It is difficult to say anything about the quality of the information obtained on Teufelsberg as there are insufficient sources on this matter. It can only be speculated whether there were any important messages intercepted and deciphered that helped overcome a political crisis during the Cold War. Nevertheless, there is one indication of the effectiveness of Teufelsberg. The U.S. Department of Defense has awarded the prestigious Travis Trophy every year since 1964 to the unit that has made the most important contribution to strategic reconnaissance. All intelligence units in the army, navy, and air force are considered. Field Station Berlin on Teufelsberg is the only unit that has received this trophy four times—1973, 1981, 1985, and 1989.[23]

What did the East know?

Code name 'Relais' and a traitor in Gatow

The East German regime was naturally very interested in finding out about the efficiency and the function of the listening stations of the Western powers in West Berlin. It generally did so, on the one hand, through precise analysis of the equipment that was externally visible and, on the other, through spies who sold information from Teufelsberg and Gatow. Both methods will be described briefly. 'Relais' was the code name for helicopter flights over West Berlin whose purpose was to observe the antennas set up by the Western powers. Making use of helicopters belonging to the Soviet armed forces, Main Division III of the Stasi undertook these reconnaissance flights from 1982. In 1986, for example, a Soviet Mi-17 transport helicopter clocked up 84 hours in the air exclusively for this task. The objective of these flights was described as the 'visual, photo-optical, and video-technical reconnaissance and documentation of operationally important and technologically developed enemy areas and facilities in the territory of West Berlin'.[24] Teufelsberg, of course, was one of those facilities. The Stasi accepted the fact the Western powers would object to these reconnaissance flights.

Field Station Berlin was regarded as an important base of the global radio reconnaissance system of the United States. Its geostrategic location was highly advantageous for the Western powers, standing as it did 115 metres above sea level in the middle of West Berlin and only seven kilometres from the East German border.

Some of the FSB antennas were installed under so-called radomes, which are shaped like oversized golf balls. Although the radomes served to protect the highly sensitive equipment from bad weather and enemy observation, the Stasi was fully aware of the antennas that had been installed underneath. According to the assessment of the Stasi, the installations used by FSB on Teufelsberg included passive radio reconnaissance systems, active radar systems, directional radio reconnaissance systems, and direction finders for the ultrahigh frequency and very high frequency ranges. The data was transmitted to both the NSA and, in part, to the British electronic intelligence service known as the Government Communications Headquarters (GCHQ).

It was the belief of the Stasi that the West had the capacity to listen to and record: (a) the military and political radio and telecommunications traffic of East Germany; (b) the electronic emissions of the fire control and weapons systems of the NVA and the GSFG; and (c) other forms of radio, directional radio, and telecommunications traffic in East Germany.[25] In other words, this meant the Americans and British were able to intercept radar transmissions from the NVA, the GSFG and the Polish People's Army at a distance of 250 to 500 kilometres. Movements in the air within a radius of 500 kilometres could be detected, meaning the West possessed what was in effect an early-warning system. In addition, the communications of the land and air forces of the NVA and GSFG could be intercepted, while the locations of their transmitting radio stations could be determined. The most important ability in case of an emergency was probably the detection and manipulation of the fire control and weapons systems of the NVA and the GSFG.[26] NATO plans sold to East Germany and the Soviet Union by the American spy James Hall in 1986 revealed exactly this strategy of manipulating enemy weapons systems.

The most effective, albeit seldom, way in which the East could obtain information was through traitors in the West. An employee at the British listening station in Gatow and, later, one at the American listening station on Teufelsberg offered their services to the East as spies. Nobody is born a spy or a traitor. It is usually personal or financial circumstances that motivate someone to become a spy. The preparedness to engage in espionage often fades due to the challenges involved in actively making contact with the other side. Nevertheless, Berlin was unique. Nowhere else could members of the military or even ordinary citizens offer themselves to the other side with such ease. As British double agent George Blake reported in his memoirs, this was a phenomenon already widespread in Berlin in the 1950s.

An example of this is the case of British wireless operator Geoffrey Prime. Because of his knowledge of the Russian language, Prime was posted to the Royal Air Force base in Gatow in 1964 and worked in signals intelligence. He was able to listen in on Soviet conversations, and he offered his services to the Soviets as a spy during his years in Berlin. The way he made contact was quite simple. He threw a note with his contact details at the feet of a Russian soldier at the checkpoint station in Marienborn.[27] It was not long before he was recruited by the Soviets, equipped with a small Minox camera, and trained in various techniques for passing on intelligence. He was stationed in Gatow for four years, during which time he had access to information that had come from the British department on Teufelsberg. He was then transferred to England and worked in a variety of positions at GCHQ. He remained a double agent during his time there and, until 1977, he photographed countless documents for the Soviets. He sold his last photographs to the KGB in Vienna in 1980.[28]

Prime was arrested in 1982 for the sexual assault of a minor. His espionage activities for the KGB were unearthed as a part of the investigation process and he made a full confession in June 1982. He was sentenced to 38 years in prison: 35 for espionage and three for the sexual harassment of a minor. The length of the prison sentence is a clear indication of the severity of his espionage activities. He was released early, after 19 years, in March 2001.[29]

BE
SECURITY— CONSCIOUS

OR THIS FOUR
POWER CITY

MIGHT BECOME A
ONE POWER CITY

Poster of the U.S. military government in Berlin in the 1980s.

Dream duo of the East, nightmare for the West

Hall and Yıldırım in Berlin

In 1982, for financial reasons, James W. Hall decided to offer his services to the Soviet Union. The way in which this American soldier, stationed in Berlin, made contact was just as simple as it was for Geoffrey Prime two decades earlier. Hall wrote of his willingness to cooperate in a letter which he then dropped in the mailbox of the Soviet consulate in Berlin.[30] The KGB was naturally interested in working with the then 25-year-old sergeant, for he worked on Teufelsberg at that time. The infiltration of this facility was high on the list of the KGB in Berlin, and they now had an application in their mailbox from someone who worked there. The KGB and Hall quickly came to an agreement, as the Soviets were willing to pay Hall well for conducting espionage.

Hall initially photocopied secret documents at his workplace. When measures were introduced that exercised greater control over photocopying, he started smuggling documents out of the field station so he could photocopy them elsewhere. He was given an extra-large, double-bottom sports bag for this purpose. American soldiers were never checked when they left the field station. Hall then slipped the photocopies through the slightly open side window of a parked car at an agreed meeting point—a dead letter box on four wheels, so to speak. During his years of service in Berlin,

Hall sold several thousand documents not only to the KGB but also to the Stasi. These documents contained details on the technical and personnel capacities of the Americans and the British in Berlin.

Hall's connection with the Stasi came about by pure chance. In 1982, a few weeks after Hall offered his services to the KGB, he was approached by the Turk Hüseyin Yıldırım. Yıldırım was a master mechanic at a U.S. Army vehicle repair shop in West Berlin, where soldiers were able to repair their own vehicles under professional guidance, and his contacts with the Stasi went back to 1979. In that year, he had simply turned up at the headquarters of the Stasi and had said he wanted to do business. However, Yıldırım was of no interest to the Stasi. After a number of conversations, he was told that, although there was no use for him at that stage, he should get in touch again if he had contact with one of the occupying powers in West Berlin.[31] He did so, once he was working at the repair shop several months later, and the Stasi saw by then that there was potential for cooperation.

The repair shop was housed in Andrews Barracks and was frequented by soldiers from Field Station Berlin. It was an ideal place to socialise. Yıldırım possessed not only extraordinary skills as a mechanic but also an understanding of human nature and an ability to be convincing. His nickname in the repair shop, 'the Master', also caught on outside it. The code name he was given by the Stasi was 'Blitz'. In the process of helping Hall repair his vehicle over the course of several days, the two started talking. Hall had already been working for the KGB for a short time and he was happy to be recruited by Yıldırım for the Stasi. Yıldırım and the Stasi did not know at that moment that Hall was working for the KGB. Hall later reported the encounter was a godsend for him and that it enabled him to make money quickly. He made two copies of all the documents he smuggled out—one for the KGB, which he supplied directly, and one for Yıldırım. Yıldırım delivered the documents to the Stasi, received money for them, and gave Hall his share. Hall had little to take care of, and Yıldırım, who acted solely for financial reasons, haggled over the price of the documents. It was like a bazaar at times.[32]

The KGB, which had become aware in 1985 that Hall was also working for 'the Master', and thus for the Stasi, requested he give up this extra work on the grounds that it was too risky. Hall decided not to follow this advice. He found the meetings with the KGB, which placed great emphasis on the security and protection of their source, to have become too complicated and time-consuming, so he chose instead to work only for the Stasi from then on.[33] The all-round carefree package offered by Yıldırım brought in less money, but it was much easier.

Hall was transferred back to the United States in 1985. After a few months, he applied for a post in Frankfurt am Main. Since Hall was married to a German woman, no one in the personnel office regarded this as unusual. He was posted, in the spring of 1986, to the 205th Military Intelligence Battalion, which was

He turns cars into masterpieces

"He taught me how to work with metal to form new parts myself and how they should be in place," said Maj. Larry D. Seals. "My Ghia is actually better now than it original was."

The man Seals was praising is Hüseyin Yildirim, meister mechanical engineer at the Andrews Auto Craft Shop.

Born in 1928 in Istanbul, Yildirim served in World War II as a tank mechanic for the Turkish Army and later achieved the rank of lieutenant in his field artillery unit. After the war he spent a decade working for a firm in Turkey as a mechanical engineer.

In the 1960's Yildirim owned and operated his own mechanical tools shop. Since 1974, he has been in Ger-

many where he received his first meister certificate in mechanical engineering while working for Borch Industries. From Borch he was recruited by Mercedes Benz where he continued to work as an engineer for eight years. Here, he received his second meister's certificate and three coveted suggestion awards.

Today, Yildirim devotes his skills to Americans in the craft shop at Andrews. He gladly passes on his talent and knowledge to anyone who is interested. "I have much to teach you," he says, "if you're willing to listen to me." In addition to teaching and helping those working in the craft shop, he also teaches the skills of welding twice a week in regular class sessions.

Welding and body work are special skills of the meister and according to Seals the rebuilding of his 1971 Karman Ghia would have been impossible without the meister's help.

MSgt. Cling Hyder, a part-time assistant in the shop, says, "The meister teaches me something new everyday that I'm here. I try to absorb

as much as I can from him so that when he isn't here I can fill in for him."

The meister welcomes everyone to the shop whether they are skilled mechanics or novices wanting to learn the basics of auto repair. Turning automobiles into masterpieces is what he does best.

JUST MAKE A NEW PIECE—Tom Colin is an eager listener to the words of the meister. Having problems with a part on his motorcycle he checks with him to find out if the clutch can be fixed without buying a new one.

A LITTLE ADJUSTMENT—The meister checks over some of the work being done on an engine in the auto craft shop. Photos by Frank Jones

Newspaper report in the *Berlin Observer* in June 1982 about Hüseyin Yıldırım's work in the American vehicle repair shop.

directly subordinate to the headquarters of the U.S. V Corps in Frankfurt. The documents he photocopied there were of far greater importance than those in Berlin. Yıldırım, who remained Hall's contact for the Stasi, sometimes visited Frankfurt to collect the documents personally and photocopy them himself. The quantity and the quality of the documents supplied by the Hall-Yıldırım duo was extraordinary. They delivered a total of approximately 10,000 documents, among which were top-secret plans developed by NATO for offence and defence. Markus Wolf, who was head of the foreign intelligence branch of the Stasi from 1952 to 1986, described the duo as a 'miracle source that can only be dreamed of in the intelligence service'.[34]

The Stasi dream team split up in 1987, which in effect also initiated the subsequent unmasking of the two spies. Yıldırım had met a wealthy American woman and left his family in Berlin to go to America with her. He was 'decommissioned' by the Stasi and instructed to make no further contact with Hall whatsoever.

Hall was eventually exposed by his new contact, Manfred Severin. This was because Severin offered his services as a double agent to the United States in 1987, and he was able to put American counterespionage on Hall's trail. Hall himself sold two more documents to the Stasi before being transferred back to the United States in 1988. It was not until December 1988 that the American Counterespionage Section, in

Poster of the American Counterespionage Section in the 1980s.

cooperation with the CIA and the FBI, succeeded in convicting Hall and Yıldırım of espionage. Both men were arrested in the United States.

The case of the Hall-Yıldırım duo was particularly instructive and, at the same time, sobering for American counterintelligence. The duo had in fact attracted the attention of investigators at an early stage. Yıldırım, in an extramarital relationship with an American woman, was denounced by the ex-boyfriend of his lover. This was in 1982, by which time Yıldırım had already been working for the Stasi for several years. An official investigation by American counterespionage authorities in Berlin was launched and Yıldırım was questioned; Yıldırım protested his innocence and insisted he undergo a lie detector test. It did not come to that. The counterespionage agents knew 'the Master' well from the evenings they spent together while repairing their vehicles. Nobody wanted to believe he was a Stasi spy, so the case was closed.[35]

An internal investigation of Hall was conducted in Frankfurt in 1987. A colleague to whom he had lent his car found wads of money in an envelope in the back seat and reported this to his superior. Hall was asked about it and was able to extricate himself with spurious explanations. His colleagues also noticed he was living beyond his financial means. He justified this with different stories, usually to the effect that his German wife had rich relatives. No effort was made to verify this claim. Although there was sufficient evidence, the internal investigation failed to do its job properly.

James Hall after his arrest in December 1988.

It was the Stasi double agent Manfred Severin who brought about the fall of Hall and Yıldırım. After months of being observed in the United States, Hall eventually fell into the trap investigators set for him. With the help of Severin, Hall was recorded on film and audio as he received U.S. $60,000, in a motel near his home in Savannah, Georgia, for his espionage services. He was arrested on 21 December 1988 and Yıldırım a day later. Hall confessed and cooperated with the investigative authorities. He made extensive statements about, and thereby incriminated, Yıldırım. A few months later, Hall was sentenced to 40 years in prison. Yıldırım did not confess and always denied having been a spy for the Stasi. However, so overwhelming was the evidence against him that he was sentenced to life imprisonment in May 1989. Under the circumstances that prevailed at the time, he could hope that he would be set free if captured spies were to be exchanged between East Germany and the United States, but this possibility disappeared after the fall of the Berlin Wall in 1989 and the reunification of Germany in 1990.

Yıldırım's Turkish family—the wife and children he had left—fought for his release for years. They were supported in this regard by the American lawyer Jamie Nichols, who even appealed, without success, for clemency from Presidents Bill Clinton and George W. Bush. In November 2003, the judicial authorities of the United States agreed Yıldırım could be transferred to Turkey to serve the remainder of his sentence. Yet, after 15 years in American custody, he arrived in Turkey and did not spend a single day in prison. Instead, he was released immediately. Markus Wolf had been a steadfast advocate for the release of Yıldırım and had presented the Yıldırım case in his books and articles as an example of victor's justice in the wake

Helmut Trotnow, Hüseyin Yıldırım and Markus Wolf at the documentary film event at the Allied Museum in Zehlendorf, Berlin, in April 2004.

of the Cold War.[36] It is therefore of no surprise that Wolf went to meet Yıldırım when the latter visited Berlin in April 2004 for the showing of the documentary film *Deckname Blitz: Der Spion vom Teufelsberg* at the Allied Museum. Through his presence, the most powerful man in the Stasi demonstrated he held great esteem for his spy.

At Field Station Berlin, appropriate measures were taken in response to the James W. Hall espionage case. When questioned after his arrest, Hall said he would not have spied for the KGB or the Stasi if he had undergone polygraph tests while doing his work. As a result, every soldier at FSB with access to sensitive data was subjected to a lie detector test before being transferred from the listening station.[37] Although Hall was sentenced to 40 years in prison, he was released, after 22 years, from the U.S. Disciplinary Barracks at Fort Leavenworth, Kansas, in September 2011. He changed his identity and now has a regular job. Only his boss and a few colleagues are aware of his past. He avoids contact with the press and, having signed a confidentiality agreement while in custody, to this day does not talk about his work as a spy for the East.[38]

Nevertheless, we now know more about Hall's activities and the damage he did in the 1980s. He photocopied around 13,000 pages for the Stasi, including the 4,000-page National SIGINT Requirements List (NSRL). This was a document containing all the espionage objectives of the NSA, and it fell into the hands of the East.

The 'Kid'

Becoming a spy to live in East Germany

The youngest spy from the American armed forces in Berlin who worked for the Stasi was Jeffrey M. Carney. The young Jeffrey from Ohio recognised his love of Germany while at school. He read history books and achieved good results in the German language. At the age of 17, having had enough of his broken family and home, he joined the U.S. Air Force. In recognition of Carney's knowledge of German, the air force provided him with further language training for more than a year and then posted him to Berlin. He became a radio intelligence officer with the 6912th Electronic Security Group at the listening station in Marienfelde. He and his colleagues listened to the radio traffic of East German aircraft and were to report anything they noticed. Carney was good at his job and was nicknamed 'Duden' due to his listening skills, his memory, and his grammatical knowledge. Despite the excellent results of his work, Carney did not feel properly understood and appreciated by his colleagues. He had doubts about American policy during the Cold War and believed NATO wanted to provoke a conflict with the East. When he was scolded one day for making a mistake, the young soldier, in anger, made a momentous decision. After drinking several beers that evening, he went to East Berlin via the border crossing at Checkpoint Charlie. Carney told the border guards on the other side that he

wanted to live in East Germany and had no desire to go back to West Berlin. His interlocutors did not know whether they were dealing with a potential spy or just a drunken young man.[39] They convinced him that he would have to return to his station if he wanted to be able to change the situation he was complaining about. They photocopied his papers, warned him not to tell the Americans what he had been up to, and requested he bring something from his workplace on his next visit. The 19-year-old returned to West Berlin, having taken his first step towards many years of spying. In the following weeks, Carney met several times with his superiors in East Berlin and handed over the first documents. They were surprised this young soldier, with the Stasi code name 'Kid', was able to provide them with so much valuable

The young soldier Jeffrey M. Carney in uniform.

material. Carney was able to gather the most important documents at his workplace as they often lay freely accessible on the desks there. His Stasi superiors asked about the poor security precautions. 'Is it really that lax?' they asked in disbelief. 'Yes, it is!' was Carney's reply.[40]

Carney's regular visits to East Berlin were too risky, however. Several meetings with Stasi agents in 1982 and 1983 therefore took place in the Berlin exclave Eiskeller, where the less secure border between East and West Berlin ran through a forest near a dirt road. Carney would ride his bike there and go into the forest on the western side of the exclave to deposit his documents in a dead letter box that had been prepared under a tree. So that he could work as effectively as possible, Carney was equipped with a small camera and a special thermos flask. This enabled him to copy even more documents without having to remove them from wherever they were lying. He frequently visited East Berlin in his spare time and his Stasi superiors introduced him to East Germany and its people. This was a clever move by the Stasi. Its agents were fully aware their spy's greatest wish was to live in East Germany. At each meeting in East Berlin, Carney received money for his espionage activities. He did not want to accept it at first, as money had never been his motive, but his case officer explained to him a spy who did not accept any money might appear suspicious to senior Stasi officials. Carney was therefore paid around 300 West German marks at each meeting in recognition for his work.

The U.S. listening station in Marienfelde, Berlin, at the end of the 1980s.

At the same time, Carney continued to play his role as a good and brave American soldier in West Berlin. He was even selected as a representative of the air force to attend, alongside a representative of the army, the Christmas dinner with the mayor of West Berlin, Eberhard Diepgen. Yet Carney's masquerade became ever more complicated, for he had to hide not only his work for the Stasi from the air force but also his homosexuality. It did not make his role as a spy particularly easy. After finding a microfiche database containing innumerable files, he and the Stasi had to figure out the best possible way to make copies of them. However, he was soon transferred and did not have a chance to complete this task. He was to go back to the United States and work at San Angelo Air Force Base as an instructor. On his last day at Marienfelde, he put everything on the line and smuggled dozens of documents, hidden in his underwear, out of the listening station. He intended this as a farewell gift to the Stasi, as he had no idea whether he could continue to be of use at his new base. The Stasi did not know either. Nevertheless, arrangements were made so Carney could meet with Stasi agents in the vicinity of the United States. Mexico was chosen as the rendezvous and Carney had to inform his colleagues in East Germany about two weeks in advance of any meeting he wanted to have happen. From 1984, he mainly copied documents from the technical library at the base. There was nothing that was top secret.

Carney became increasingly mentally unstable in the months following his return to the United States. He felt overwhelmed and started to plan his escape to East Germany. He wanted it to be a farewell without return this time, quite unlike his outing past Checkpoint Charlie a few years earlier. Carney packed and fled to Mexico in September 1985, going to the East German embassy in Mexico City. The staff there did their best to try to get him out of the country unnoticed. He was eventually flown to East Germany via Havana. The Stasi gave him an apartment in Marzahn, Berlin, as well as a new identity. He had finally achieved, in 1985, what he had striven for years before: to live in East Germany as an East German citizen. He was even allowed to choose his new name. He opted for Jens Karney, a pseudonym that was far too similar to his real name. His new identity card had his correct date of birth, which was, in retrospect, a careless decision by a top spy and the senior officials looking after him. Jens Karney had imagined a quiet life as an East German citizen, but, after a few months, the Stasi had new tasks for him. The second part of his career in espionage would therefore be carried out from East Berlin. The Stasi provided Jens Karney with tapes of conversations that had been recorded in West Berlin, including calls made on the car telephone of the commandant of the American sector of Berlin. Karney would be the specialist who was to find out if there was anything of significance on those tapes. English was his mother tongue, and, unlike other Stasi language experts, he knew the jargon and abbreviations of the U.S. military. Karney evaluated the tapes the Stasi brought him every day with great success. There was even information about who at the U.S. embassy was in love or having an affair. The Stasi was specifically interested in women who had been cheated on so that Stasi agents could be assigned to them as 'Romeos'. Karney continued in his new role until November 1989 when the Berlin Wall and the East German regime, and his ideal world, collapsed.

Karney received a final payment of 15,000 East German marks when the German Democratic Republic was in the process of being dissolved. Now on his own, he decided to stay in East Berlin and wait to see what would happen. He was unemployed at the beginning of 1990. He travelled abroad that year with his partner for a few weeks and, in the following months, found a job with the Berlin Transport Company. His past in espionage caught up with him on 22 April 1991. He was seized that day, upon leaving his apartment in Friedrichshain, Berlin, by agents of the U.S. Air Force Office of Special Investigations. He was interrogated for some time in Tempelhof and then flown to the United States via Frankfurt. Neither Berlin nor German authorities were informed their citizen had been arrested, detained, and flown out of the country.

The trial of the former Stasi spy took place in the United States and was closed to the public. He faced the possibility of a life sentence four times over. The official verdict before the military tribunal in December 1991 was 38 years in prison.[41] A subsequent out-of-court settlement in which Karney assured his full cooperation reduced the sentence to 20 years. He did not end up serving the full sentence, being released from Fort Leavenworth after 11 years and seven months. The abduction of Karney had become public in Germany in 1998 when Focus TV reported about it twice. After his release in 2003, Karney tried in vain to renew the German passport, now expired, that he had received after reunification or apply for a new one.[42] He was forced to recognise that the age-old saying about espionage also applied to him: everyone loves treason, but no one loves the traitor.

Unremarkable end

Teufelsberg after the withdrawal of the Western powers

The fall of the Berlin Wall, the reunification of Germany and the end of the Cold War also meant the end of Field Station Berlin. It was in January 1992 that the task of the field station was declared over. The Americans and the British vacated Teufelsberg in the months that followed. Only empty rooms, a few signs, and the protective covers for the antennas—the oversized golf balls on the roofs—remained.

The Teufelsberg Investor Consortium acquired the site in 1996 with the idea of building a luxury hotel and apartment complexes. It was also intended the special history of the site during the Cold War would be remembered with an intelligence museum. Negotiations with the authorities in Berlin and the search for investors took up much time.

A single conference on the history of Berlin during the Cold War was held on Teufelsberg in 1999. It was organised by the Teufelsberg Investor Consortium, the historical department of the CIA, and the Allied Museum. In attendance were historians, intelligence agents, spies, former double agents, politicians, and many other people whose careers had been shaped by the Cold War.

For various reasons, the plan of the investor consortium could not be implemented in the end. The building permit was withdrawn and, from 2003, the site was no longer guarded. In the following years, the former listening station on Teufelsberg only ever made headlines due to vandalism. The site received media attention at the beginning of 2009 because American film director David Lynch wanted to build an esoteric university there, but it was just a publicity stunt.

There has been a much more serious discussion about Teufelsberg in recent years at the district office of Charlottenburg in Berlin. The owner and investor of the property tried again to obtain a building permit for the purpose of attracting tourists, but without success. Even so, since 2011, professional tours have been offered at the site of the former listening station. This allows visitors to walk around the site legally and to learn something about its history. In addition, since 2011, it has been a meeting point for street artists who have found surfaces there for their art. The remains of the buildings on Teufelsberg were listed for preservation in 2018 and there has been, since the beginning of 2021, a renewed effort by investors to establish offices, restaurants, and a museum on the site. Whether it will succeed this time is questionable.[43]

CHAPTER THREE

Digging for gold

An underground thriller

The Berlin spy tunnel from Rudow to Altglienicke

The most spectacular operation of the Western intelligence services in Berlin was the construction of an approximately 450-metre-long spy tunnel from the American sector of the city to the Soviet sector. It was planned and built at the beginning of the 1950s. Due to the fact that eyewitnesses from the Western secret services are sworn to secrecy and that sources from the Soviet side are lacking in transparency, the spy tunnel has given rise to speculation, myth and legend ever since its discovery. It even inspired Hollywood to make *The Innocent*, a romantic thriller starring Anthony Hopkins and Isabella Rossellini, in the 1990s. At the beginning of 2007, the CIA report on the Berlin spy tunnel—the most important document on this subject—was almost completely declassified and made publicly available on the CIA website.[1] One of the most surprising revelations from this document was the real code name of the operation, which had previously been known as Operation *Gold* and had been referred to as such in numerous documents and publications. The code name for this Anglo-American secret operation was in fact 'PBJOINTLY.'[2] Astonishingly, parts of the declassified CIA report were blocked and removed from the internet a few months later.[3] It seems the spy tunnel is still surrounded by an aura of mystery 52 years after it was built.

The primary objective of the Western intelligence agencies in Berlin was to obtain secret political, economic, or military information about the Soviet Union and East Germany. In the years that followed World War II, this objective was pursued by relying on spies and listening to telephone conversations. However, at the end of 1948, the Soviet Union ceased transmitting telephone and telegraph traffic by radio and started using landlines and long-distance cables. This made Western espionage activities more difficult. The cable connections, some of them dating back to the 19th century, were safer for communications, as they were not easy to manipulate and monitor. After the outbreak of the Korean War (1950–1953), finding out the intentions of Moscow was of top priority. The arms race between the two superpowers—the United States and the Soviet Union—increased the likelihood there would be military conflict not only in Korea but also in other parts of the world.

Front page of a small brochure produced in East Germany in the summer of 1956 and offered for sale to the many thousands of visitors to the excavated Berlin spy tunnel.

The massive military presence of the Soviet Union in Europe meant the West greatly feared the possibility of a surprise attack on German soil. The American intelligence services, especially the CIA and the NSA, were urged to assess what Moscow was up to and to provide early warning of any possible attack.

How were the secret services to obtain relevant information? The conversion of Soviet communication methods theoretically made it possible to uncover and tap the long-distance underground cables. The prerequisite for this, however, was that the cables used by the Soviet side ran through an area that could be accessed by the Western intelligence services without being observed. There were only two locations in Europe where this was possible: Vienna and Berlin.

Like Berlin, Vienna had been divided up by the four victorious powers at the end of World War II and was under Allied administration. This made Vienna, like Berlin, a stronghold of espionage.[4] Peter Lunn became station chief of the British Secret Intelligence Service (SIS) in Vienna in 1948. It was there he had the idea of tapping the telephone lines of the Red Army, some of which ran through the British sector of Vienna. By 1955, the SIS had built at least four spy tunnels in the city for this purpose. As most of the cables ran underground, and were easily accessible, little construction work was necessary. The tunnels, with their wiretapping equipment, were only a few metres in length. American intelligence had been informed by the British of the wiretapping operations in Vienna at the beginning of the 1950s. Although the Americans had not been involved in the tunnelling in Vienna, the experience gained there provided the impetus for planning a similar tunnel in Berlin.[5]

The idea of a spy tunnel in Berlin was developed and promoted on the American side by William Harvey and Frank Rowlett. William Harvey was in charge of the CIA Office of Special Operations in Washington and was the driving force behind the tunnel project on the part of the CIA. In the autumn of 1952, Harvey was transferred to Berlin to assume responsibility for the final planning phase. So closely was he associated with the project that the operation was nicknamed 'Harvey's Hole' within the CIA.

The other driving force behind the project was Frank Rowlett, who was one of the best American decoding specialists of the 20th century. He worked for the CIA

William Harvey (left) was awarded by CIA director Allen Dulles for his work on the Berlin spy tunnel.

from 1952 to 1958 and for the NSA afterwards. He was responsible for the overall management of the tunnel project and coordinated it from the headquarters of the CIA. He was one of the proponents of a joint operation with British intelligence and was the head of the CIA delegation in its meetings with the British.[6] This was because he regarded the experience of the British in Vienna as essential for carrying out the project. The British therefore transferred Peter Lunn in the middle of 1953, assigning him head of the SIS station in West Berlin.

The more concrete the plans for the tunnel project became, the more important it was to find out where precisely the cables ran and which of these cables might be of interest. Berlin had been a point of intersection for European communication lines in the late 1930s. These lines were later used by Soviet authorities for military and civil communications. The CIA succeeded in recruiting a number of people who worked for the postal and telecommunication services in East Berlin. These people provided information about the locations and users of the various long-distance cables in and around Berlin. According to the assessment of the information that had been gathered, there were only two places in the city through which important lines ran: one was near Anhalter Station and the other in the immediate vicinity of the sector border in Altglienicke.

Lunn and Harvey decided to build their tunnel in Altglienicke, probably because such an operation near the border in the southwestern part of Berlin would draw less attention than it would in the city centre. In January 1953, one of the agents who had been recruited by the CIA tapped a line in an East German telephone exchange and recorded 15 minutes of conversation. The SIS evaluated the recording and came to the conclusion the content was unique and of great interest.[7]

Once the best location for the operation had been determined, a detailed presentation was prepared for the then director of the CIA, Allen Dulles. The plan, which was approved by Dulles, envisioned digging a tunnel from a warehouse within the American sector of Berlin to the long-distance cables in the eastern part of the city. So extensive was the scope of the project that spending cuts had to be made elsewhere. We know today that it swallowed up at least U.S. $6 million. This was a lot of money for a secret operation in the mid-1950s and demonstrates the importance attached to it by Western intelligence.

The British contribution would not be financial. The SIS would instead carry out the important task of wiretapping as the Americans lacked the necessary expertise. It was agreed that both the British and the Americans would share access to the intelligence that was gathered.

A CIA delegation visited London on 22 October 1953 to discuss the details of the project with its British partners, and another meeting took place in the same city from 15 to 18 December. Based on the experiences gained by the British in Vienna, several details had to be sorted out. It was decided that all recorded telephone conversations would be evaluated in London while all telex messages, some of them encrypted, would be examined in Washington. In addition, a small team was to monitor the most important lines on site in Berlin so that, if necessary, a report could be made without delay.

The planners originally estimated at least 158 people would be needed for the evaluation of the material obtained. This number ended up being closer to 600 across the United States and Great Britain. The declassified CIA report on the Berlin spy tunnel sheds light on an important matter in this regard. Both the CIA and the SIS were concerned about how secrecy was to be maintained among the many translators required to evaluate Russian-language communications. During the tunnel operation in Vienna, the British had relied upon a few civilians from Poland and Belarus for the translation work but, for the quantity of material the Berlin operation was expected to produce, the number of personnel would need to be far greater. It was feared a traitor might be hidden among the newly recruited translators. This was one of the problems discussed at the meeting in London in December 1953 but, as it turned out, it was not the translators that would be the problem. The traitor had already been present at the negotiating table, where only 14 people had been in attendance. His name was George Blake.

In March 1954, four Americans met the landowner Hermann Massante in Berlin and requested he let his property at Schönbergweg 11 in Rudow, in the district of Neukölln, to the American occupation forces. Within 24 hours, a generously remunerated 10-year lease was signed for the 37,000-square-metre site. In the

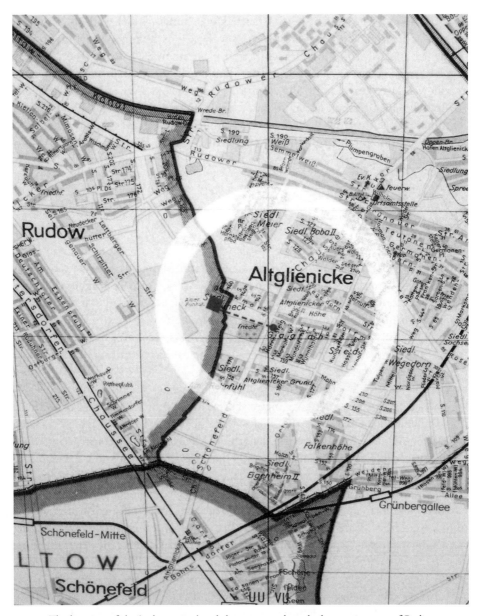

The location of the 'radar station' and the spy tunnel marked on a city map of Berlin.

following months, the Americans constructed three buildings there. The sector border lay only approximately 150 metres away. As was usual with the construction projects of the Americans in Berlin, companies and civil engineers based in the city were involved in the construction of these new buildings. The normal procedure was to be followed so as to avoid drawing attention. Nevertheless, an oversized cellar in one of the buildings became a topic of conversation among the construction workers.[8] By August 1954, the three buildings were complete. The site was publicly described as a 'radar station', something that was perfectly plausible given Schönefeld Airport lay not too far away. The Americans would naturally be interested in aerial activity in the area.

Master craftsmanship

The construction of the tunnel

The largest of the three buildings of the 'radar station' resembled a warehouse, and it was from there that specialists from the U.S. Army Corps of Engineers started digging the tunnel in the autumn of 1954. A vertical access shaft was to lead to a horizontal tunnel, and this tunnel had to be almost two metres in diameter. For every 50 centimetres of the length of the tunnel that was dug, five prefabricated curved steel segmental liners were bolted together, thereby forming a tube whose inner diameter was 1.94 metres. Loose earth was pressed into the small cavity between the steel segments and the soil to ensure greater stability. The tunnel was lengthened in this way metre by metre. It was hard work in cramped conditions. The tunnel workers had to be supplied with sufficient fresh air, for which reason a ventilation pipe extended the entire length of the tunnel. After construction work had been completed, the temperature in the tunnel was regulated through this pipe. An air-conditioning system was installed in an approximately 2.5-metre-long chamber at the end of the tunnel.

There were further challenges during construction. It was originally intended the tunnel would lie 5.2 metres under the surface. However, after only a few days, the tunnelling team came across groundwater at roughly that depth. The Allies therefore decided to renew their efforts at a depth of just 2.7 metres. This meant greater care would have to be taken with regard to soundproofing and air-conditioning. On 28 February 1955, work was complete. More than 3,000 tonnes of earth had been removed and replaced with 125 tonnes of steel.[9] The tunnel was approximately 450 metres long. It started under the warehouse of the 'radar station' and ended directly underneath Schönefelder Chaussee. More than 300 metres of the tunnel lay in the Soviet sector and thus in East German territory.

Now the installation of the listening equipment could commence. This equipment was kept in a chamber, known as the preamplifier room, located in the last 20 metres of the tunnel. All of the technical equipment needed to amplify the tapped signals

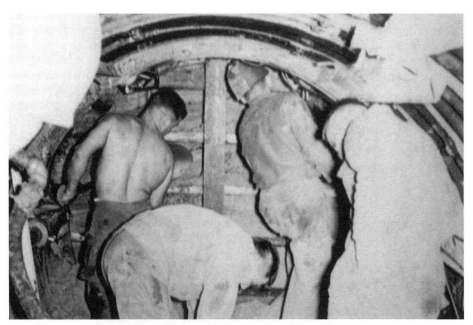

American special units built the Berlin spy tunnel from the autumn of 1954 until the spring of 1955.

Photo of the interior of the preamplifier room in the Berlin spy tunnel immediately after its completion in 1955.

An American Ampex 350 tape recorder. It was this type of device that was used to record the information obtained from the Berlin spy tunnel.

was installed in this room, which looked like a cross between a submarine's interior and a telecommunications office. The installation work lasted until 28 March; at the same time, the inside of the tunnel was covered and insulated so as to prevent high humidity and subsequent equipment failure.

Once the American pioneers had completed their work, the British pioneers took on the task of digging a vertical shaft from the end of the tunnel up to the point where the three long-distance cables were to be tapped. According to the assessment of the Americans, this was by far the most delicate job of the entire operation. The cables lay just 70 centimetres below the surface. The shaft had to be large enough for a man to work in and strong enough so the earth around it would not cave in. The British had been seeking a solution to this problem since the end of 1953 and had dug multiple test shafts on English soil. One method of shaft construction, nicknamed 'mole', was further tested at the British airbase in Gatow in the summer of 1954 to see whether it would work in the soil of Berlin.

In parallel to the insulation work on the preamplifier room, the British commenced construction of the vertical shaft in March 1955. Three weeks were needed for the British to gradually work their way up to the cable harnesses.[10] It had taken seven months for the horizontal tunnel, the preamplifier room and the vertical shaft to be completed. The task of tapping the cables would be the next challenge. The tapping method used in the Berlin spy tunnel was capacitive coupling, a technically complex technique in which the derived signals had to be amplified. The preamplifiers therefore had to be in close proximity to the tapped cables.[11]

The first long-distance cable was successfully tapped on 11 May 1955 and the second on 21 May. The third, designated FK150, was in poor condition and could not be tapped until 2 August. The three cable harnesses together contained a total of 184 telephone lines: 93 for public telephone traffic, 39 for Soviet communications and 52 for special purposes. In addition, 89 telegraph lines ran through the cable harnesses: 42 for public communications, 36 for Soviet authorities and 11 for special purposes.[12] All lines, aside from a few for public telephone traffic, had been tapped, and the information was recorded in the basement of the warehouse. At least 200 Ampex 350 tape recorders had been set up there.

During the construction and operation of the tunnel, various precautionary measures were taken due to the fact that the 'radar station' lay within visual range of the East German security forces that routinely patrolled the frontier. The many tonnes of tunnel segments, and the large numbers of personnel, were transported to the site, often at night, in covered trucks. An observation post at the site watched the area along the course of the tunnel around the clock. All activity on the eastern side of the border was documented so that any potential problems could be identified in advance. In the tunnel itself were two lockable steel doors, one in front of and the other behind the preamplifier room. Finally, and perhaps most importantly, attached to the tunnel was an explosive cord 12 metres long and about as thick as a garden hose. Should the tunnel be discovered, it was to be detonated at the point where it crossed the border so the ground around it would cave in and crush anything of importance.

The ace of trumps of the East

The double agent George Blake

George Blake was born in Holland in 1922 to a Dutch woman and a Turkish man. He was active in the Dutch resistance from 1940 to 1943 and then fled to Great Britain. From 1944, he worked for British intelligence and was committed to operations abroad. He was posted to the British legation in South Korea in 1948 and taken prisoner by the North Koreans when the Korean War broke out in 1950. Unbeknown to his fellow prisoners, Blake offered his services to the Soviet Union. This was not the result of money or coercion. He took this step because he believed in the idea of communism and felt he had been on the wrong side until then.[13] He continued to work for British intelligence when he returned to England in 1953 but, in the years that followed, he revealed to the KGB the details of all the operations in which he was directly involved or about which he could obtain information.

George Blake and his new Soviet case officer, Sergei Kondrashov, met for the first time in London at the end of October 1953. Kondrashov had been transferred to the Soviet embassy in London to look after the new double agent whose code name was 'Diamond'. Blake provided his case officer with lists and documents at this first meeting, among which were details of Operation *Silver*—the British tunnel project in Vienna. Afterwards, Blake and Kondrashov rendezvoused regularly, in the utmost secrecy, and it was on 18 January 1954 that Blake handed over the minutes of the meeting that had taken place between the CIA and the SIS in December 1953. He delivered a full report on the Anglo-American tunnel operation on 12 February 1954. The KGB had thus been informed of the plans for the Berlin spy tunnel even before the site for the 'radar station' had been leased.

The KGB decided to take no action against the construction of the tunnel to begin with, as it wanted to protect its spy in England.[14] Only a handful of Soviet officials were aware of the project. It was only when Blake left the technical department of the SIS at the beginning of 1955 and was, by coincidence, transferred to the SIS station in Berlin that the Soviets considered taking measures against the tunnel. Yevgeny Pitranov, the head of the Soviet station in Karlshorst, Berlin, and an officer with considerable experience in counterespionage, only learnt of the existence of the tunnel when it was put into operation. In order to find out what information the West could actually obtain by tapping the telephone lines, Pitranov went to the Soviet telecommunications centre and recorded some of the telephone traffic himself. He then played back these recordings for Marshal Andrei Antonovich Grechko, who was the commander in chief of the Group of Soviet Forces in Germany (GSFG). The marshal was horrified by what military intelligence could be gained from randomly recorded telephone conversations. He immediately saw to it that countermeasures were taken. First, a general order outlining security regulations for telephone calls was issued to the troops. Although such regulations already existed, this new order was intended to reinforce awareness of possible problems in security when communicating over the telephone. Second, Pitranov had to formulate a plan to seemingly discover the tunnel by chance.[15] The final decision on this matter would, of course, be made in Moscow. At no point though was serious consideration given to the idea of transmitting false information through the wiretapped cables. This was confirmed and justified most clearly by Kondrashov in a 1997 interview.[16] The deliberate production and targeted distribution of false information would have required tremendous effort. In addition, the West had other sources of information, so any false information might have been recognised as such at quite an early stage. This would have put Blake in danger. Kondrashov emphasised in the interview that Blake was of great importance to the KGB and that his protection was therefore given the highest priority.

After the first cable in the tunnel had been tapped in May 1955, the tapes with the recorded material were flown out of Berlin every two days. The material was then

The former Soviet case officer Sergei A. Kondrashov speaking about the spy tunnel during an interview at the Allied Museum in Zehlendorf, Berlin, in September 1997.

evaluated in London and Washington. The team in London, which comprised more than 300 specialists, occupied itself in the following months with the transcription and translation of the recorded matter.

The tunnel is busted

The discovery of the tunnel from the point of view of the East and the West

It had been clear to the British and the Americans from the very beginning of Operation *Gold* that the tunnel would remain undiscovered for only a limited time. Whether it was a matter of months or years could not be predicted. The two greatest security issues were, first, the many hundreds of workers in London and Washington who were involved in the evaluation of the recordings and, second, the physical instability of one of the three cable harnesses. The harness designated FK150 had been troublesome from the outset and had required more time to be tapped successfully.[17] The Americans expected that one of these two issues would eventually lead to the discovery of the tunnel.

That time came in April 1956. Heavy rainfall had rendered several telephone lines inoperable, and 3,000 metres of defective line between Karlshorst and Mahlow had to be replaced on 16 April. More lines failed in the days of rain that followed. These included the lines of communication between Moscow and the early warning air-defence system in East Germany, in addition to the numerous lines leading to and from the Soviet military headquarters in Wünsdorf. The authorities in East Berlin identified significant problems with FK150 on 18 and 19 April and partially resolved them on 20 April. The CIA and the SIS learnt about all of this from the conversations they were listening to and from their contacts at the telecommunications office in

East Berlin. It was also clear from the recorded conversations that problems with communications persisted and that further failures and repairs could be expected. The Western intelligence agencies in Berlin could only hope the technicians tasked with searching for defective cables would not stumble across the tunnel.

However, in the early hours of Sunday 22 April, towards 1am, a platoon of approximately 40 men appeared near Schönefelder Chaussee and dug up the road with hoes and shovels. This activity was spotted from the 'radar station', so the head of tunnel operations, William Harvey, was alerted immediately. Shortly before 2am, the workers reached the point where the cables had been tapped, although they did not know at that stage precisely what it was that they had unearthed. The conversations that took place between the Soviet and East German workers upon their discovery could be overhead at the 'radar station' through microphones that had been installed in the shaft and in the preamplifier room. While Harvey and his colleagues would have been keen to know what was being discussed, one thing was already clear in those early morning hours—after 11 months and 11 days, the operations of the spy tunnel had come to an end.

The Anglo-American team wanted to find out from the discussions of the workers whether it was chance or treason that had led to the discovery of the tunnel. Those discussions indicated that neither the East German technicians nor the Soviet officers knew what they had come across in the process of searching for defective lines. More high-ranking Soviet officers arrived over the course of the next few hours. By 4:15am, it had become clear to the discoverers that the exposed cables had been tapped. It would only be a matter of hours before the unearthing of the vertical shaft and then the tunnel.

The security of the 'radar station' was threatened, as the tunnel led directly to the basement of its warehouse. It had been in preparation for such a situation that the CIA had rigged the tunnel with explosives. William Harvey sent his close associate Hugh Montgomery that Sunday morning to the commandant of the American sector of Berlin, Major-General Charles Dasher, to ask for permission to detonate the explosives. Montgomery found Dasher at the yacht club in Wannsee and described the situation to him. Dasher wanted to know whether the detonation might wound or kill Soviet soldiers or East German telecommunications technicians. Montgomery could not rule out that possibility. Given such uncertainty, Dasher denied the request to blow up the tunnel. Montgomery returned to the 'radar station' and conveyed the news to Harvey.[18] As a result, Harvey decided a large-calibre machine gun would be positioned on the American side of the tunnel to act as a deterrent against any advance towards the 'radar station'.

The vertical shaft under the tapped cables was discovered towards 11:45am on 22 April, as were the tunnel and the preamplifier room an hour later. The East Germans and Soviets could hardly believe what they saw. 'I'm at a loss for words!' or 'It's incredible!' were statements that could be heard by the CIA staff at the

Bernd von Kostka in conversation with Hugh Montgomery (centre), who worked for the CIA in Berlin and was present when the spy tunnel was discovered in 1956.

'radar station', who were still able to listen to what was being said thanks to the microphone within the preamplifier room.[19] At 3:35pm, all communication lines in the preamplifier room were cut. Fifteen minutes later, the microphone was discovered and disconnected. No more information flowed through the tunnel.

As Harvey had foreseen, Soviet soldiers followed the course of the tunnel in the hours that followed. They approached the American side of the tunnel but turned back when told to do so at gunpoint. Harvey had even seen to it that there could be no mistake as to the location of the sector boundary inside the tunnel. Sandbags had been piled on top of one another with a cardboard sign attached to them which stated: 'You are entering the American sector.'

'PBJOINTLY' was over. The tunnel had been operational for more than 11 months and had probably been the most extensive and most important source of intelligence on East Germany and the Soviet troops stationed there during that time. The CIA and the SIS had been convinced the discovery of the tunnel had been brought about by the heavy rainfalls in April and the poor condition of the telephone lines. It did not appear as if treason had played a role.

Even during the planning phase, the Anglo-American team had considered the consequences of a discovery of the tunnel. It had taken the view the Soviet Union would be extremely unlikely to admit publicly that its telephone lines in East Berlin had been tapped. The assumption was that the Soviet Union would want to avoid embarrassment on the world stage. However, to the surprise of the West, the Soviets would initiate a propaganda campaign in the following weeks.

A small number of people in Moscow and East Berlin had been aware of the spy tunnel from the moment it had been planned. To protect their source of information—the top spy George Blake—the Soviet side had to find a suitable time to make a seemingly accidental discovery. That time came on 18–19 April 1956 for two important reasons. First, a number of telephone lines had been damaged in the rainfalls in the middle of April, and not only those that had been tapped. The British and the Americans were aware from the telephone traffic they monitored that faulty lines of communication were not unusual. It made perfect sense that the lines would need to be checked and repaired. Second, the discovery of the tunnel had become desirable at that moment from the point of view of Soviet foreign policy. Nikita Khrushchev, as later confirmed by Sergei Kondrashov, personally gave his approval for the discovery of the tunnel to go ahead on 22 April 1956. Why did Khrushchev need to be involved in the making of this decision at all? The Soviet leader was, at that moment, on a state visit to Great Britain for several days. The delegation that accompanied him included Kondrashov, who was Blake's superior. The talks being held in London had been prompted by the Suez Crisis, which, as it turned out, would worsen throughout 1956 and escalate into an armed conflict that autumn. Kondrashov described the talks in Great Britain as very difficult. The decision to discover the Berlin spy tunnel was a part of the Soviet strategy for their negotiations with the British.[20] Specifically, even though both sides knew the British had been involved in the construction and operation of the spy tunnel, the Soviet Union sought to gain an edge in the talks by resisting the urge to pull the British into the espionage spotlight.

The 'accidental' discovery of the tunnel had been carefully thought-out. The Soviet ambassador in East Berlin, Georgy M. Pushkin, was told on 22 April to prepare to make an official protest to the Americans. Detailed instructions on how to deal with the spy tunnel arrived from Moscow the following day. Points 2 and 5 of those instructions should be highlighted here. Point 2 stated that correspondents from East and West Berlin should be invited to inspect the tunnel, and point 5 made it clear that, even though the tunnel had been equipped with British technology, blame was to be directed solely towards the Americans. In accordance with Soviet information policy, the commandant of the Soviet garrison in Berlin, Colonel Ivan Kotsyuba, deliberately made no mention of the British in his statements to the press.

Kotsyuba, on the instructions of Moscow, held a press conference in Karlshorst, Berlin, after which the members of the national and international press that had been invited went by bus to the point on Schönefelder Chaussee where the tapped lines had been exposed. Lothar Löwe was the Berlin correspondent for a British newspaper at the time. He had been rather surprised to receive an invitation to a press conference in Karlshorst. Nothing like this had ever happened before and all the journalists were eager to find out what the press conference would be about.[21] When Heinz Junge, one of three official photographers who were supposed to take photos for the East German press, arrived in Karlshorst, he was asked several times by a Soviet officer whether he had his flashlight with him. As it was as bright as day, Junge could not understand why he would need his flashlight, but the answer to this question became clear when he and the other representatives of the press were led into the tunnel.[22] While the preamplifier room was brightly lit by neon tubes along its 20-metre length, this was not the case for the rest of the tunnel. It was only sparsely illuminated by light bulbs.

The representatives of the press were filled with excitement. It was not every day they could report a story quite like this. The media coverage in the days that followed was extensive. Further press meetings were held at which Soviet representatives were shown the tunnel and the tapped lines. The international press also showed great interest in the tunnel, with stories appearing in *Le Figaro*, *The Times*, *Life*, and the *New York Herald Tribune*, as well as many other publications. The most detailed, and of course most contradictory, reporting took place in East

> In accordance with the chain of command, Kotsiuba, the deputy of our commandant, yesterday attempted to meet with the American commander General Dasher, who refused a meeting at that time. The meeting took place today. Kotsiuba issued a verbal protest to the Americans.
>
> Dasher became extremely irritable. He said, "We did not construct the underground tunnel. Only ordinary military communications installations are located in this district."
>
> When Kotsiuba disputed the veracity of this version, Dasher said that they would establish a commission and conduct investigations, and promised to inform our commandant on the progress of investigations.
>
> We would like to present the following recommendations for your consideration:
> 1. The chief of staff of the Soviet army should file a written protest to the headquarters of the American army in Europe, including a publication of it in print.
> 2. Invite accredited correspondents from East as well as from West Berlin to observe the object.
> 3. Give permission to our German friends to comment in print on this issue, but not before the publication of our protest.
> 4. It would be advisable to dispatch a group of our experts to investigate the equipment.
> 5. Regardless of the fact that the tunnel contains British equipment, all accusations in print should be addressed exclusively to the Americans.
>
> Your orders to invite the American commander to the object and the creation of a joint commission according to the policy of the commandant's office have been enacted.
>
> A. Grechko
> G. Pushkin
> E. Pitovranov
>
> 23 April, 1956
> Sent to Comrades

Soviet telex message of 23 April 1956 which contains recommendations on how to handle the discovery of the spy tunnel.

and West Berlin. *Neues Deutschland*, the official newspaper of the governing Socialist Unity Party of Germany (SED) in East Germany, denounced the underground activities of the Americans for days on end.

Western newspapers were dependent on information and speculation from the East, as there was only one response they could obtain from American officials: 'No comment!' CIA files reveal that the Americans and the British were completely unprepared for the Soviet press offensive. Nevertheless, the CIA could be reasonably satisfied with the reporting in the Western press, which tended to be quite favourable. 'The Tunnel of Love', 'Wonderful Tunnel', and 'Money Well Spent' were some of the headlines at that time.[23] The American people generally seemed to be happy that their intelligence service was capable of carrying out a spectacular and successful operation in the midst of the Cold War.

The Eastern propaganda campaign did not end with the reporting in the daily press. In the weeks that followed, the entrance to the tunnel was enlarged and an exit was created at roughly the 180-metre mark along the tunnel. This made the tunnel accessible to larger groups of visitors. Companies and political groups made day trips to the Berlin spy tunnel during the summer months of 1956. By the time this tourist attraction closed that autumn, tens of thousands of visitors, including West Berliners, had viewed the interior of the tunnel.

After that, approximately 300 metres of the length of the tunnel on the eastern side of the frontier were completely unearthed and disposed of. This work required trucks, excavators and heavy equipment. The damage thereby caused to the ground above the tunnel was considerable. The property under which the tunnel ran in East Berlin belonged to farmer Paul Noack, who had planted 1,100 saplings in his orchard there in 1954. A large part of the orchard was destroyed during the removal of the tunnel. Noack was faced with the prospect of financial ruin. Who was to pay for the cost of the damage? An unofficial agreement was reached whereby Noack would receive 6,500 marks from the East German government if he agreed to sue the Senate of West Berlin.[24] It was not necessarily the need to compensate Noack that was the issue for the East German government. Rather, given there were bound to be further costs incurred for the disposal of the tunnel, the purpose of the agreement that had been made with Noack was to test whether further demands for compensation from the West could be made with success. The introduction of this legal aspect into the story of the tunnel meant there remained plenty for the

Collage of various newspapers from the time of the discovery of the spy tunnel in April 1956. The press around the world reported on the event.

press to report, and the legal proceedings that followed were taken very seriously by the East German government. The renowned lawyer Dr Friedrich Karl Kaul took on the case on behalf of Paul Noack. The lawsuit was filed in January 1957 and rejected that November on the grounds that the defendant—the Senate of West Berlin—had possessed no knowledge of the tunnel. Dr Kaul lodged an appeal with the Berlin Supreme Court in February 1958, which demonstrates the persistence with which the East approached the question of the spy tunnel. With the rejection of this appeal in July 1958, publicity surrounding the tunnel quickly came to an end.

Everyone enjoys success

The value of the information and the fate of George Blake

By the time the tunnel operation came to an end on 22 April 1956, 368,000 telephone conversations in Russian, and 75,000 in German, had been sent to London for evaluation. In Washington, 350 people concentrated on the evaluation of telex messages—18,000 tapes in Russian and 11,000 in German. The analysis work lasted until September 1958.[25]

The intercepted information was varied in content. In addition to the many private conversations that enabled conclusions to be drawn about the morale of the troops, much information of military value was gathered, and it is this by which the success of the tunnel can be measured. In the mid-1950s, the tunnel was the most important and most reliable source of information for Western intelligence on the activity and organisation of Soviet and East German forces in East Germany. The names of thousands of Soviet officers and the units to which they belonged

The British *Daily Express* reports on the conviction of George Blake on 20 June 1961.

could be ascertained. Many of those units had never previously been identified, but the information from the tunnel enabled their locations to be determined. The training schedules and deployment plans of Soviet formations were now known. Information was obtained on the equipment and weaponry of Soviet air forces in East Germany and Poland. People and sites associated with the Soviet nuclear energy programme were identified, and knowledge was gained on Soviet intelligence and communications in East Germany.[26]

While the vast quantity of information gave the British and the Americans a better understanding of the Soviet armed forces, it was also possible to draw conclusions from what did not flow through the tunnel. For example, there was nothing in the intercepted traffic indicative of Soviet plans for an offensive from East Germany against West Berlin or West Germany.

George Blake worked at the SIS station in Berlin, which was located at the headquarters of the British military occupation forces at the Olympic Stadium, from 1955 to 1959. The SIS had approximately 100 people in Berlin at the time. Blake worked in a department that was responsible on the one hand for obtaining political information and on the other for infiltrating the Soviet headquarters in Karlshorst. This role enabled him to continue working safely as a double agent for the KGB. No one at that stage made a connection between him and the discovery of the spy tunnel.[27] Blake returned to London in 1959 and was transferred to Lebanon in 1960.

He was recalled to London around Easter 1961 for important talks. Upon his arrival, he was confronted with charges of espionage for the Soviet Union. A defector had informed British intelligence of Blake's activities. Blake denied the charges at first, but eventually confessed to having worked for years as a double agent. He was tried in England a month later and sentenced to 42 years in prison, the longest sentence ever handed down in the country.

Ironically, this long sentence in a British maximum-security prison earned Blake the sympathy of fellow inmates who would later help him escape. That escape took place in 1966.[28] He hid from the authorities in England for some time before escaping to East Berlin and being taken from there to Moscow. Blake lived in Russia until his death on 26 December 2020. A pension from the KGB enabled him to make a good living. He had been unable to return to Great Britain even after the end of the Cold War. There had still been a warrant for his arrest, which would have required he serve the remainder of his sentence.

On 11 November 2012, Russian state-owned television broadcast a documentary about George Blake. It was a kind of homage from Russia to its top spy on the occasion of his 90th birthday. The Russian television team had conducted research and shot footage in and around Berlin several months beforehand, uncovering details on the tunnel operation that had not been available in Russia. President Vladimir Putin, who had himself been a KGB agent for several years, conveyed his congratulations in a personal message and paid tribute to Blake's services. Perhaps the Russians remained thankful even after so many years due to the fact that Blake had conducted espionage not out of a desire for money but rather from a sense of political conviction. This makes him stand out among the many spies of the Cold War era.[29]

The secret passage lies dormant

Operation Radar *in 1967 and the rediscovery of the tunnel in 1997*

In contrast to the spectacular discovery of the tunnel in 1956, an operation was planned by the Stasi at the beginning of 1967 that was not intended to be brought to public attention. It was called Operation *Radar*. Main Division I of the Stasi wanted soldiers armed with submachine guns and hand grenades to infiltrate the section of tunnel that was still expected to exist immediately beneath the sector border. The objective of this operation was to secure the border inside the tunnel, as the Stasi suspected that 150 metres of it still lay in the territory of East Berlin. The soldiers were to be prepared to encounter enemy troops and to force them back to the sector border.[30] When the operation was finally carried out between 17 and 20 July 1967, the result came as a surprise to the Stasi.

The first day was taken up with the task of drilling into the ground in an effort to find the tunnel. Its precise location was determined on 18 July. The remnants of sandbags had gotten caught on the large drills. Larger holes were thereupon dug so a clearer picture of the situation could be obtained; all that was found was loose soil, muddy earth and rotten sandbags. The planned infiltration of the tunnel and the underground advance to the sector border could not be conducted, as almost the entire length of the tunnel in the territory of East Berlin had been removed from the ground in 1956. This fact became apparent, to those who had planned Operation *Radar*, by 20 July 1967.

This episode reveals how little the Stasi had been involved in the discovery of the tunnel and how little it was aware of Soviet activities. It was only after Operation *Radar* in 1967 that Main Division I could be certain there no longer existed an underground tunnel leading from Rudow to Altglienicke. Interestingly, the Stasi report on the operation created the impression that there had still been a tunnel and that it had been rendered inaccessible. Great care had been taken in the writing of the report to avoid portraying the operation as a failure.[31]

Following the discovery of the tunnel, and the removal of that part of it in East Berlin, the entrance in the basement of the warehouse at the site of the American 'radar station' was filled in. Nevertheless, the Americans continued to carry out operations on the site and only gave it up in 1983. From October of that year, it was once more at the disposal of Hermann Massante, the original owner of the land. Over the course of the next four years, a legal dispute arose between him and the building and housing inspectorate of Neukölln because, contrary to what had been requested of him, he did not want to demolish the three buildings at the site.[32] They were only demolished once the property was sold to a real estate investor in 1989, although nothing was done to remove and dispose of the tunnel. It therefore remained where it was.

Only after the reunification of Germany did the Senate of Berlin, in 1992, plan to undertake construction work on the site of the former American 'radar station'. It was not until 1997 that this work began. When it did, parts of the tunnel were uncovered. The Allied Museum immediately expressed its interest and managed to secure a large segment of the tunnel. Sergei Kondrashov, who had been George Blake's KGB case officer, and David Murphy, who had worked for the CIA, launched their book *Die unsichtbare Front* on 22 September 1997 in front of the uncovered tunnel. The segment secured by the Allied Museum was approximately seven metres long and was soon transported to the museum for restoration. It has been on display there since 1998 as part of an exhibition on the Berlin spy tunnel. A few more years passed before further sections of the tunnel were uncovered. This was when work was being done on extending the motorway to Schönefeld. The Allied Museum once more expressed its interest, obtaining a roughly six-metre-long segment of the

The last segments of the Berlin spy tunnel were removed during the construction of the A 113 motorway. Aerial view from 2005.

tunnel in 2005 and storing it in a depot. This second segment was put on display for a special exhibition at the Allied Museum in 2006. The remaining steel segments dug out of the ground, in what had once been the American sector, were disposed of. With that, the last remnants of the tunnel had been removed from Berlin soil. In 2010, the Senate of Berlin erected a column where the spy tunnel had once been in Altglienicke, reminding cyclists and pedestrians of what had been a spectacular episode in the history of the Cold War in Berlin.

Sensational discovery

The second life of the tunnel in Mecklenburg-Vorpommern

It seemed as if the story of the Berlin spy tunnel had come to an end once its remnants had been removed from the ground. That changed in August 2012. Werner Sobolewski from Pasewalk phoned the Allied Museum and said: 'I think there are parts of the Berlin spy tunnel in Pasewalk Forest.' This statement seemed strange at first but the more Sobolewski spoke of the buried tunnel elements, the more credible the story became. The tunnel expert from the Allied Museum visited the forest with Sobolewski a few days later and examined the elements of the tunnel that had been partially exposed by heavy rain and inclement weather a year or two earlier. There was no doubt they were original parts of the Berlin spy tunnel. It was a sensational discovery, all the more so because no one could explain how the tunnel elements had ended up there. This unexpected development was reported in several national and international newspapers. Research undertaken by the Allied Museum since then has revealed the details of what happened.

Remains of the Berlin spy tunnel lying in Pasewalk Forest.

The removal of the tunnel in Altglienicke in 1956.

In the autumn of 1956, the East German National People's Army (NVA), which had only been founded that year, assigned five officers and 45 enlisted personnel the task of removing and disposing of the tunnel. According to Harald Freitag, a non-commissioned officer involved in the removal of the tunnel between 10 October and 30 November 1956, these were hand-picked soldiers from the 2nd Pioneer Regiment. As the tunnel segments were uncovered by excavators and lifted out by cranes, the pioneer troops immediately recognised the solid components could be of military use. Although photographs of the tunnel were not allowed, the soldiers took some pictures anyway. Freitag commented in 2012 that the tunnel struck him as an outstanding and exemplary piece of construction and that he regarded the ability of the Americans to build it in complete secrecy as even more impressive.[33]

Once the tunnel in Altglienicke had been removed, its parts were cut into smaller pieces for transportation. These pieces, two to four metres long, were loaded onto trucks and taken to the various pioneer units in East Germany so they could be reused in the construction of emplacements, shelters and command centres. Several segments arrived at the garrison of the 5th Pioneer Regiment in Pasewalk, at least two of which were buried in the forest in order to serve as permanent command shelters for pioneer exercises.

East German pioneer units bury parts of the spy tunnel during an exercise in the forest in 1960.

According to Freitag, the removal and transport of the tunnel segments was closely monitored by the Western military liaison missions. The vehicles belonging to the military missions even followed the trucks as they made their way to the pioneer units. The Western powers were therefore fully aware of what was going on, but it somehow seems as if this awareness faded in the decades that followed. The final CIA report on the tunnel makes no mention of this militarily relevant information, and the historical department of the CIA only learnt of it from the newspapers in 2012.

The buried tunnel segments were forgotten after the fall of the Berlin Wall and remained so until discovered and recognised by Sobolewski in 2012. Sobolewski had been a workman at an NVA garrison in the 1980s, and one of his tasks at that time was to ascertain whether some of the segments there could be used as cement silos for planned construction projects. He remembered this when he later saw the partially exposed segments in the forest. A few months after that, two of those segments were removed from the ground in Pasewalk and transported to the depot of the Allied Museum in Berlin.

Even these elements of the tunnel were not the last to be found. Two more segments were discovered in storage in Mecklenburg-Vorpommern at the end of 2013. They were in private ownership and their owner had no idea of their significance until he saw the story in the newspapers about the discovery in Pasewalk. He had been planning to build a house at the time of reunification and had acquired the segments with the idea of assembling a cement silo. That did not come to pass, and the segments were instead used, in stark contrast to their original purpose, for storing wood and enclosing geese for almost 20 years. The International Spy Museum in Washington, which regards the spy tunnel as an important topic in the history of espionage, acquired these two elements so it could put them on display in a permanent exhibition.

CHAPTER FOUR

Licence to spy

Legal espionage behind the Iron Curtain

The emergence of the Allied military liaison missions in Potsdam

Glienicke Bridge extends over the Havel River and connects the cities of Berlin and Potsdam. It became known as the 'Bridge of Spies' during the Cold War. Here, at the point of intersection between East and West, three prisoner exchanges took place between the Soviet Union and the United States: the first in 1962, the second in 1985, and the third in 1986; Steven Spielberg did a Hollywood Blockbuster on the famous 1962 exchange in 2015. But it was also called the Bridge of Spies for another reason. After the construction of the Berlin Wall in 1961, the bridge was closed to all traffic and guarded by security units. Well into the 1980s, the small group of those permitted to pass through the checkpoint at the bridge included diplomats who had been approved by the East German government as well as members of the Western military liaison missions.[1] Many of them had to travel from West Berlin to East Germany via this checkpoint on a daily basis. In an interview in 2007 on the ARD television news programme *Tagesthemen*, the minister president of Brandenburg, Matthias Platzeck, remembered how he saw the bridge every day in his youth and watched the vehicles passing through the checkpoint. It was a remarkable sight for him as well as for those who lived nearby.[2]

The establishment of the military liaison missions goes back to the time of World War II when the three Allied Powers—the United States, the Soviet Union, and Great Britain—decided to force the German Reich and the Axis Powers to surrender unconditionally. The plans for the subsequent occupation of Germany were discussed by the Allies at that time. Article 2 of the Agreement on Control Machinery in Germany, which was signed on 14 November 1944, laid the foundation for the missions. It stated that each commander in chief of a zone of occupation would have attached military representatives, from each of the other zones of occupation, for liaison duties.[3] This was an idea that made perfect sense from the point of view of the wartime alliance.

After the surrender and occupation of Germany in 1945, however, a good year passed by before the first bilateral agreement between Great Britain and the Soviet Union was concluded. The Robertson-Malinin Agreement came into force on 16 September 1946 and provided for the exchange of military liaison missions, each

Philippe Mariotti takes photos for the French military liaison mission from the roof of his tour vehicle in 1983.

with up to 31 members. The British military liaison mission was officially called the British Commanders'-in-Chief Mission to the Soviet Forces in Germany (BRIXMIS). The next mutual establishment of military liaison missions was that between France and the Soviet Union in the Noiret-Malinin Agreement of 3 April 1947. The French mission was known as the Mission Militaire Française de Liaison près du haut Commandement soviétique en Allemagne (MMFL) and had a maximum of 18 members. Shortly afterwards, on 5 April 1947, the Americans and the Soviets concluded the Huebner-Malinin Agreement, according to which each mission would consist of only 14 members. The American mission was called the United States Military Liaison Mission to the Commander-in-Chief, Group of Soviet Forces (USMLM). Each of these bilateral agreements were negotiated with Mikhail Malinin, a Soviet general, and they regulated the presence and rights of the military liaison missions.[4]

The three Western missions were based in Potsdam, with the Americans in a villa on Lehnitzsee, in the district of Neu Fahrland, and the British and the French on Geschwister-Scholl-Straße in the historic part of the city. When anti-British protests outside the BRIXMIS residence in 1958 led to damage being done to the building, Soviet authorities provided the British a new villa on Seestraße, also in the historic part of Potsdam.[5]

The residence of the British military liaison mission in Potsdam between 1958 and 1990. The villa was owned by designer Wolfgang Joop from 1999–2017.

The Soviet Military Missions (SMM) were housed with the commanding officers of the three zones of occupation in West Germany: with the Americans in Frankfurt am Main, the French in Baden-Baden, and the British in Bad Salzuflen and later in Bünde.

It is noteworthy that the staff and catering of the three mission residences in Potsdam were provided by the Soviet Union. The caretakers and kitchen hands were all East German citizens. The missions always took it as given that these people would pass on any information they might overhear to the Stasi. This assumption was proven to be correct after the collapse of the East German state, when some of the mission members looked through their own files at the Stasi Records Agency in the late 1990s.

Not only were the buildings, maintenance, staff and catering provided by the Soviets, so too were the fuel vouchers needed for inspection and reconnaissance tours in East Germany. Passports for mission members were issued by the Group of Soviet Forces in Germany (GSFG). Nevertheless, it was the Soviet External Relations Branch (SERB) that was responsible for maintaining official contact between the Western military liaison missions and the Soviet side.[6]

Changing with the times

The evolving role of the military liaison missions

Article 2 of the Agreement on Control Machinery in Germany was intended by neither East nor West to create nests of spies in their zones of occupation, and it was the case that the work carried out by the missions in the first few years of their existence had little to do with intelligence and espionage. Indeed, the establishment of a military liaison mission during World War II had improved the effectiveness of two-way communications and it was foreseen that also setting up such liaison missions immediately after the war would resolve a number of practical problems. The members of these missions would ideally be military 'diplomats' who would maintain contact and foster relations with the commanders-in-chief to whom they had been assigned. Accordingly, mission members and their residences in Potsdam were granted quasi-diplomatic status to improve communications and fulfil tasks more easily. The representative nature of these missions, whereby mission members were invited to ceremonies and official occasions by the Soviet occupation authorities in East Germany, should not be understated. Soviet representatives were naturally also invited to the mission residences in Potsdam on holidays celebrated by the Western powers. An important responsibility of the missions was to safeguard the interests of their own citizens who were in other zones of occupation. Specifically, in the first few years following the end of the war, this meant, but was not exclusive to, the search for missing persons in the Soviet zone of occupation, the repatriation of the dead, and various activities associated with de-nazification. Such work was supposed to be facilitated by the

Ceremonial cutting of a cake by Soviet generals, on Torgau Day in 1976, at the villa of the American military mission.

rapport between representatives, which itself was to be fostered by conducting joint military activities and celebrating national holidays.[7]

However, the role of the military liaison missions soon changed with the beginning of the Cold War. It was against the backdrop of the Soviet blockade of Berlin in 1948 and 1949, the founding of the two German states in 1949, and the Korean War in 1950, that the nature of the tasks to be undertaken by the missions evolved. Gathering intelligence in East German territory would be one of those tasks in the decades that followed. That this was already the case as early as 1952 is demonstrated by a top-secret document delivered that year to the head of BRIXMIS. In it, the British high commissioner in West Germany wrote simply and succinctly that the head of BRIXMIS would report directly to him and that his task would be twofold: liaising with Soviet military authorities and gathering intelligence.[8]

This shift in the nature of the task necessitated mission members be better trained and equipped. While the BRIXMIS tour reports at the end of the 1940s and at the beginning of the 1950s contained imprecise drawings of the military equipment spotted in East Germany, those produced in the following years demonstrated a significant increase in professionalism. The missions were soon equipped with high-quality cameras, so there was barely any more need for sketches and drawings.

Mission personnel were specially selected and trained for duties in East Germany. With the increasing importance of intelligence in the Cold War, the training of the small number of representatives each country was permitted to send to Potsdam had to be improved. Good knowledge of Russian or German was a priority. By the end of the 1950s, the three Western military missions in Potsdam were regarded as an outstanding and reliable early warning system for any possible surprise attack by the Soviet Union in Europe.[9] They were, so to speak, the eyes and ears of the Western powers in East Germany.

Reconnaissance work was made possible thanks to the almost daily inspection tours carried out in East Germany. These tours started in West Berlin; a meeting took place before each trip so that the vehicle crews could be provided with the latest information. BRIXMIS, with its large staff of 31, usually allocated three people per tour vehicle. The French MMFL did the same, but its smaller size in terms of personnel meant fewer vehicle teams were able to be formed. The Americans often opted for inspection teams of two people so that more vehicles could be dispatched.

The uniform insignia of the French, British, and American military liaison missions in Potsdam.

For the purposes of their inspection tours, the three Western powers divided East Germany into three large operational areas designated A, B, and C. There was also one small local area surrounding Potsdam. Each large area was allocated to a different Western power with each sending two teams to patrol its allocated area. One team would be assigned to the observation of ground objectives and the other to air objectives. This meant all three Western powers together had three ground teams and three air teams covering most of East Germany. The area around Potsdam was shared on a rotating basis.[10] Responsibility for the large areas also switched once every few weeks. As a result, each Western military liaison mission had an opportunity to observe all operational areas in East Germany.

This system could only work if there was good cooperation between the three missions.[11] They maintained telephone contact with one another almost daily and held meetings once a week to ensure they did not duplicate their efforts. Each end-of-year report prepared by a mission was sent not only to its parent institutions but also to the missions of the other Western powers. Such exchange of military information could not be taken for granted, especially given that France withdrew from NATO in 1966. Yet this did not in any way impact on the bond of trust the Americans and British had developed with their French counterparts in Potsdam.

Radar and radio antennas were important objectives of the reconnaissance tours undertaken by the military liaison missions.

While on their inspection tours in East Germany, the members of the military liaison missions had to take note of any facts of military value. Where were units stationed? What was their strength? What equipment did they have? Were there any modifications to equipment that was already known to exist? Photographs of vehicles or aircraft were of particular interest, especially if they possessed new components. The pictures could then be sent to military specialists in the West for analysis. There were other questions that were obviously important from a military standpoint. Were Soviet and East German ground troops on the move? Was a member state of the Warsaw Pact conducting manoeuvres on East German soil? Where did the tactical strengths and weaknesses of the enemy lie, and what routes of advance did he use in his manoeuvres?

A valuable task carried out by the military liaison missions was the inspection of manoeuvre areas once they had been vacated by Soviet troops. Although, according to former mission members, the best-equipped and most powerful units of the Soviet armed forces were to be found in East Germany, the Western powers were able to obtain much information due to the carelessness of personnel. For example, mission members searched vacated manoeuvre areas for papers and ammunition, and even medical waste was collected in order to ascertain if any illnesses were plaguing the Soviet Army.

The teams allocated to spotting air objectives positioned themselves near the approach corridors of airfields so as to be able to take good photos of aircraft. They also drove to and photographed radar and radio transmitter installations.

When the military liaison missions were first established, the treaty partners had considered it necessary and had agreed that the mission members were to be given significant freedom of movement in each other's occupation zone for the performance of their duties. This freedom of movement was increasingly restricted the more the missions undertook intelligence activities. Even at the outset, it had been stipulated that some areas, designated Permanent Restricted Areas (PRAs), would be out of bounds to mission personnel. In East Germany, PRAs included the entire coast of the country, major areas devoted to military exercises, and the zones where air bases and large barracks lay. In the 1950s, the PRAs in East Germany covered approximately a quarter of the country. Also introduced were Temporary Restricted Areas (TRAs), which

ATTENTION ! PASSAGE OF MEMBERS OF FOREIGN MILITARY LIAISON MISSIONS PROHIBITED !

ATTENTION ! PASSAGE AUX MEMBRES des MISSIONS MILITAIRES ETRANGERES de LIAISON est INTERDIT !

ПРОЕЗД ЧЛЕНАМ ИНОСТРАННЫХ ВОЕННЫХ МИССИЙ СВЯЗИ ЗАПРЕЩЕН !

DURCHFAHRT für das Personal der ausländischen MILITÄRVERBINDUNGS - MISSIONEN ist VERBOTEN !

One of many thousands of Mission Restriction Signs in East Germany.

usually comprised zones where military exercises and manoeuvres would be held for a short time. These zones became accessible to mission personnel after the manoeuvres had drawn to a close.

Updated information on TRAs and PRAs was officially communicated to the Western missions by SERB. The extent of these restricted areas varied over the decades, but it usually amounted to between 25 and 33 per cent of the total area of East Germany.[12] The more territory restricted, the more difficult it was for the missions to do their work. The Western military liaison missions protested against the significant degree to which East German territory was off limits. When this did not help, it was decided the territory accessible to the Soviet missions in West Germany would be reduced. This approach, whereby the treatment of the Soviet missions would mirror that of the Western missions, proved to be the most effective countermeasure in dealing with the Soviet Union, as it was often the case that restrictions in East Germany would be eased shortly thereafter.

Another means by which East German authorities restricted the freedom of movement of the Western missions was to put up what were called Mission Restriction Signs. These signs first appeared in East Germany in the mid-1950s and declared in four languages that the passage of personnel of the foreign military liaison missions was forbidden. The number of such signs increased considerably over the course of the following three decades. Mission members tended to ignore them as they had no legal basis and had not been agreed on at the time the missions had been established. Some members even regarded the signs as souvenirs, unscrewing them or sawing them off and throwing them into the boots of their tour vehicles.

The equipment of the military liaison missions changed over time. The vehicles in particular were frequently modified so they could continue to cope with the demands of the reconnaissance tours. Cars made by Opel and Mercedes were often used in the 1970s, while off-road vehicles built by Range Rover or Jeep were also occasionally seen. The vehicles were usually four-wheel drives and were optionally fitted with large fuel tanks. At the beginning of the 1980s, the three Western military liaison missions primarily employed Mercedes off-road vehicles, and this continued to be the case until the missions were disbanded in 1990. This vehicle was the Mercedes-Benz G-Class; the Americans had 16 of them in the mid-1980s. In addition to the optional extras offered by the manufacturers, further modifications were made by each of the three Western missions. For example, a towbar coupling and an electric winch could be attached to the front bumper of a vehicle, both of which would be protected by a ram bar. A modified lighting system enabled external lights to be switched on or off individually and headlights to be dimmed gradually. A round or square hatch in the roof made it possible to pop out and take photos quickly. Roll bars and additional components that strengthened the roof helped to improve safety in the event of an accident and provided footholds for climbing onto the roof; even the chassis and undercoating were reinforced. Additional fuel tanks were installed so longer trips could be made without the need to refuel. The Americans and the British also saw to it that their vehicles were equipped with infrared technology for night-time driving.[13]

Even though the three Western military liaison missions had residences in Potsdam manned day and night, West Berlin remained their main base of operations. Vehicles were repaired, and sometimes even modified, in garages in West Berlin. Furthermore, the military liaison missions possessed additional personnel who were not assigned to reconnaissance tours in East Germany; these people lived in West Berlin with their families. As had been stipulated in the agreements that had been made, a total of only 63 soldiers from the West could be assigned to the military liaison missions to the GSFG. That was, therefore, 63 who were permitted to conduct inspection tours in East Germany. Those who remained in West Berlin—sometimes up to 50 people per occupation sector—analysed and passed on the intelligence that had been gathered. The Americans were based at Föhrenweg 19–21 in the locality of Dahlem; the French in House 8 at their headquarters, 'Quartier Napoleon', in the northern part of Berlin; and the British on the top floor of the 'London Block' at the British headquarters at the Berlin Olympic Stadium.[14] This integration into the military structures of the Western powers in West Berlin was an important feature of the intelligence activities of the missions.

For BRIXMIS, there was another reason why Berlin was important as a base of operations. Members of the Royal Air Force assigned to the Berlin base of the British military liaison mission carried out reconnaissance flights within the Berlin control zone almost every day in their small Chipmunk aircraft. The control zone covered an area whose radius was 32 kilometres and whose centre was situated at the Berlin Air Safety Centre near Kleistpark in Schöneberg. Western aircraft could move freely within this control zone, which extended several kilometres into East Germany.

An exhibition room in the Allied Museum in 2005 with an original Mercedes-Benz G-Class of the French military liaison mission.

Chipmunk aircraft stationed at Gatow, Berlin, were regularly used by BRIXMIS for taking aerial photographs of military objectives.

The Chipmunk was a two-seat, piston-engined aircraft that could fly at low altitude and at low speed. This meant military activities within the control zone could be easily observed and photographed. Any observations of potential interest were conveyed to the personnel of the BRIXMIS inspection tours.[15] The American and French armed forces in Berlin also had small aircraft at their disposal so they too could take aerial photos within the control zone.

A good example of the work undertaken by the missions, and of the observations they made, is demonstrated by their efforts during the East German uprising of 1953. Demonstrations in East Berlin developed into a people's revolt across East Germany whose climax occurred on 16 and 17 June that year. The immediate deployment of Soviet troops to East Berlin provided the military missions an opportunity to learn about the way in which Soviet formations would move in an emergency. There had been neither plans for manoeuvres nor forewarning of an uprising. Soviet forces were responding to a situation that had arisen suddenly.

A top-secret BRIXMIS report that summarised the intelligence gathered from 16 June to 10 July 1953 concluded that Soviet armoured and vehicle columns possessed poor transit discipline.[16] Some vehicles drove too close to one another and collided; others were so far apart from each other that they lost their way in Potsdam. A burning vehicle had to be extinguished by the soldiers with sand because there were neither fire trucks nor fire extinguishers available. According to the BRIXMIS report, the number of broken-down vehicles on the road to East Berlin was exceptionally high.[17]

However, over the course of the next couple of days, many of the broken-down vehicles were back in action. Defective T-34 tanks were towed to East Berlin or were repaired in the shortest possible time. As a result, all of the vehicles that had initially set off still managed to reach their destination within 48 hours.[18] By exploiting the opportunity that had arisen due to the uprising, the missions obtained important information on the operational preparedness and discipline of Soviet formations and on the ability of Soviet troops to make unserviceable vehicles left behind ready for combat within a short period of time.

Fair game in East Germany

The first firearms casualties

The inspection tours in East Germany were not at any stage without danger. As will be discussed, there were a number of incidents in which mission vehicles were fired on or were damaged by roadblocks. East Germany, which gained no advantage whatsoever from the bilateral agreements between the Soviet Union and the Western powers, regarded the military liaison missions as 'a thorn in the flesh'. The legal presence of the mission vehicles made it obvious to East German citizens that their state did not enjoy full sovereignty and therefore did not have the power to prevent the reconnaissance tours. Nevertheless, despite the fact the existence of the missions had to be accepted, the Stasi did everything possible to make their work more difficult.

Upon being informed the PRAs in East Germany would cover more territory from 20 October 1959, the three Western missions decided they would each send five teams to those soon to be restricted areas in the hope of obtaining valuable information. They wanted to know what was special about these new exclusion zones, all of which lay near the East German border. The French sent four of their teams directly into those areas, while the fifth was given the task of identifying any regiments and troops that might be on their way. The tour officer of this fifth team was Lieutenant Moser, the observer was Lance Corporal Marchand and the driver was Lance Corporal Choquet. They set off on 19 October from West Berlin for the area around Frankfurt an der Oder and Prenzlau.[19] After a journey of several hours, they neared an observation post at night in the Angermünde-Templin area. They left later that night and passed a group of Soviet soldiers, having failed to notice them in the darkness until the last moment. Moser watched the soldiers in the rearview mirror and suddenly saw muzzle flashes. A bullet struck the rear of the vehicle, so Moser had to make a split-second decision. They could stop the car and identify themselves as members of the French military liaison mission. Not being in a prohibited area, they need not have feared any consequences. However, they would have been delayed by several hours and would have had little chance to complete their planned tour. The other option was to try to move out of range of the bullets as quickly as possible. Since the car was only a short distance away from the next corner, Moser ordered the driver to accelerate.

Then there was machine gun fire. Moser was hit in the leg and bled profusely[20] but the car was soon out of range and the team decided to head for the next town

A vehicle of the French military liaison mission in the 1950s. Number plates at that time were considerably larger than they were in subsequent decades.

so Moser could receive medical attention. He was given first aid at Zehdenick, after which the team made its way to West Berlin unhindered.

Moser had expected there might be difficulties as they approached West Berlin, but it seems the Soviet soldiers had not reported the incident that had occurred a few hours earlier.[21] The head of the French mission lodged a complaint with SERB the same day. Soviet General Kozlowski apologised for the incident by saying the Soviet soldiers did not think they had injured anyone. While Moser was the first mission member to be injured by gunfire, it would not be the last time mission vehicles and their unarmed occupants were shot at.

On the evening of 10 March 1962, the BRIXMIS duty officer in Potsdam, Nick Brown, set off with his driver, 26-year-old Lance Corporal Douglas Day, on a local tour which would take them to Kleinmachnow. There they drove along Ernst-Thälmann-Straße, which lay only a few hundred metres from the border. The Berlin Wall had been built along that border in August 1961, but refugees had continued to escape to the West in the seven months that followed. This situation played a decisive role in what happened that evening. The occupants of the BRIXMIS vehicle did not know a unit of East German border guards had set up a checkpoint at short notice. Its purpose was to prevent East German citizens from fleeing to West Berlin.

Late in the evening, instead of refugees, the border guard unit saw the BRIXMIS vehicle. According to the version of events described by the British, the vehicle was lost and had therefore come to a stop.[22] Brown checked the map and told Day to

Bullet holes in the rear of Douglas Day's British mission vehicle, 1962.

turn around. They were then fired on without warning, and Day was hit in the foot. Further shots were fired as the vehicle continued driving. Day was hit again, this time in the torso, and the car came to a standstill. A total of 37 shots had been fired. Brown was unharmed.

The border troops surrounded the vehicle, called an ambulance, and confiscated papers and maps in the car and those on Brown's person. The severely wounded Day was taken to an East German hospital. A week passed before he could be safely transported to the British hospital in West Berlin. The British complained strongly to Soviet authorities about this incident. The Soviets responded to the effect that although the mission vehicle had not been in a restricted area, it had nevertheless been unwise for its occupants to ignore the calls of the border guards while in the immediate vicinity of the frontier in the middle of the night.

It had become clear to the Western missions that neither Soviet soldiers nor East German border troops would shy away from opening fire on mission vehicles, even if this meant inflicting casualties.

A big fish on the line

A Soviet warplane crashes in Spandau

From the point of view of British intelligence, an explosive situation arose on 6 April 1966 when a Soviet warplane crashed in West Berlin. The presence of Soviet aircraft in the airspace of West Berlin had been a terrible nuisance to the Western powers for quite some time. A year earlier, several fighter jets had flown overhead and had massively disrupted a session of the Bundestag in the Berlin Congress Hall.

On the late afternoon of 6 April, towards 3:30pm, Berliners were startled by the news that an aircraft had plunged into Stößensee. The British arrived at the crash site at approximately 6pm, and a Soviet delegation of around 20 appeared roughly an hour later. The delegation demanded all activities cease until Soviet units arrived to recover the aircraft. Unsurprisingly, the British rejected this demand. The wreck of the aircraft lay in a lake in the British sector of Berlin, so there could be no question the matter fell within British jurisdiction.

After nightfall, the BRIXMIS air force officer, Squadron Leader Maurice Taylor, went out with a small boat and a lamp to the aircraft wreckage, of which only a small part of the tailplane was to be seen above the surface of the water. The nose of the aircraft was at the bottom of the lake. The British naturally wanted to know what type of aircraft it was. Taylor could only make out parts of the machine and took a number of photos.[23] The overnight analysis of those photos revealed the crashed aircraft was a Yakovlev Yak-28P, a type that had only been introduced to Soviet Air Force units in East Germany a few weeks earlier. The Yak-28 was a swept wing, turbojet-powered aircraft introduced in 1960 and withdrawn from service in 1992. It was produced initially as a tactical bomber and also manufactured in reconnaissance, electronic warfare, and interceptor versions. The last of these, the Yak-28P, was known by the NATO reporting name Firebar and was of particular interest to the British at that time because of its Oriol-D radar equipment. The American mission in Potsdam had only managed to take some photos of a Yak-28P in flight over East Germany two weeks before the crash.[24] Now, one of these aircraft had come down in British territory.

The pilot, Boris Kapustin, and the navigator, Yuri Yanov, had taken off in their machine from Finow, which lay approximately 40 kilometres from Berlin. They were to make their way to the Soviet air base in Köthen, having already made a failed attempt to do so on 3 April. On that day, they had returned to Finow with engine problems and the mechanics had worked for three days after that to repair the interceptor.[25]

About 12 minutes after takeoff on 6 April, both engines failed in quick succession. The aircraft dropped like a stone. The pilot and navigator had little more than 30 seconds. They were over West Berlin and given permission over the radio to eject. Neither Kapustin nor Yanow did so. Kapustin wanted to maintain control of the aircraft long enough to avoid a series of apartment blocks, guiding it towards Lake Stößensee, which lay in the British-controlled sector of West Berlin in the district of Spandau. Only a few seconds later, the 21-metre-long interceptor plunged into the lake.

Even as late as 10:30pm on 6 April, the British did not know what type of aircraft had crashed or whether the crew was still in the machine. The initial dives carried out by Berlin police units and fire services a few hours later had no success in finding the crew in the muddy water. American helicopters and British military police units searched the surrounding area throughout the night.

Royal Navy divers from Portsmouth arrived in Gatow on the morning of 7 April so recovery efforts could be conducted properly.[26] The British were keen that the salvage operation run smoothly, for they knew by then what type of aircraft had crashed in their territory. It was possible the wreck would be the most significant intelligence discovery in years.

Yet when work at the crash site began on 7 April, the main concern was to recover the bodies of the two crewmembers. It was beyond doubt by 5:45pm that both men were dead and still in the cockpit. Great care had to be taken in pulling them out, for the ejection seats, though they had not been fired, could very well have been rendered defective by the crash. On 8 April, towards 3pm, the bodies were handed over to the Soviet delegation with full military honours. With that, the compassionate aspect of the operation came to an end.[27]

The British divers had also recovered items of military interest. This included the radar equipment, which was sent to England for examination. It had been intended the work in England be done quickly, for the wreck was to be returned to Soviet authorities on 13 April. The parts that belonged in the cockpit would need to be reinstalled before then if the British wanted to leave no evidence they had been

The first parts of the wreckage of the Soviet combat aircraft were transferred from a British ferry to a Soviet one on 13 April 1966.

examined. However, the electronic equipment from the nose cone did not end up being sent back to Berlin by the time the fuselage was handed over to Soviet authorities on the Havel on the afternoon of 13 April. This meeting point on the river had only been agreed on after tough negotiations with the Soviets. The wreckage was transported by a British ferry to a point near the East German frontier and was then loaded onto a Soviet ferry. General Vladimir Bulanov, who had been entrusted with conducting the negotiations on the part of the Soviet Union, took receipt of the wreckage. It was agreed a further search would be carried out for the remaining elements of the aircraft, for there were important parts like the radar and engines that were missing. More significant, however, was the absence of the identification friend or foe (IFF) set from the returned wreckage.[28] It was a severe blow to the Soviet military leadership that its IFF system no longer remained a secret!

The next part of the recovery operation was to find the wings and the engines. These components had been torn off on impact and were now widely scattered in the lake. The Soviet representatives at the crash site, aware this part of the operation would take more time, had moved into quarters near the lake on 6 April. It was the idea of the commandant of the British sector of Berlin, Major-General Sir John Nelson, to delay the return of the engines so they could be thoroughly examined. The only problem was that the British had yet to find them. How much time would be needed for the examination of the engines, and for how long could the Soviet

AM 6.APRIL 1966 STEUERTEN DIE SOWJETISCHEN PILOTEN
HAUPTMANN
BORIS WLADIMIROWITSCH KAPUSTIN
UND OBERLEUTNANT
JURI NIKOLAJEWITSCH JANOW
IHR DEFEKTES KAMPFFLUGZEUG IN DEN STÖSSENSEE UND
VERLOREN DABEI IHR LEBEN. DURCH IHREN SELBSTLOSEN
EINSATZ VERMIEDEN SIE EINE UNABSEHBARE KATASTROPHE
IM NAHEN WOHNGEBIET. DIESE TAFEL GILT DEM GEDENKEN
AN DAS OPFER DER SOWJETISCHEN SOLDATEN ALS EIN
ZEICHEN DER MENSCHLICHKEIT IN ZEITEN DES
"KALTEN KRIEGES".

Commemorative plaque on the bridge over Stößensee in Spandau, Berlin, for the Soviet pilot and navigator who lost their lives when their Yak-28P crashed in 1966.

military be kept waiting without arousing suspicion? The Western forces in Berlin did not know anything about General Bulanov, so they were unable to assess how he might react to the planned intelligence manoeuvre.

The first engine was salvaged on 18 April, although the British kept it a secret and took it to the Royal Air Force base in Gatow when an opportunity presented itself to do so surreptitiously on 20 April. As a precaution, Nelson had sought the permission of his superiors at the Foreign Office in London beforehand to pursue this course of action and he had been given the green light. In the following days, the engine was examined in detail in a remote hangar by British experts who had been specially flown in. During that time, the Soviet representatives, in the belief that neither engine had been found, complained daily about the inefficiency of the British.

When the second engine was discovered on 25 April, the British gave the Soviets the impression it was only the first one they had found. However, time was running out. It had been decided in London that the equipment being examined in England would arrive back in Berlin on 1 May. The British therefore announced on 28 April that they had discovered the second engine, even though it had in fact been in Gatow for a week.

Both engines were finally handed over on 2 May. General Bulanov wrote to the British and pointed out that an important part was still missing, although he did not describe in detail what it was. It is doubtful whether he believed the British claim that any components that had not been returned must still be at the bottom of the lake.

One particularly critical situation arose almost immediately after the crash. On 7 April, a Soviet amphibious vehicle crossed Checkpoint Charlie and headed in the direction of Stößensee. Up to 40 Soviet soldiers set up camp in the immediate vicinity of the crash site to observe the recovery operation. Had the amphibious vehicle proceeded into the lake towards the wreck, the British would have had to stop it by force, thereby triggering an armed conflict. This did not happen, so the British concluded the Soviet Union was not prepared to provoke a military confrontation for the sake of preventing the examination of the equipment from the wreck.[29]

Willy Brandt, at that time the governing mayor of Berlin, found the most fitting words when he spoke of the crash a few days after it had taken place. He acknowledged the bravery of the Soviet pilot and navigator for sacrificing their own lives in order to avoid a disaster.[30]

Boris Kapustin and Yuri Yanov were hailed as heroes in East Germany and the Soviet Union for having manoeuvred their interceptor over the residential areas of West Berlin and into the lake. A memorial was erected in their honour in the municipal park of Finow in Brandenburg. After the reunification of Germany, the district of Spandau unveiled a commemorative plaque for both men on the bridge over Stößensee in 1992. Their story is kept alive in Russia to this day, with sculptures depicting Kapustin and Yanov still being created as part of an effort to commemorate the Cold War and its heroes. As recently as 2020, a German radio documentary was produced in which the families of the two men were visited in Russia and interviewed.[31]

It had to happen sometime

Fatalities on the road and murder in the forest

On 13 April 1969, the commandant, Claude Legendre, and his adjutant, Lebert, were being driven by Tiberi in French mission vehicle no. 33. They had been followed for some time by a Stasi BMW and were unable to shake it off. According to the French account, the mission vehicle was travelling at the speed limit in the left lane of Motorway 170 towards Dresden at around 7:30pm. Slightly ahead in the right lane were three motorcycles. When the mission vehicle and the motorcycles were almost level, the rear of the three motorcycles accelerated to overtake the two in front of it. During this overtaking manoeuvre, the rear motorcycle swerved into the left lane immediately in front of the faster-moving mission vehicle. A collision occurred, with the motorcyclist being thrown against the windscreen, over the mission vehicle, and onto the road.[32] The members of the French mission stopped immediately and the BMW came to a halt in front of them. Neither the mission members nor the

A team of the French military liaison mission on a reconnaissance tour in East Germany in 1967.

Stasi employees provided first aid to the victim. He either died immediately or at the scene of the accident. To the astonishment of the French, East German police and ambulance units arrived very quickly, whereupon the BMW departed.[33]

The mission car was towed to Dresden. Legendre and his team were interrogated overnight at the Soviet headquarters in the city and were held there for a few days. The head of the French mission, Colonel Rohé, was only informed of the whereabouts of his staff two days after the accident had taken place. SERB asserted the occupants of the mission vehicle were murderers and threatened to put them on trial in East Germany. According to Soviet authorities, the motorcyclist was killed because the mission vehicle had been driving too fast.[34] However, on 19 April, SERB suggested the three prisoners could be released for a payment of 27,000 East German marks. The French military liaison mission agreed to this payment provided it was understood it was made not as a punishment but as a gesture for the bereaved.

The three prisoners were released on 26 April and declared *personae non gratae*. On the same day, in the presence of the head of MMFL and that of SERB, all documents and film that had been in the mission vehicle were burned. The money for the 'ransom' had been gathered by the colleagues and families of the prisoners. Legendre stated many years later that he was grateful to the donors, although he felt as if he had been left in the lurch by the French authorities.[35]

Not only firearms but also vehicles were increasingly used as weapons against the military missions. East German security units employed trucks as ramming vehicles to cause accidents or to stop or block mission vehicles. In 1979, a truck of the East German National People's Army (NVA) rammed into a USMLM vehicle, seriously injuring one of the occupants. A BRIXMIS car was also rammed and wrecked by an NVA truck in 1983.[36] Many more incidents involving the vehicles of the military liaison missions took place during this period. It was particularly bad for BRIXMIS in the 1980s with its members involved in 137 incidents.[37] Fortunately, most of these only resulted in minor damage or injuries, but that changed in March 1984.

On 22 March 1984, a French mission vehicle set off to observe army activity in and around Halle. In the Mercedes limousine sat Captain Jean-Paul Staub and Sergeant Jean Marie Blancheton with their driver, Sergeant Philippe Mariotti. Their route would take them through the district of Lettin, near the Otto Brosowski Barracks, and East German forces were already waiting for them. An exercise was being conducted there by the NVA in cooperation with Division VIII of Main Division I of the Stasi from 19 to 23 March. Six NVA vehicles, including three trucks with trailers, waited around the clock during those five days for any mission vehicles that might approach. Any such mission vehicles were to be blocked and disrupted.

Based on observations it had made in the past, the Stasi considered it highly likely the French would approach the barracks on this occasion. As a result, the East Germans positioned themselves on all three routes that led to the barracks.[38] When the French drove past the main gate of the barracks in the late afternoon, one of the trucks started following them. The mission vehicle increased speed and, although a truck and trailer soon appeared in front of them, Mariotti did not hesitate. They would be cornered if he did not manage to manoeuvre the Mercedes past the oncoming truck. As the driver of a mission vehicle, it was his job to weigh up the risks and to try to avoid being trapped. At the wheel of the oncoming NVA truck was 20-year-old Lance Corporal Baumann. Beside him sat a Stasi agent in the uniform of an NVA sergeant. Contemporary documents refer to him under the code name 'Paul Schmidt', and it was his intention to stop the mission vehicle precisely as foreseen in the operational plan.

The situation ended in tragedy a few seconds later. The truck rammed the Mercedes on the driver's side and Mariotti was killed instantly. Staub was seriously injured and driven to a hospital, while Blancheton, whose injuries were less severe, remained with the vehicle and his dead comrade.

It is of no surprise that the sequence of events leading to the accident was subsequently described differently by both sides. Each blamed the other for the death of Mariotti. According to the East German account, the Mercedes had swerved from side to side as it hurtled towards the truck, making it impossible for the truck to avoid a collision. In the record of the interrogation that took place on the evening of the accident, the truck driver stated that he only saw after the collision that the car was an MMFL vehicle.[39] This was obviously a lie. Neither the truck driver nor

The completely destroyed French mission vehicle of Philippe Mariotti and the injured Sergeant Jean Marie Blancheton approximately 30 minutes after the accident of 22 March 1984.

his passenger mentioned their objective had been to disrupt the military missions. According to the French account, the mission vehicle wanted to pass the truck on the right, but the truck driver swung the wheel at the last moment and rammed into the side of the Mercedes at full speed. The French version of events is, in this case, more credible.[40]

Worth pointing out in this context is the fact that on 27 March 1984, only five days after the fatal collision, 'Paul Schmidt' and his observation team were decorated with medals and awarded money for blocking the French mission vehicle and thus also for the death of Mariotti.[41] That money was offered in reward for an intended collision resulting in death is an unmistakeable indication of the inhumane attitude of the East German regime.

Almost all reconnaissance tours conducted by the military liaison missions in East Germany started in West Berlin. So it was that Major Arthur D. Nicholson and Sergeant Jessie Schatz set off from the West Berlin site of the U.S. mission on Föhrenweg in Zehlendorf on the morning of 24 March 1985. After a stopover at the mission base in Potsdam, they continued their journey in their Mercedes off-road vehicle at 10am with the objective of visiting a former training area of the Soviet armed forces. Nicholson and Schatz completed this task more quickly than expected, so Nicholson decided they would conduct an inspection tour of the training ground of the Soviet tank regiment in Techentin, Mecklenburg-Vorpommern.[42]

Two Soviet military vehicles block a car of the French military liaison mission, c. 1980.

It was in this area on the night of New Year's Eve in 1984 that Nicholson had been successful in infiltrating a vehicle depot and even in taking interior shots of a T-64B main battle tank.[43] This was a daring exploit for which he and those involved had been awarded, yet he had been aware all the while that French mission members had been fired on at this location in October 1984 while they had been inspecting concealed Soviet tanks. The French had been unharmed, but, as can be imagined, this incident heightened the alertness of the Soviet guards.

On 24 March 1985, at approximately 3:30pm, the USMLM tour vehicle arrived at the tank firing range, which could be accessed from several sides via dirt roads. Not seeing any guards, Nicholson and Schatz headed towards and stopped in front of the tank depot. Nicholson left the Mercedes off-road vehicle with his camera equipment, while Schatz opened the roof hatch of the vehicle and observed the surrounding area. Schatz suddenly spotted a Soviet guard, with a Kalashnikov at the ready, running directly towards them from a distance of only 70 metres. He shouted out a warning to Nicholson just as the Soviet soldier fired a shot. He started the car and reversed so that Nicholson could reach it more quickly. Two more shots were fired. Nicholson fell to the ground. Schatz continued to reverse until he was level with Nicholson. He got out with the first aid kit, but the Soviet guard, Sergeant Alexander Ryabtsev, appeared at that moment, threatening Schatz with his weapon and pushing him back into the vehicle. The guard called for reinforcements, but no one looked after the injured American officer. Nicholson died on the spot. It was determined that the time of his death was roughly an hour after the shots had been fired.[44]

About two hours after the shooting, the head of the USMLM, Colonel Roland Lajoie, was informed that an 'accident' involving mission vehicle no. 23 had taken place. He arrived at the scene of the crime towards 10pm and was immediately confronted with allegations by the Soviet side. He was stunned that one of his men had been shot and that he had been met with accusations of wrongdoing rather than expressions of regret.[45]

None of the incidents involving the Western military liaison missions attracted as much attention and media interest as the death of Nicholson. President Ronald Reagan protested personally to the Soviet Union about this incident.[46] The West German press, not to mention the American and international press, reported extensively on the transportation of the body over Glienicke Bridge and on the burial at Arlington National Cemetery in Virginia.

Portrait of Arthur D. Nicholson. The library of the U.S. garrison at Clayallee in Zehlendorf, Berlin, was named after him in 1986.

The death of Major Nicholson marked a turning point in the work of the American military mission. The Americans officially referred to this incident as a case of 'murder'. Nicholson and Schatz had been in neither a PRA nor a TRA. The Americans wanted to ensure something like this could never happen again. If this were not possible and the safety of mission members could not be guaranteed, the Americans were prepared to consider the idea of closing the mission in Potsdam. Soviet authorities would have been fully aware that a natural consequence of such a course of action would have been the closure of the Soviet military mission in Frankfurt am Main. There followed months of difficult negotiations with a specially established American-Soviet working group whose task was to investigate and deal with the incident.

These negotiations were particularly difficult due to the fact there were only two witnesses of the sequence of events. The Soviet witness was Sergeant Ryabtsev. This important witness did not appear at any stage during the bilateral negotiations and therefore could not be directly questioned by the Americans. The Americans had to rely completely on the statements made by their driver, Jessie Schatz. He was the main witness, but his credibility was by no means out of question. Schatz had personal traits and tendencies that made him an excellent target and, it seems, easy prey for the Stasi and for Soviet intelligence. He had been under constant surveillance by the Stasi since joining the USMLM in 1979.[47] In addition to his passion for gambling, his excessive consumption of alcohol, and his unsuccessful financial transactions, Schatz had been charged with tax evasion and fraud in 1982. Astonishingly, he was once more recruited for the USMLM in 1984 and completed a second period of service in Potsdam. During that time, he was again under constant surveillance by the Stasi[48] and it was on the account provided by this man alone that the Americans had to draw for conducting their negotiations with the Soviets.

The lengthy American-Soviet negotiations essentially revolved around the following points. The Americans took the view that the mission vehicle had not been in a restricted area and that it therefore ought to have been allowed to stop there. The Soviet Union argued that the site was covered by Article 10 of the Huebner-Malinin Agreement, which prohibited any visit to military zones classified as Troop Garrison Areas. The Americans responded to the effect that every depot where a military vehicle was parked might be construed as falling under Article 10. This would render the work of the missions in East Germany impossible and would therefore make the dissolution of the Huebner-Malinin Agreement a logical consequence.

The discussions lasted for months, but little meaningful progress was made. The Western military liaison missions in Potsdam continued to exist on the basis of the old agreements until they were closed after the reunification of Germany in 1990.

The missions in Potsdam played a significant role during the years of the Cold War. They could legally obtain information on East German territory and could pass it on to Western military authorities and intelligence agencies. Yet the missions

Nicholson's body was transported to West Berlin over Glienicke Bridge on 25 March 1985.

were also an instrument for defusing crises. Its members were able to gain an idea not only of what the potential enemy was up to but also of what he was not up to. Furthermore, the existence of the missions ensured the Western powers were in constant contact with the Soviet Union even in times of crisis. The same was the case for the work of the Soviet military liaison missions in West Germany. It is worthy of note that not a single Soviet mission member received a gunshot wound during the more than 40-year presence of the Soviet missions in West Germany. The Soviet missions also suffered neither fatalities nor serious injuries whenever they were observed, pursued, or, if necessary, blocked by Western troops.

PART II: GERMAN INTELLIGENCE SERVICES

SVEN FELIX KELLERHOFF

CHAPTER FIVE

Early confrontation

The beginnings of the secret war

The Ulbricht Group in action

The fighting in Berlin came to an end on 2 May 1945 and, although Hitler's war would last for another six days, it was only a few hours after the guns had fallen silent in the ruins of the capital of the Reich that Walter Ulbricht, sitting approximately 40 kilometres to the east in a country house adorned with pillars at Buchholzer Straße 8 in the Brandenburg village of Bruchmühle in Strausberg, declared that the next war had begun. He only did so in secret and commented to his closest confidants about his vision for a new German state: 'It must look democratic, but we must control everything.'[1] Two days earlier, on 30 April 1945 at 6am, the 10 members of the Ulbricht Group had departed Moscow for Germany to begin the Stalinist transformation of the country immediately after victory had been achieved over National Socialism. Wolfgang Leonhard, who at the age of 24 was the youngest in the group of exiled communists, later remembered the first assignment he and his returning comrades had been given: 'We were to set up the administrative districts in Berlin and select suitable anti-fascist individuals for this purpose. Each administrative district would consist of 16 departments. As many "commoners" were to be sought out as possible, especially social democrats, centrists, those not attached to any party, and even academics.'[2] Concealed beneath this assignment was a hidden agenda to be pursued by the communist cadre. The Communist Party of Germany (KPD), which was only formally re-established five weeks later, would pursue the shrewd tactic of claiming for itself just three posts in each city council, albeit always the most important ones: all deputy mayors and all those posts responsible for personnel and public education. Even if there were plenty of qualified personnel who were communists, Ulbricht stipulated they were to make up no more than one third of each district council.

Ulbricht's men headed to Berlin every day to establish district authorities which, though dominated by communists, were to appear non-partisan. Leonhard spoke of the first trip he made:

It was a hellish scene. Everyone thinks only of the ruins and the destroyed houses. That was by no means the worst thing. What was worst was the smoke. It was unbelievably dreadful. You could hardly walk across Alexanderplatz without going through smoke. The underground train tunnels were flooded due to ground water and bombed water pipelines, and German soldiers looked and walked around in bewilderment, not at all understanding what was going on. There were some jubilant Soviet soldiers. And the most haunting picture: the lines in front of the pumps. No one had any water. There was no light or gas either. There was nothing, but you absolutely needed water. The people standing before the pumps looked worn out. And then you looked around and saw the white flags hanging from windows everywhere as if to say: 'We surrender! Regardless of who surrenders what or when, we want no more!' And you could see that many also wore white armbands: 'I surrender.'[3]

The Berlin-based collaboration between German communists and Soviet intelligence had its beginnings in Bruchmühle and lasted until 1989. It was not by chance that this village in Brandenburg had been chosen as the initial base of operations for the Ulbricht Group. This was where the military administration of the 1st Belorussian Front, commanded by Marshal Georgy Zhukov, had set up its headquarters during the Battle of Berlin. As a result, in addition to pursuing their main objective, the communists were to carry out a number of other tasks that, while smaller in scale, were regarded as being of great importance from the point of view of Soviet intelligence. Once, for example, Leonhard had to drop everything because it was rumoured a Trotskyist group had been founded in Reinickendorf, Berlin: 'It was

Berlin, May 1945, and Adolf Hitler's bust is only good for recycling. The guns had barely fallen silent before a new contest on an invisible front began.

just a few days after the collapse of the Third Reich that we had to search for Trotskyists in the middle of a destroyed and hungry Berlin— a grotesque situation!'[4] Real or alleged Trotskyists—in reality a collective term for possibly non-conformist communists who refused to submit to the absolute authority of the party leadership—had been one of the main targets of the various Stalinist intelligence agencies inside and outside the Soviet Union since the end of the 1920s. A second and particularly important secret assignment given to the Ulbricht Group was to drive to the Haus des Rundfunks on Masurenallee in Charlottenburg and take possession of the recordings kept in the archive there of the talks that took place in October 1940 between Soviet foreign minister Vyacheslav Molotov and Nazi leaders. These recordings could not be allowed to fall into the hands of the Western Allies. When Leonhard and his comrades arrived at the archive, they discovered the assignment had already been carried out by some unnamed Soviet institution.

After six days in Bruchmühle, Ulbricht moved the headquarters of his secret organisation to Lichtenberg at Prinzenallee 80 (today Einbeckerstraße 41). The work continued from there. Once the district authorities had been established, various municipal posts needed to be filled in accordance with the criteria of a conspiratorial seizure of power. The Ulbricht Group completed this task within one week. The non-affiliated engineer Arthur Werner was appointed the first mayor of Berlin. Although he had no idea about what was involved in political administration, 'his manner and appearance' made him look like 'a typical commoner'. As Ulbricht later sneered: 'Of course, we often found it quite amusing.'[5] No less than three of Werner's four deputies were communists, and five of the 15 municipal departments were under the control of former KPD members. Those five were the departments for personnel, finance, public education, social welfare, and employment. The most important criterion in the selection of personnel was dependability in the power-political contest, which is why Ulbricht had two of his men join the municipal council.

From the outset, Ulbricht kept a tight rein on all communists who had not been in exile. When he met with former KPD members in Berlin in the first two weeks of May 1945, many of whom had been imprisoned or even held in concentration camps during the Nazi era, the meetings

Wolfgang Leonhard was exceptionally good looking during the time he carried out his first assignments for the Ulbricht Group. He was even supposed to bewitch the wives of reluctant SPD functionaries.

Walter Ulbricht was a loyal student of Stalin. As an apparatchik, he brought anything that might have developed a life of its own into line with the party.

resembled not friendly reunions of political friends but rather appointments between a manager and his subordinates. Ulbricht issued clear, brief and harsh orders that were to be obeyed immediately. He rejected the anti-fascist groups organised by Hitler's opponents in nearly all districts after the fighting had come to an end. These groups were self-help initiatives that carried out emergency measures like putting out fires, cleaning streets, and providing medical care. Their secondary purpose, as opponents of Nazism, was to politically enlighten and influence their neighbours. Wolfgang Leonhard expected the Ulbricht Group would work on friendly terms with these obviously KPD-dominated committees, but he was mistaken: 'Ulbricht intransigently demanded of us that we dissolve these committees.' Only much later, after he had broken away from the cadre of the Socialist Unity Party of Germany (SED), did he understand the reason for Ulbricht's approach: 'Ulbricht deeply distrusted all independent movements and initiatives. Indeed, he distrusted anything over which he did not have full control.'[6]

The struggle for the police

Why Karl Heinrich 'disappeared'

While the creation of an administrative authority was necessary for ruling Berlin, almost as important was the founding of a police force. The Soviet occupation forces, which bore sole responsibility for security in the capital of the Reich until the Western Allies marched into the city as planned at the beginning of July, quickly set up a new German police force. Paul Markgraf, a former regimental commander in the Wehrmacht and a recipient of the Knight's Cross, became its first chief on 19 May 1945. This appointment was one of the first acts of the municipal council, although the new chief of police was in fact directly subordinate to the Soviet commandant in Berlin. Markgraf had been taken prisoner in early 1943 after the Battle of Stalingrad and had decided to join the National Committee for a Free Germany, a communist-dominated group in the Soviet Union committed to the resistance against National Socialism. After partaking in several re-education courses, Markgraf drew the attention of the Soviet People's Commissariat for Internal Affairs (NKVD). He was earmarked for important tasks in a future Soviet Germany, and it was in the wake of the Ulbricht Group that he and nine other re-educated prisoners of war were flown from Moscow to Berlin. The initial task of the new chief of police was to bring under a united command all of the German police forces that had been set up by Soviet commanders in various districts since the beginning of May.

Seeking to restore order in Spandau as quickly as possible was a man by the name of Karl Heinrich, a social democrat who had been a police major until 1932 and who, as a committed defender of democracy and the rule of law, had spent eight years in various prisons and concentration camps. He had been set free in the autumn of 1942 after being deemed medically unfit to be kept in prison and had secretly established contact with social demo-cratic resistance circles. Once the war had come to an end, he began to assemble trustworthy police officers and, under the supervision of the local commandant, worked with them to ensure

Traces can be seen in Karl Heinrich's face of the eight years he spent in prisons and concentration camps during the Nazi era. He was also fiercely opposed to the KPD.

public safety. In a matter of days, Heinrich rose to the position of district chief, a role he had undertaken in Dortmund in 1926 and 1927, and by the end of May 1945 he had been appointed commander of the uniformed police in Berlin. In effect, he was second only to Chief of Police Markgraf. A career such as this was surprising given that Heinrich, as head of the uniformed police in the government quarter between 1929 and 1932, had repeatedly put a stop to unauthorised demonstrations, be they Nazi or communist. This earnt him the derogatory nickname 'Truncheon Heinrich'.[7] Even though he joined the re-established Social Democratic Party of Germany (SPD) after the war, this did not prevent him from ending up in charge of 180 police stations and of all uniformed police forces. Nevertheless, he was monitored by Soviet intelligence. His personnel officer Hans Seidel, his secretary Hildegard Tepper, and possibly also his deputy Rudolf Wagner acted as informers for the NKVD.

These informers had much to report, as 'Heinrich collected material on cases of corruption that involved police officers who were members of the KPD'.[8] He was not happy with the large intake of communists, pushed for by the chief of police, into the ranks of the uniformed police. He wanted to change the political orientation of the organisation. Some of the affected communist police officers sought to defend themselves by making complaints about Truncheon Heinrich to the NKVD, but the Soviet commandant in Berlin did not yet have any interest in getting rid of Karl Heinrich, for the British occupation officers who had arrived in the city in the meantime held the commander of the uniformed police in high regard. The situation became acute when Erich Mielke, without the knowledge of Heinrich, was appointed head of the police station in Lichtenberg in July 1945. It is likely Heinrich was aware of certain details from Mielke's past. Mielke and another member of the 'self-defence unit' of the KPD had shot dead police officers Paul Anlauf and Franz Lenk on 9 August 1931. The names of the murderers had been known since September 1933, and it would have been quite strange if the well-connected Heinrich had not been aware of them. It raises the question as to whether Heinrich made preparations for the removal of Mielke.[9]

In any case, Heinrich's career with the police ended abruptly and in a manner that was typical of secret service activity: he disappeared without a trace. Heinrich was summoned to a meeting with Markgraf at police headquarters on 2 August 1945. In the middle of this meeting, a Soviet major burst in and asked the head of the uniformed police to accompany him to the headquarters of the NKVD in Berlin. Heinrich did not detect that anything ominous was going on. He forgot his glasses, which remained on the table in Markgraf's office, and left his briefcase in the anteroom. A pistol and three loaded magazines were later found in that briefcase, a fact that would subsequently be provided as the reason for the arrest of Heinrich. He was locked in a cell in the basement of the NKVD headquarters in Elsässer Straße and interrogated and tortured. He was accused of illegal possession of weapons, for it was the case in the summer of 1945 that German police officers in Berlin were not even allowed to carry batons, let alone firearms. Heinrich's arrest was not officially confirmed by Soviet intelligence to begin with. However, given that the head of the uniformed police was one of the most well-known social democrats in the city, Soviet authorities eventually had to respond to queries from the commandant of the American sector, Floyd Parks. Six days after the disappearance of Heinrich, his arrest was justified with the claim that, based on the testimonies of several former inmates of concentration camps, he was suspected of having been a Gestapo agent. Although Heinrich himself had been imprisoned in concentration camps, it is of no surprise, given his career, that many would seek to defame his character. The NKVD interrogator recommended the arrested police officer be charged with armed resistance against the Soviet Union and with counterrevolutionary sabotage. According to Article 58 of the Penal Code of the Russian Soviet Republic, both crimes were punishable by death, but a trial never took place. Heinrich had suffered for eight years under Nazism and was now being tortured by the NKVD, the result of which was that his health deteriorated rapidly. He was transferred to the sickbay of NKVD Special Camp No. 3 in Hohenschönhausen where he died on 3 November 1945. 'He was buried unwept and unsung like all the other deceased inmates in the carbide-lime pits near the goods yard, about 600 to 800 metres from the tracks,' reported an anonymous source, possibly a surviving fellow inmate, in a letter to the West Berlin newspaper *Telegraf*.[10]

The public did not immediately learn of the death of Karl Heinrich, and his family did not hear of it either. Instead, the KPD henchman Markgraf cynically ordered: 'For as long as the current commander of the uniformed police is unable to perform his duties, it has been decided in accordance with the order of the Allied command in Berlin on 10 January 1946 that Mr Johannes Kanig will be entrusted with the conduct of business.'[11] The SED was not to be outdone in such cynicism. In June 1947, the communist press published excerpts from two petitions for clemency, one from 1940 and the other from 1941, that had been presented by Karl Heinrich to the Reich minister of justice and to Adolf Hitler. Although the Gestapo had rejected these petitions, the newspapers *Neues Deutschland* and *Berliner Zeitung* failed to mention this. In their deliberately shortened accounts, Heinrich was portrayed as a Nazi collaborator rather than as an opponent of Hitler. The reaction of social democrats in Berlin was rather restrained. The air of suspicion was too oppressive, even if based on manipulated evidence.

The snare of Hans Kemritz

A double agent on Schadowstraße

The offer was so tempting that Erich Klose, a former German officer, did not think to question it. In the winter of 1945–1946, barely six months after the end of the war, he had received a letter from Hans Kemritz, a comrade from the days they had worked together in the high command of the army. Officially, Klose had worked there as a civilian employee in the personnel department, but he had in fact been a member of the Abwehr, the intelligence organisation of the Wehrmacht. The letter was an invitation for Klose to visit Kemritz's office on Schadowstraße in Mitte, Berlin. Kemritz, a former major who had now been admitted to the bar, wrote that he had an interesting job offer for Klose. Unemployed at that time, Klose was overjoyed and went to see his comrade without first writing a reply. Kemritz quickly dismissed him and requested he make an appointment. Not suspecting anything was amiss, Klose did as requested and even put on his best suit for the next meeting in order to make a good impression. That meeting turned out to be seemingly unproductive, but as he was walking back towards the boulevard Unter den Linden, two men appeared and arrested him. A few metres away stood a covered truck which Klose was forced to get into. They waited there for a long time until another arrested person was bundled into the vehicle—someone who, like Klose, had worked for German intelligence during the war. With that day's targets apparently achieved, the truck drove off and arrived at an NKVD basement in Weißensee, Berlin. Erich Klose was never seen again. He is said to have died of tuberculosis in the special camp in Hohenschönhausen on 10 February 1946—or that was at least the information the Soviets provided his wife three months later. As with almost anything relating to Kemritz, the details of the disappearance of Klose are not entirely clear. Even the exact date of this incident is unknown. Some sources state the arrest took place on 16 November 1945, while others consider it to be sometime in January 1946.[12]

Also unclear is how many other people were snared by Dr Hans Kemritz and the reasons for this. Was it really just seven people, all of them former members of the Abwehr, as alleged years later by senior American officials in a confidential meeting with representatives of the West German government?[13] Or were there at least 23 victims, including not only former general staff officers but also a teacher named Heinrich Wöhlert, a district judge by the name of Kossak, and a woman called Miss Berg? A Miss Flehr disappeared after an appointment with Dr Kemritz in November 1945, as did Mr and Mrs Gollert a few weeks later. Martin Rieckenberg, who had scheduled a meeting with the lawyer at the beginning of December 1945, likewise went missing. It seems that Rieckenberg had been promised being given responsibility for the management of 40 apartment buildings. Whether he kept this appointment is unknown, but he was never seen again. Kemritz had invited a physicist by the name of Klarett to a Christmas party in December 1945. Shortly thereafter, the scientist was sitting in his tuxedo in a Soviet basement prison. Kemritz did not even spare his closest friends. Walter Wiegand visited Kemritz in his office on 24 January 1946 and, instead of returning to West Berlin, spent several years in a prison in the Soviet occupation zone. Moritz Becker, a former lieutenant-colonel in the Abwehr, disappeared in March 1946 after a visit to Schadowstraße and is said to have died in Bautzen in November 1948. The former businessman Hans-Jürgen von Hake also went to see Kemritz in early 1946. Hake had lived in Denmark since 1933, gathering information there for the Abwehr and performing a subordinate role as a captain in the occupation administration from 1940 to 1945. As a suspected war criminal, he had been on the wanted persons list of the Danish authorities since the end of the war. He did not return from his meeting with Kemritz. It was only in April 1946 that Hake's wife, Elly von Hake, received a letter in which he stated in few words that a Soviet military court had found him guilty of espionage and had sentenced him to 10 years in prison. She soon learnt from a German prisoner who had been released from the internment camp in Sachsenhausen that her husband had fallen into a trap set for him by Kemritz. It would be another four years before she received a second letter from her husband. In it, he wrote that he had been transferred to a prison in Luckau. According to the available records, he died there on 4 July 1950. Another Kemritz victim was engineer Reinhard Danneberg, who had been released from American internment in June 1946. He found a letter from Kemritz waiting for him in his apartment and arranged a visit to Schadowstraße for 2 July. When Danneberg did not return to his fiancée after this appointment, the young woman approached the lawyer, who replied tersely: 'I think there is a 95 per cent chance that the Russians have Mister Danneberg.' Ill at ease when the bewildered woman asked him how he could know that, he responded: 'Mister Danneberg looks like a former officer.

It's just his appearance.'[14] It was of course the case in the first half of 1946 that thousands of officers, who had been released from internment by the Western powers and returned to their homes in the Soviet-occupied part of Germany, were immediately arrested once more and sent to the camp in Sachsenhausen. However, Danneberg had lived in the western part of Berlin.

Suddenly, a few months later, the snare in Schadowstraße ceased to exist. Kemritz usually maintained contact with a single NKVD interpreter, but, on 28 October 1946, several Soviet intelligence officers arrived at his office. He was questioned for more than three hours, after which the intelligence officers took away a large quantity of files. The lawyer knew he had to act quickly. He gathered up the remaining papers and set off as quickly as possible to his house in Dahlem, a stately villa on Kiebitzweg (now Otto-von-Simson-Straße). He never went back to his office in Mitte, instead making arrangements to head to West Germany. He and his wife were picked up by American officers in a service jeep at the beginning of November 1946, taken to Tempelhof, and put on a plane to Heidelberg. Kemritz soon found a new place to stay in Bad Homburg, was admitted to the bar in West Germany, and had a luxurious house built in 1948 for the enormous sum of 80,000 West German marks, the new currency that had just been introduced.[15]

Hans Kemritz had always been adept at looking out for himself. Born in 1888, he was the son of a senior police officer at police headquarters in Berlin. He completed a law degree and graduated with good grades in the first and second state examinations. He was awarded a doctorate at Friedrich Wilhelm University for his dissertation on the entitlements of parents in the event of their child being injured or kidnapped. He served at the front during World War I, not as a volunteer like many his age but rather as a conscript. Leaving the army during the Christmas season of 1918, he briefly worked for the magistrate of what was at that time the still independent municipality of Neukölln and then started his own law firm in 1919. He specialised in industrial property protection—i.e., the enforcement of patents—and earnt a lot of money in doing so. His law firm was located on Schadowstraße from 1930, and he acquired his villa on Kiebitzweg shortly thereafter. Kemritz returned to military service as a lieutenant in August 1939, but at the age of 51 he was assigned an administrative post at the military district command in Berlin. He clearly performed this role well, for he eventually became the head of the branch of the Abwehr responsible for the Berlin district and held that position as a major until the spring of 1945. When the Red Army commenced its assault on the capital of the Reich, Kemritz had to partake in the hopeless defensive fighting. The result was his capture by the Soviets on 1 May 1945 but, even though, as a former intelligence officer, he would have been on the list of those who were to be arrested automatically, the Soviets released him from the camp in Landsberg an der Warthe in October 1945 and even allowed him to resume his work as a lawyer on Schadowstraße.

The only known photo, not dated, of Hans Kemritz, the people snatcher for Soviet intelligence in Berlin and a double agent for the American CIC.

Before Kemritz had been released, an officer of the Soviet Main Intelligence Directorate (GRU) had spoken to him and presented him with two alternatives: either to return to prison or engage in espionage on behalf of the Soviet Union. It is evident Kemritz's task from the outset was to throw former Abwehr personnel and other Germans of potential interest to the wolves. At that point in time, the NKVD did not have enough people in Germany to conduct systematic searches, and the Soviet Union did not particularly want to cooperate with the Western powers in this regard. Only in the hunt for war criminals was there such cooperation. Otherwise, the Soviets much preferred to press-gang specialists into service. Kemritz's circle of acquaintances was large thanks to his service in the Berlin district of the Abwehr and his ability to make a trustworthy impression on those he met. This made him ideally suited to establishing initial contact with many of the Germans the Soviets were interested in, and it seems his approach usually followed the same pattern. He received lists of people the NKVD had their sights on. Most of those people lived in West Berlin and therefore needed to be lured to the Soviet sector of the former capital of the Reich. Kemritz would pick his target and find out as much as possible about them, after which he would write them a letter with an offer designed to attract their attention. An invitation to his office on Schadowstraße would follow and it was there a tentative discussion would take place. Standing by during the meeting was a Soviet arrest squad and vehicle. According to the description of a sensational magazine article, the manner in which Kemritz bid farewell to the visitor would determine for the NKVD men the course of action to be followed. Anyone with whom he shook hands for a long time and to whom he also waved goodbye was to be arrested immediately upon leaving the office.[16] This was what happened with Erich Klose. How many other visitors there were and how many of them were not arrested, either because they turned out to be of no interest to the Soviets or because they responded favourably to an offer of recruitment, is pure speculation. There is no known case in which an arrest was not made.

Hans Kemritz was certainly one of the most important Germans in the service of the NKVD in 1945 and 1946. Nevertheless, he was fully aware of the dangers involved in the work he was doing and tried to make sure he was ready for all eventualities. He had already contacted American officers in December 1945 and had met with representatives of the U.S. Army Counter Intelligence Corps (CIC) in his house in Dahlem in January 1946. What precisely he had offered the CIC is unknown. In any case, he continued his work for the NKVD while also passing on copies of their lists to the CIC. This enabled American intelligence to anticipate the intentions of the Soviets and to choose which people on those lists should be discouraged from going to the eastern part of Berlin. It was, of course, necessary that many Germans still be allowed to fall into the trap so there would be no cause for the NKVD to become suspicious. This meant that American officers indirectly sanctioned the abduction of an unknown number of people by the Soviets.

What happened next demonstrates the iron loyalty with which the United States, right up to the top, stood by its double agent. The activities of Kemritz came to light at the end of 1950, as Elly von Hake had initiated civil proceedings against the lawyer upon learning of the death of her husband. This also triggered criminal proceedings. She accused Kemritz of deliberately luring her husband to East Berlin for the purpose of giving the Soviets the opportunity to kidnap him. From a legal perspective, Kemritz, who was reported to be in Bad Homburg, was accused of being involved in false imprisonment, so the public prosecutor's office in Frankfurt soon issued a warrant for his arrest. The arrest was made, but it was at that moment that John McCloy, the U.S. high commissioner for Germany, intervened. He saw to it that the criminal proceedings were discontinued, arranged for the release of Kemritz, and removed the case from German jurisdiction. He could do this quite easily due to the occupation statute in force at that time, although he had certainly not imagined what the consequences might be. There was widespread protest in the increasingly self-confident free press of West Germany and significant debate in its federal parliament, the Bundestag. A whole series of highly confidential and extremely difficult negotiations took place between German and American jurists; it was even necessary for personal discussions to be held between McCloy and Chancellor Konrad Adenauer and between McCloy's chief political advisor and German Minister of Justice Thomas Dehler. In the middle of June 1951, most German newspapers strongly criticised the violation by the Americans of the independence of the German judiciary. In the Bundestag, the social democrat Otto Greve spoke in an impassioned manner: 'Ladies and gentlemen, we are still waiting today for the facts of the Kemritz case!'[17] By that time, Mr and Mrs Kemritz had moved from their house in Bad Homburg to live on an American military site, but the West German press and federal government did not let the matter rest. They probed into the matter once more in the spring of 1952 and demanded the allegations be dealt with in a German court. However, McCloy enjoyed the full support of Washington, with U.S. Secretary of State Dean Acheson regarding the matter as done and dusted. The exposed double agent and his wife were flown to the United States at the end of March 1952, and it is there the trail goes cold.

Why did the U.S. government risk putting a severe strain on its relations with Bonn for the sake of Hans Kemritz, especially at a time the United States wanted to facilitate the rearmament of West Germany? As a defendant, he certainly would have been able to reveal unpleasant details regarding his arrangement with the CIC, albeit not without also incriminating himself, for there would have then been no doubt whatsoever that he had worked as a decoy for the NKVD before offering his services to the Americans. The American historian Arthur L. Smith has extensively researched the Kemritz affair and has come to a conclusion that, though unsubstantiated, is easily imaginable:

John J. McCloy, the U.S. high commissioner for Germany, regarded Hans Kemritz to be of such great importance that he openly snubbed Chancellor Konrad Adenauer whenever the question was raised of bringing the people snatcher to justice.

> It is difficult to accept that a rather low-ranking ex-major of the Abwehr could have possessed such highly sensitive information that the United States would be ready to protect him at any cost. However, a logical explanation did emerge in the debate in the Bundestag. The suggestion was made there that Kemritz had helped the Americans monitor the Soviet nuclear programme in East Germany. Considering all the facts in relation to Kemritz, this seems to be a logical assumption'.[18]

It is possible the double agent for the CIC had a ring of informants working for him in the uranium mines of the Ore Mountains. This would explain why the Americans found him to be of sufficient interest in early 1946 and why they were happy for him to remain in his precarious position as a people snatcher for the NKVD. Furthermore, the haste with which he was whisked away from West Berlin the moment the suspicion of the Soviets had been aroused makes sense in this context. However, it is hardly to be expected more precise information on this matter will ever emerge. If Smith's conclusions are correct, it means that, in less than a year after the end of World War II, the Kemritz affair was the first major intelligence operation of the Cold War. It is of no surprise that it took place in Berlin.

The division of the police forces

The rise of Erich Mielke

After the disappearance of Karl Heinrich, the Western powers lost all confidence in the will of the Soviets to jointly build a functioning police force in Berlin. On 18 May 1946, the commandant of the American sector of the city took the unusual step of issuing an order to Chief of Police Paul Markgraf to the effect that police officers were to be forbidden from participating in party politics. The party that the

Americans specifically had in mind was the SED, which had been founded a few weeks earlier in the eastern part of Berlin through the forced union of the KPD and SPD. It seems Markgraf did not comply with this demand, for it was only five months later that the military headquarters of each of the four occupying powers, still meeting regularly with one another at that stage, decided the reorganisation of the police in Berlin was in order. A sectorial police chief was appointed in each zone of the former capital of the Reich. These four sectorial chiefs were subordinate to the chief of police and his deputies on the one hand and to the officers responsible for public security in each zone on the other.[19] The resources and experience at the disposal of the three sectorial chiefs in the western zones were limited. Furthermore, decisions could only be made in cooperation with the occupying powers. The effect was the effective division of the police forces in Berlin. This was exacerbated by the constant and systematic attempts by the communist-dominated Berlin Presidium of the People's Police to utilise the police for political ends. Its preference for police officers who supported communism and its full exploitation of the methods of espionage were inextricably linked. Any undesirable police officers were denounced, truthfully or otherwise, as war criminals. With the first and, until 1990, the only, free elections for the whole of Berlin soon to take place in October 1946, the sometimes subtle yet often brutal instrumentalisation of the Berlin Police in the interests of the SED and the Soviet occupation forces became a political issue.

The election result was disappointing for the communists. The SPD received 48.7 percent of the vote, while the Christian Democratic Union (CDU) and the Liberal Democratic Party (LDP) together received 31.5 percent, but the SED achieved only 19.8 percent. It was clear from this that the division of the city would not be far off, especially given the determination of the communists to hold on to power. The personnel policy of Markgraf at that time was designed to bring the police forces of Berlin into line with the politics of the SED. SPD leader Franz Neumann criticised Markgraf's tactics in a speech he gave at a meeting of the city council. According to his research, the chief of police had managed, despite the existence of the sectorial police chiefs, to fill 15 of the 21 departmental posts of the criminal investigation department with SED members. Almost all detective superintendents, 14 out of 21 inspectorate chiefs, and two thirds of all district chiefs were communists.[20] In contrast to the non-communist police officers, these cadres always made their services available to the communist cause, thereby meeting the expectations of the chief of police.

These events occurred in the context of the de-nazification of Germany, a process that all victorious powers had decided on but whose implementation was handled in different ways. In the British and American zones, Nazi functionaries and other former state officials, even those of low rank, were automatically interned. In contrast, the Soviet Union was from the outset more interested in the radical transformation of its zone of occupation along the lines of its own model of society. Those who fully submitted to the will of the KPD or, from 1946, the SED had the best prospects for a new career, while those who opposed the claim to power of the communists would be labelled as fascists and would fall into the clutches of the NKVD. Soviet authorities in Berlin often relied on Germans as confidants and informants, with the number of such collaborators rising from approximately 2,300 in 1946 to approximately 3,000 in 1949. Rebellious young people would often be arrested on the grounds they had supposedly been members of Werewolf, the chimerical Nazi guerrilla group. Also arrested were Wehrmacht officers who had returned from captivity in the West and social democrats who had resisted the forced union with the KPD. Allegations of war crimes or espionage were usually levelled at them, yet it was almost always the case that neither serious investigations nor proper trials were conducted. Instead, those who were arrested often disappeared for years in special camps, reactivated concentration camps like Buchenwald and Sachsenhausen, or other former Nazi detention centres like forced labour and prisoner of war camps. Conversely, the British and the Americans carried out extensive investigations and numerous courts martial in their internment camps, although the number of those facing serious charges who were acquitted or released rose in parallel with the increase in tensions between East and West.

By the end of 1945, the Soviet military administration in Germany set up a political commissariat and attached it to the criminal investigation department. Soon known as Kommissariat 5 (K-5) and with departments in the states of Brandenburg, Mecklenburg, Saxony, Saxony-Anhalt, and Thuringia, its task was to support Soviet authorities in their supposedly anti-fascist, but in reality, pro-Stalinist, purge, specifically by reinforcing the relatively small number of NKVD personnel in East Germany, carrying out interrogations and taking on administrative tasks. The German Administration of the Interior was formed on 30 July 1946 to centralise the control of the rapidly growing police forces in the Soviet zone of occupation. Its first president was the communist and former Buchenwald prisoner Erich Reschke, and one of his deputies, Erich Mielke, became the head of what was in effect the first secret service of East Germany, the Committee for the Protection of the National Economy. Its headquarters was situated in Wilhelmsruh, Berlin, and its employees were involved in the persecution of real or imagined spies and saboteurs.

In a presentation on 30 October 1946 to the chiefs of police of the five states established in East Germany by the Soviet military administration, Mielke outlined the tasks to be carried out by his new committee: '(1) the creation of democratically united and reliable organs, and (2) the utilisation of those organs to protect democratic reconstruction and peaceful development as well as to liquidate and suppress fascist remnants. The second task can only be carried out once the first task has been completed. The liquidation of fascist remnants is to be achieved (1) through the re-education of the masses, (2) through the physical liquidation and punishment of active fascists and their accomplices, and (3) through the replacement of that which is old by that which is better.' Mielke was more explicit towards the end of his presentation:

> Despite the fundamental political and social changes that have taken place in the Soviet zone, there are still a large number of people—fascist enemies of democratic reconstruction—who have slipped through the cracks and who can only be liquidated through the creation of a truly effective organ. Most of the gangs and criminals are organised. These gangs, seeking to disrupt democratic reconstruction, are political in character, especially when it is remembered that the gang leaders are Hitlerites who exploit every opportunity to prove that the new people of today are incapable of establishing and safeguarding security and order.[21]

Rather in keeping with communist tradition, Mielke's statements were based on an idiosyncratic perception of reality. When he spoke of 'democratic', what he meant was the absolute rule of the SED, while 'gangs' for him included the social democrats in West Berlin who had vehemently and successfully opposed the union with the KPD.

Mielke was initially unable to manage things as he pleased in East Berlin. Beside Paul Markgraf at police headquarters on Keibelstraße was the social democrat Johannes Stumm, who had been a leading figure of the Berlin Police until being demoted and then dismissed by the Nazis in the early 1930s. In January 1947, the city council had assigned Stumm responsibility for a planned Department for the Security of Democracy, but the Allied commands, facing Soviet pressure, did not confirm this appointment. It was insufficiently clear against whom this new department was supposed to protect democracy. As a result, the attempt by the city council—which was dominated by the SDP, CDU, and LDP—to establish a counterweight to Paul Markgraf had failed.[22] In October 1947, after much toing and froing, Stumm finally renounced the appointment, which had not in any case been fully thought through, and returned to his post as a departmental head at police headquarters. In the meantime, the three Western sectorial police chiefs chose to limit their efforts to organising their uniformed police forces and criminal investigation departments to the best of their ability.

Berlin was finally divided when the Soviet Union, on the night of 23/24 June 1948, cut off the supply of electricity to the western part of the city and then, on the following morning, put a stop to the westward flow of road, railway, and inland waterway traffic. For the next 322 days, until 12 May 1949, the movement of people and goods from West Germany to the western sectors of Berlin was prohibited by Soviet authorities. This blockade was in a sense the first battle of the Cold War, as the United States, Great Britain, and France decided to undertake the enormous task of supplying not only the troops they had stationed in the city but also the approximately two million inhabitants there. The three Western sectors were by no means entirely cordoned off from the surrounding area or from the Soviet sector, for, even though there were checkpoints, there were neither fences nor walls of the sort that existed after 1961. Nevertheless, the Soviets and their collaborators in the SED put the people of West Berlin under a tremendous amount of pressure. Their goal was to compel the Allies to withdraw by inciting the animosity of the population against them. Stalin's measure was a miscalculation, though. The immense logistical efforts of the British and the Americans meant they were perceived by West Berliners no longer as occupiers but rather as protectors.

In this extremely tense situation, there remained only one step before the division of the police was fully complete. It came in the form of the reinstatement of Karl Heinrich's former personnel officer of the uniformed police, Hans Seidel, who had been removed from his post in March 1947 by the SPD-dominated city council due to his party-political activity for the East. Notwithstanding this dismissal, Paul Markgraf, backed by the Soviets, chose to assign Seidel a leadership position in July 1948. The city council thereupon suspended the chief of police. Although this decision was rejected by the commandant of the Soviet sector of Berlin, the city council nonetheless appointed Johannes Stumm as the new chief of police for the three Western sectors. This SPD man set up his new police headquarters in a former barracks on Friesenstraße in Kreuzberg, Berlin. It was there that the first democratically legitimate state police protection system was established in post-war Berlin, the antecedent of an intelligence agency whose objective would be the protection of the constitution. However, in comparison with the intelligence network that had already been set up in East Berlin, the measures that had been taken in the western sectors of the now clearly divided city were marginal.

CHAPTER SIX

Mielke's men

A secret service for the SED

Partial success for Walter Ulbricht

By July 1948, East German communists did not have any need to conceal their intentions. Soviet authorities decreed that the political dominance of the SED would be enforced. The open confrontation that had arisen due to the Berlin Blockade and that had intensified due to the unexpected and creative response that was the Berlin Airlift meant there was no longer any reason for the Soviet Union to show consideration towards its former partners in the anti-Hitler coalition. Walter Ulbricht announced the new party line at a state political conference at the end of July: 'Our interests are absolutely the same as those of the Soviet Union!' Erich Mielke clarified what that meant in practice:

> The state apparatus must be made entirely free of certain people who have snuck in, especially agents, Schumacher men, spies, and saboteurs. … In order to carry out the cleansing properly, we must also identify the incompetent bureaucrats who inhibit our work and who cite all sorts of objective difficulties in an attempt to water down the tasks set for us by the two-year plan. … Ultimately, even those who are not enemies and whose intentions are honourable must be removed if they are not up to the tasks assigned to them. Care must be taken to ensure that these people do not just receive promotions, which is something that seems to happen far too often.[1]

Yet purging the brand-new state apparatus of unadaptable social democrats—the so-called 'Schumacher men'—was a task that overtaxed the secret police that existed in East Germany at that time. As a result, Walter Ulbricht, in the second half of 1948, sought permission from Moscow for an independent secret service that would be under the direct control of the SED. Serving as a basis for the new secret service would be the political commissariat K-5, whose departments with the state police forces throughout East Germany had in the meantime expanded significantly, as well as the Committee for the Protection of the National Economy. On 28 December 1948, although Soviet Minister of State Security Viktor Abakumov advised Stalin against it, the Politburo of the Communist Party of the Soviet Union approved the request officially made by Wilhelm Pieck in Moscow. Abakumov was ordered to send additional specialists to East Germany to support the establishment of the new secret service. With around 700 employees of the Committee for the Protection

East German border guard personnel (in uniform) and Stasi specialists (in civilian clothing) excavate an unsuccessful escape tunnel under Heidelberger Straße in October 1962.

of the National Economy in East Berlin, as well as roughly 1600 members of K-5 spread out across East Germany, there were sufficient personnel for the new agency. In addition, there were more than 4,000 politically reliable old communists or young cadres among the ordinary police. In May 1949, Erich Mielke was appointed interim head of the secret service, which was named the Main Directorate for the Protection of the National Economy. In cooperation with Soviet officers, he immediately set about selecting trustworthy personnel. He proved to be highly selective: of the 6,670 people who were eligible, only 772 were initially assessed as suitable. A mere 10 per cent of the former K-5 employees were allowed to join the new secret service.[2] This process of selecting personnel was quite a challenge for Mielke, as it was required that 2,950 people be hired before the autumn of 1949. Subsequent historical accounts produced by the Stasi itself described this phase in the following manner: 'Under the leadership of our comrade Erich Mielke, an apparatus was set up in the course of the year of 1949 which after the formation of the German Democratic Republic was initially known as the Main Directorate for the Protection of Public Property.'[3]

Although Mielke, given his previous achievements in the creation of the East German People's Police, appeared predestined to become the head of the secret service of the SED, this was not what ended up happening. Moscow's two highest representatives in the newly founded German Democratic Republic, Vasily Chuikov as head of the Soviet Control Commission and Vladimir Semyonov as chief diplomat, wrote to Stalin on 7 January 1950 and advised against the appointment of Mielke. Chuikov and Semyonov were concerned about the lack of clarity regarding what Mielke had been up to after his time as a KPD secret agent in the Spanish Civil War. Particularly problematic in their view was the speculation about his work for the Nazi Organisation Todt in France up to 1944. Perhaps also in their minds was the fact that Mielke was a disciple of Ulbricht rather than a mere functionary who listened to Moscow. In any case, Stalin himself reached the decision to appoint Wilhelm Zaisser as the first Minister for State Security. Zaisser had been a communist since 1919 and an agent for the KPD since 1920, and he had soon thereafter started working for the Soviets as well. As 'General Gómez' from 1936 to 1938,

Erich Mielke in the 1950s. The hope of this double murderer to become the head of the secret service of East Germany was initially unfulfilled. Even the Soviets treated him with suspicion.

Zaisser had been one of the most important commanders of the Communist Party of the Soviet Union in the Spanish Civil War. After that, he had proven his worth in various leadership roles in the Soviet Union. His loyalty to Stalin was beyond question. The inauguration of Zaisser was followed by his admission into the party executive and politburo, which meant that he immediately became a part of the inner leadership circle of the SED. The result was that although Ulbricht had been successful in establishing an East German secret service, its chief had the authority to act completely independently of Ulbricht's influence.

Bumpy start

The creation of the Stasi

On 8 February 1950, the rubber-stamp parliament that was the People's Chamber in East Berlin formally voted for the establishment of the Ministry for State Security (the Stasi), confirming a decision that had already been made by the SED. The party newspaper *Neues Deutschland* announced the parliamentary decision on the following day: 'On account of its great importance and significance, the law was passed unanimously in its first and second readings without prior referral to the committee, without discussion, and with tremendous applause from the house.'[4] The short length of time in which the decision was made was matched by the short length, not even 70 words, of the law itself: '§1 The Main Directorate for the Protection of the National Economy, previously subordinate to the Ministry of the Interior, is to be reorganised into an independent Ministry for State Security. The law of 7 October 1949 on the Provisional Government of the German Democratic Republic (*Gesetzblatt*, p. 2) will be amended accordingly. §2 This law will come into force upon its promulgation. Berlin, 8 February 1950.'[5] The legal basis for the work of the Stasi was to be found in Article 6 of the Constitution of the German Democratic Republic of 7 October 1949, in which the second section of the chapter 'Rights of the Citizens' stated:

> Campaigns to boycott democratic institutions and organisations; campaigns to murder democratic politicians; expressions of hatred of faith, race, and people; military propaganda and incitement to war; as well as all other acts directed against equal rights are crimes according to the criminal code. The practice of democratic rights within the meaning of the constitution does not encompass carrying out boycott campaigns.[6]

Since 'democracy' in East Germany always meant the absolute rule of the leadership of the SED, the Stasi had the power to treat opposition or even internal dissent as criminal.

The appointment of Zaisser was a bitter disappointment not only to Ulbricht but also to Mielke, who had worked with great determination since 1945 towards becoming the head of the secret service. As consolation, Mielke was appointed state secretary in the newly established ministry, although he did not by any means regard this as a milestone.[7] Nevertheless, as the second-highest official of the secret police in East Germany, he threw himself into his work and had Bundestag member Kurt Müller arrested on 23 March 1950. The day before, after a specially arranged meeting with Ulbricht in the building of the Central Committee of the SED on East Berlin's Torstraße, Müller, who was the deputy chairman of the West German KPD, was abducted and taken to the remand prison on Magdalenenstraße, directly opposite the office building of the Stasi in Lichtenberg. Mielke interrogated Müller per-sonally, and it is apparent from the transcript that the former wanted to prove the latter had deviated from the party line: 'We know that you are a member of a Trotskyist organisation.' Müller denied this, but his interrogator did not give up. The conversation focused on people who Müller

Wilhelm Zaisser was the first Minister for State Security. As a true follower of Stalin and his direct representative in the politburo of the SED, he fell out of favour after the death of the Soviet dictator and the events of 17 June 1953.

had been in contact with two decades previously and who had at that time been a part of the leadership of the KPD. These people had spoken out against party leader Ernst Thälmann and had therefore at a later stage been branded as deviationists. Müller maintained he had never belonged to a Trotskyist group.[8] Years later, after an odyssey through various prisons and penal camps, Müller returned to West Germany and reported:

> In one of the first interrogations that he personally conducted against me, Mielke explained to me that he was acting on instructions from Moscow and with the approval of the SED leadership. He boasted that he was an old chekist and a student of Beria, that he used to work in the Lubyanka Building, and that I would not be the first one he had dealt with.

According to Müller, Mielke resorted to brutal methods:

> From the end of March to the middle of August 1950, Mielke only conducted his interrogations at night. They started every day at ten o'clock at night and ended between four and six in the morning. I had to remain standing as he questioned me every night during those five months. And during the day, after six in the morning, I was not allowed to sleep.[9]

Müller suffered from sleep deprivation for weeks on end, and it was not entirely by chance that there was always water on the floor of his cell. In the wall of a basement cell of the prison on Dircksenstraße, where Müller had once been brought from his normal cell in order to serve three days of penal detention, the former KDP functionary scratched the following quote from Josef Stalin: 'Terror is a sign of weakness.'[10]

Müller's disappearance was noticed in Bonn seven weeks after he had been arrested. As if in an attempt to justify this disappearance, Heinz Renner, the KPD leader in the Bundestag, declared his party had evidence Müller had worked as an agent for the British and that he had been in constant contact 'with the secret service of a foreign power'.[11] In contrast, the SED announced Müller had maintained contact with the Lenin League, a communist opposition group that had in fact not existed since 1930. At any rate, Zaisser's ministry officially confirmed that Müller had been arrested in East Germany.[12] On the following day, a letter purportedly from Müller was delivered to President of the Bundestag Erich Köhler in which the KPD deputy chairman renounced his mandate. The letter was without a letterhead and clearly a forgery. The abduction of Müller exacerbated the tense political situation that had arisen in the summer of 1950 as a result of the attack by the communist regime in North Korea on South Korea. The prominent SPD parliamentarian Heinrich Ritzel was met with applause in the Bundestag when he stated: 'I think the house would certainly not object if the East were carrying out some sort of partial dismantling of the communist parliamentary group.'[13] The United Nations Commission on Human Rights looked into the matter, albeit without success. A Soviet military tribunal sentenced Müller to 25 years in prison for espionage. He was released in October 1955 and returned to West Germany. Whether Mielke's personal mistreatment of

Müller was designed to make an impression on his superior or whether it was simply a result of his frustration must remain a matter of speculation.

In fact, the second man of the Stasi would have had far more important things to do at that time because the agency was in the process of expanding. The number of full-time personnel had tripled by the end of 1952. Many people who would have been unsuitable by Mielke's standards benefited from this expansion. The result was that roughly one third of those employed by the Stasi in 1953 had to resign, mostly involuntarily, after he eventually became the Minister for State Security in 1957. Clearly illustrating the 'remarkable level of internal chaos' is the fact that, between 1950 and 1953 alone, 44 active and 38 former Stasi agents defected to the West.[14] This figure amounted to one per cent of all Stasi employees, a devastating record for a secret service. In an attempt to counteract this, Zaisser and Mielke enacted draconian measures. They saw to it that 26 of the defectors were kidnapped from West Berlin or West Germany and punished severely, with some of them even being put to death. This created an atmosphere of uncertainty within the Stasi, which, in turn, may have had an impact on its efficiency.

Indeed, the Stasi proved to be a complete failure during the East German uprising of 1953. Its informers did not report the change in the mood of the working class to party leaders in good time, and, by the middle of June 1953, its intelligence agents had demonstrated their ineffectiveness. There were even some locations in East Berlin where angry workers chased Stasi officers down the streets. Rudolf Gutsche, head of the main division of the Stasi responsible for surveillance and investigation, got into his wine-red BMW on the morning of 17 June 1953. Accompanied by another Stasi officer, the 34-year-old drove into the city centre without hesitation. This turned out to be a bad idea, for the number plate clearly identified his car as a government vehicle. Many people had gathered at Alexanderplatz in order to protest against the SED dictatorship, and it was there, on the corner of Rathausstraße, that a truck rammed into the BMW. Construction workers immediately surrounded the vehicle, smashed the windows, and dragged out both occupants. The Stasi officers drew their service weapons. One of them fired a stray shot. They were then disarmed and beaten, and their car was set alight. The situation was similar for several other senior officers, as Zaisser and Mielke had sent all available men out onto the streets. Josef Kiefel, responsible for espionage in the West, experienced the full brunt of the anger of the workers. He suffered serious head injuries when stones were hurled at him on Stalinallee. It was worse for Heinz Kairies, head of the division responsible for university surveillance. His Saxon dialect was his undoing. 'What d'you want, Saxon copper?' shouted a demonstrator, whereupon Kairies and three other Stasi members were harassed by the crowd. He fled down a side street, fired a shot, and rushed to a building entrance that he had mistaken for a pathway. When he realised his mistake, he ran up the stairs and hid in one of the apartments. His pursuers broke down the door, chased him down the stairs, and beat him with beer bottles, iron bars, and wooden slats. Kairies somehow survived. He was diagnosed with skull fracture, spinal contusion, and several broken bones.[15]

The Stasi was unable to protect the SED dictatorship from its own people. Only the imposition of martial law over East Germany, a decision which was made in Moscow on the evening of 16 June and implemented the following day at 1pm, prevented the collapse of communist rule. Within a few hours, Soviet tanks crushed all resistance and at least 55 people lost their lives. Otto Grotewohl, who possessed little power despite officially being the second man in East Germany, stated bluntly before the Central Committee: 'The organs of the Ministry for State Security have failed.'[16] Ulbricht reached the same conclusion: 'The politburo has determined that the leadership of the Ministry for State Security has failed.' In making this statement, Ulbricht was to some degree pursuing an ulterior motive. The barely avoided revolution against his regime turned out

Ernst Wollweber was an experienced saboteur from the time of the resistance against Hitler. As the second man to become the head of the Stasi, his lack of success was a result of his disregard for the rules of intelligence.

to be a blessing in disguise, as he was able to blame Zaisser personally for the failure to anticipate the uprising. Zaisser's position had weakened since the death of Stalin and the uprising seemed to confirm his weakness. He attempted, in collaboration with the editor in chief of *Neues Deutschland*, Rudolf Herrnstadt, to overthrow Ulbricht, but the SED leader prevailed and was supported by Moscow. The logical consequence was the dismissal of the almost all-powerful head of the Stasi. It also came to light at that time that Zaisser, without permission, had approved a number of payments and credits totalling approximately 230,000 marks. The Stasi lost its status as an independent ministry, was downgraded to a state secretariat, and was incorporated into the Ministry of the Interior. Mielke, just as responsible as Zaisser for the failure of the Stasi and also found guilty of embezzlement (even if 'only' 63,000 marks), disarmingly levelled criticism at himself: 'I would like to declare to the party openly, honestly, and unreservedly that I am jointly responsible for these weaknesses and serious mistakes.'[17]

The Politburo of the Communist Party of the Soviet Union selected Ernst Wollweber as the new head of the Stasi. Wollweber had set up an organisation in Scandinavia in the 1930s whose goal was to conduct acts of sabotage against Nazi Germany and Fascist Italy. His task would be to transform the Stasi into a powerful apparatus. Zaisser's approach was now regarded as too cautious. A senior official of the U.S. Army Counter Intelligence Corps (CIC) commented at that time on the cynically positive consequences of this reassignment for his own work:

> We never knew where we stood with Zaisser. His policy was not to eliminate enemy spy networks but rather to monitor and gradually infiltrate them so that they would be rendered worthless to the enemy. In contrast, Wollweber immediately arrests anyone he suspects of being engaged in espionage, regardless of how certain he is. We can gain an idea of what the Stasi knows based on the reports we receive on who has been arrested. With Zaisser, we knew nothing.[18]

As for Mielke, Ulbricht was able to convince Moscow to allow him to remain deputy head of the Stasi.

Triumph of a double murderer

The rise of Erich Mielke to Minister for State Security

The uprising of 17 June 1953 had been a traumatic event for the Stasi. On the day before the first anniversary of the uprising, the president of East Germany, Wilhelm Pieck, expressed his concern to the head of the Stasi, Ernst Wollweber: 'Well, who knows what tomorrow will bring?'[19] Hermann Matern, one of the most powerful SED functionaries alongside Walter Ulbricht, set the agenda: 'We must strike hard and ruthlessly. There is no room in our ranks for weak-kneed pacifists and moon-gazing idiots. Comrade Ulbricht once declared at a meeting of the Central Committee: "We must make the German Democratic Republic a place of hell for enemy agents." Comrades, that is your most important task!'[20] Wollweber wanted to demonstrate the capability of the Stasi to the sceptics in the SED and in Moscow by putting into effect three major operations that were to be led by Erich Mielke personally.[21] The first of these 'concentrated strikes' was given the cover name Operation *Fireworks* and was directed against real and suspected agents of the Gehlen Organisation to be found in East Germany in October 1953. This operation was made possible through the recruitment of Hans-Joachim Geyer, who was the deputy head of a branch of the organisation in West Berlin. He had been arrested, interrogated, and turned while on a courier trip in Dresden. From then on, he provided numerous details about the work of his branch and was paid the princely salary of 10,000 West German marks, but when Geyer was in danger of being exposed, Wollweber decided the time had come to strike. More than one hundred arrests were reported to the politburo of the SED, although they were predominantly made up of insignificant informants who observed Soviet barracks, tanks, and airfields. Nevertheless, *Neues Deutschland* proclaimed a tremendous victory: 'Enemy espionage agencies in the German Democratic Republic shattered!'[22] Geyer himself moved to East Germany and, at a press conference, castigated the Western powers and West Germany for the alleged 'preparation for a new war of conquest'. He emerged once more in 1954 with the publication of an espionage novel whose title was *Am Anfang stand das Ende …* (It Ended at the Beginning …).

The second Stasi strike, Operation *Arrow*, took place in August 1954. Up to 547 Western agents were arrested throughout East Germany: 277 of those were spies for the Gehlen Organisation, 176 for American intelligence agencies, and 94 for the French. Among those arrested were several senior officials, including a departmental head in the Ministry for Heavy Industry, a director of the Waterways Directorate, and even the chairman of the union group of the railway station in Lichtenberg, Berlin, which stood opposite the Stasi headquarters. Although the people that had been arrested were accused of being 'former fascists, now spies of imperialism', only 33 of them had been members of the Nazi Party, while only another eight had served as officers in the Wehrmacht. In contrast, 48 were members of the SED.[23] Accordingly, the press campaign that followed Operation *Arrow* was more restrained than that which had followed Operation *Fireworks*.

Wollweber and Mielke regarded Operation *Arrow* as a minor success at best and wanted to follow it up with another concentrated strike as soon as possible. This strike would be coordinated by the main division responsible for the surveillance of the political underground rather than that for the conduct of counterintelligence. Operation *Lightning* was directed less against informants for enemy secret services and more against people who were in contact with organisations, especially in West Berlin, that were critical of the SED. It was planned that the operation would be fully executed on 8 February 1955, the fifth anniversary of the foundation of the Stasi, but it turned out this was not possible due to the lengthy preparations required for some elements of the operation. Intended was the abduction of more than a dozen people from West Berlin who were critics of the East German regime, including journalist Karl Wilhelm Fricke and commentator Carola Stern. Furthermore, the operation would involve the arrest and interrogation, on suspicion of espionage, of almost any non-conformist East German citizens. This meant a large number of arrests could be made and reported, thereby achieving the objective of sheer intimidation. In his final report, Mielke wrote that of the 521 'agents' who had been imprisoned, 56 had been involved with the Combat Group against Inhumanity, 32 with the Investigation Committee of Free Jurists, and 17 with the East Office of the SPD. The report also concluded that 188 of those arrested had worked for various American agencies. Such a number was reached by arresting those who not only worked at but also visited the West Berlin radio station RIAS (Radio in the American Sector). The main part of the operation was carried out in East Berlin where 159 people were arrested. Many of the suspects were soon released, for not even the SED-controlled courts could punish those against whom unfounded allegations had been made. Nevertheless, the Stasi celebrated the success of its operation and awarded 200 of its employees bonuses of between 100 and 1,000 East German marks. The grand total of those bonuses amounted to more than 63,000 East German marks. Furthermore, the Stasi, which had been downgraded to a state secretariat, regained its status as an independent ministry at the end of November 1955. Wollweber became the Minister for State Security; Mielke remained his deputy.

Despite this success, Wollweber was unable to hold onto his post for much longer. It was the era of de-Stalinisation and, on 25 February 1956, the last day of the 20th Congress of the Communist Party of the Soviet Union, approximately 1,400 delegates gathered in the Great Hall of the Kremlin in Moscow for an event behind closed doors. Party leader Nikita Khrushchev spoke of how the cult of personality that had been fostered in the Soviet Union had led to 'a whole series of extremely serious distortions of party principles, intraparty democracy, and revolutionary legitimacy'. This distancing from Stalin, the communist godfather, would have been enough on its own to cause a sensation, but Khrushchev went further. He openly criticised the methods by which Stalin had ruled since 1934: 'This terror had in fact been directed against honourable cadres of the party.'[24] This was a rather dangerous situation for Walter Ulbricht, for no leading communist in the Eastern Bloc had internalised Stalin's cult of personality as much as the General Secretary of the SED. The political thaw that had set in endangered his position of power, and it was now the Moscow-loyal Wollweber who became the beacon of hope for internal party reformers. After Krushchev sent tanks to Hungary to brutally suppress the uprising there, however, Ulbricht saw his chance. On 5 November 1956, he addressed a letter to the staff of the Stasi:

> The militarists and monopolists in West Germany, disappointed with the defeat of the Hungarian counterrevolution and foaming with rage, will leave no stone unturned in the near future to divert attention from this defeat and to stir up trouble in the German Democratic Republic. For this reason, comrades of the State Security, you will need to increase your revolutionary vigilance and fighting ability in the coming days and weeks. Do not allow waverers in your own ranks and see to it that the enemy is hit hard wherever he is to be found.[25]

Mielke now adopted a confrontational course towards Wollweber. Moscow chose not to become involved on this occasion, especially as the Stasi minister was struggling with poor health. He had already been absent for several months in 1956, and he had to go on leave in July 1957 because of a heart attack. The final blow was struck in the middle of October 1957 when Wollweber was accused of 'revisionism' before the Central Committee of the SED. This was the standard accusation made against anyone who actually or allegedly deviated from the party line. Wollweber got the drift of what Ulbricht was up to and resigned on 1 November 1957. His successor was Mielke, who had now reached the position he had been after for eight years. The Western media noticed the change that had taken place and introduced the new Minister for State Security to their readers. Among other details, it was reported a warrant had been issued for his arrest in 1931 and again in 1947.[26] *Die Zeit* succinctly stated: 'There is a double murderer on a ministerial seat in the Pankow government.'[27]

Decades later, a final sentence would be passed on Mielke for this crime alone, even though no fewer than 30 preliminary investigations were undertaken.[28]

A state within a state

The rampant growth of the Stasi and the dominance of the SED

The Stasi was already quite a large organisation by the time Mielke became its minister, with approximately 17,000 full-time employees throughout East Berlin and East Germany. Even so, its growth continued not only unchecked but also at an ever-increasing rate. During Mielke's almost 32-year tenure, the number of staff, on average, doubled every 10 years. By 1989, there were more than 90,000 full-time Stasi employees on the payroll. Accordingly, the budget grew almost every year, from well below 500 million East German marks in 1957 to more than 3.5 billion East German marks in 1988. Inflation hardly played a role in this growth, as prices were capped in the economy of short supply of East Germany and were kept relatively stable through economic subsidies. During Mielke's ministership, the expenditure of the SED on the fight against actual or suspected internal and external enemies effectively increased by 700 per cent, adjusted for the small degree of inflation. This alone is enough to demonstrate the significant growth of the Stasi. Immediately before the fall of the SED dictatorship, the Stasi had about one employee for every 170 East German citizens. In contrast, there were, at the same point in time, roughly 4,000 West German citizens for every employee of the West German intelligence agencies (including, among others, the Federal Office for the Protection of the Constitution, the Federal Intelligence Service, the State Security Division of the Federal Police, and the Military Counterintelligence Service). Absent in West Germany, yet abundant in East Germany, were unofficial collaborators. These were voluntary, hired, or blackmailed informers. By 1989, there were approximately 189,000 unofficial collaborators under the control of Stasi officers. These unofficial collaborators were quite unlike the informants, whose numbers never exceeded a few thousand, for the Federal Office for the Protection of the Constitution.

Just as the number of staff and the size of the budget of the Stasi increased under Mielke, so too did the number of tasks assigned to it. The Stasi was by no means an ordinary intelligence and counterintelligence service; one of its tasks from the very beginning was the employment of secret police for the persecution of all opponents of the rule of the SED. This was in keeping with the Soviet agencies it was modelled on: the NKVD, the MGB, and the KGB. While the focus in the 1950s was on the defence against the real and imagined activities of Western agents as well as on the suppression of any potential domestic opposition, the range of tasks changed decisively with the construction of the Berlin Wall in 1961. The Stasi became responsible for the prevention of possible 'attacks on the western frontier of the state' and was fully committed, in accordance with its motto, to its role as the 'shield and sword of the party'. A 'new form of precautionary social control' accompanied the growing power of the Stasi.[29] Its agents worked conspiratorially in a manner not to be seen in an open society with a more or less regulated market. With its enormously expanding structure, the Stasi developed into a real state within a state which replicated almost every aspect of East German society with a particular focus on those areas that might potentially be a source of concern from the point of view of security. Scientists were employed by the Stasi so they could monitor their own researchers as well as spy on their Western colleagues. The same was the case for medical professionals. The largest divisions in the Stasi were those that monitored the armed forces, the state apparatus, the churches, and any cultural or underground movements for traces of opposition.

This parallel structure did not at all mean the Stasi had detached itself from the SED. On the contrary, the state party and the state security were closely linked at all times. It was precisely this fact that Egon Krenz, the failed 'saviour' of the SED regime, tried to disguise, at all costs, at the beginning of the Peaceful Revolution of 1989 and 1990. It was his last service to the party to which he owed everything. Only the strategy of assigning blame to the Stasi allowed the state party, by then renamed the Party of Democratic Socialism (PDS), to survive the upheaval. Although Krenz was expelled from the party, his loyalty was such that he presented the following lie with the utmost vehemence:

> In reality, the Ministry for State Security developed increasingly into an externally shielded state within a state which even had members of the party under its control. ... This development was disastrous. While the cadre of the party made some decisions and investments, it was the Chairman of the National Defence Council and the Minister for State Security, in violation of every democratic principle, who alone discussed and made decisions on matters relating to the security of the state and the operations of the Ministry for State Security.[30]

Egon Krenz, who at the 11th Congress of the SED in 1986 had been selected by the Central Committee as the secretary responsible for issues of security, claimed in January 1990 that all essential questions in this area had in fact been addressed by Erich Honecker and Erich Mielke. If this were true, it would be astonishing that Krenz, regarded as Honecker's undisputed heir apparent, would have been unable to resist this encroachment by Honecker and Mielke on his area of responsibility. However, it is clear from the documents of the SED and of the East German government, now held in the German Federal Archives, that Krenz's function was nowhere near as restricted as it would seem from his portrayal. The Stasi was certainly a state within the East German state, but this does not serve to exonerate the SED, which was, and always remained, the decisive power within the dictatorship.

In the early days of its existence, the Stasi experienced a significant problem with its personnel. The number of employees fluctuated and there were many who defected to the West. It was after the construction of the Berlin Wall that Mielke managed to get this problem under control; he saw to it that there was always pressure on employees to conform and that potential recruits were carefully selected and offered opportunities that they never would have been given outside the Stasi. Just as important for the stabilisation of the Stasi as the backing of the SED were two other factors: the above-average pay and the sense of great power. According to the last surviving and almost complete payroll, the annual income of Stasi employees lay between 2,795 East German marks (modest even by East German standards, as earnt by each of the 1,636 conscripts born between 1969 and 1971 who served in the Stasi-controlled Guards Regiment Felix E. Dzerzhinsky) and a top salary of 71,250 East German marks (as received by the most important deputy minister, Colonel-General Rudi Mittig). Of the 90,597 Stasi employees listed on this payroll, one prominent name is missing: Erich Mielke. His salary was apparently so secret that not even the highly trustworthy people of the Stasi personnel administration were permitted to know what it was.[31]

The list of names, dates of birth, service departments, and annual salaries on the payroll, more than 3,500 pages of it, reveals even more about the personnel structure of the Stasi. There were entire families in Mielke's service: fathers were often high-ranking officers and mothers administrative secretaries; sons might have served in the guards regiment, in the security company, in passport inspection units at border crossings, or in Main Division VIII (responsible for surveillance and making arrests); and daughters or daughters-in-law, judging by their annual salaries, served in subordinate roles, presumably as typists or archivists. Due to the right to privacy, the names of most, and therefore probably not particularly prominent, Stasi employees cannot be published. They are protected by the very constitutional democracy they had opposed up to 1989. Even so, it does not require much effort to find this list of Stasi salaries on the Internet. The main point here is that the salaries of full-time Stasi employees were, on average, higher than those of ordinary East German citizens. The Stasi ensured the commitment of its personnel through unusually high pay. In short, Mielke purchased the loyalty of his employees. There were other incentives that guaranteed loyalty, like the privileged supply of consumer goods that were otherwise in short supply or the incorporation into a social fabric that, while similar to any other large organisation, was geared towards putting pressure on employees to conform. In this way, Stasi employees were almost always transformed into well-functioning clogs in a powerful machine. There was no room for obstinacy or deviancy. The feature film *The Lives of Others*, which won the 2006 Oscar for Best Foreign Language Film, is pure fiction in this respect. 'We do not know of a single case where an interrogator secretly sided with his victim,' said Hubertus Knabe, the director of the memorial for the victims of the Stasi in Hohenschönhausen.[32]

The Stasi was a criminal organisation on many levels. Journalist Klaus Behling and author Helmut Eikermann, alias Jan Eik, have written three volumes on the crimes of the Stasi. They emphasise that, in addition to criminal acts on behalf of the SED, like kidnappings of West German critics of the East German regime, there were a number of crimes committed by individual Stasi employees who exploited the advantage of their position of power and who had no need to fear any legal or public scrutiny. The books by Behling and Eikermann also demonstrate that the Stasi was no 'secret service like any other'.[33] It is true that intelligence agencies in any political system, be it in a democratic constitutional state or in a dictatorship, exist in a grey zone where certain individuals seek personal aggrandisement, but, as the reports on recent intelligence scandals in Germany and the United States show, such acts of indiscretion come to light sooner or later in open societies. Most well-known is the enormous, albeit for the most part feigned, uproar over the supposed revelations of the NSA traitor Edward Snowden from 2013 onwards. Nothing of the sort ever took place in East Germany. Only after the collapse of the SED regime could the activities of the Stasi be examined. In Russia, which has been under the control of former KGB officers for the last couple of decades, little has been revealed to this day of the activities of Soviet intelligence. Any attempts that have been made to find information on this matter have been systematically prevented.

'Pure Chekists'

Markus Wolf and his Main Directorate for Reconnaissance

It is said that a storm was kicked up in the headquarters of the Stasi in East Berlin on 5 March 1979. An insider later reported Erich Mielke was utterly furious; on the cover of the magazine *Der Spiegel* that Monday morning was one of his most important members of staff: Markus Wolf, the head of the Main Directorate for Reconnaissance (HVA), the East German foreign intelligence service. There had been no up-to-date picture of Wolf in the West for more than two decades, but then, without realising it, he had been photographed while on a secret trip to Stockholm. Although travelling under a false name, he had been identified by a defector. Whether Mielke, as claimed by the insider, actually berated his lieutenant-general that morning is somewhat questionable, as Stasi functionaries after 1990 would have had many reasons to portray the relationship between the two as one that was inharmonious. Wolf did so himself following the reunification of Germany, for example, in a book, published after his death, of conversations with the PDS journalist Hans-Dieter Schütt:

> Today, before you came to talk to me, I reread my diaries. I came to 1974, a year in which I was regularly in conflict with Minister Mielke from month to month. By that time, I was already on the verge of taking the decision to give it all up. My diary entries from that time clearly show how difficult it was to deal with that man.[34]

This statement is not entirely convincing given Wolf continued to work under Mielke until 1986. However, it was only by exaggerating any such conflict with the primitive Mielke that Wolf was able to maintain an image of himself as a 'pure Chekist'.

Markus Wolf was without doubt one of the most intelligent minds produced by German communism. Born in Hechingen in 1923 as the son of the doctor and playwright Friedrich Wolf, the young Markus had to leave Germany with his family at the age of 10. Friedrich Wolf had been a member of the KPD since 1928 and had been labelled by the Nazis as a 'Jewish Communist'—a twofold deadly enemy. The Wolfs arrived in Moscow as exiles in 1934, and it was there that Markus and his younger brother Konrad, who would later become a film director, spent their youth. They received the best possible education, with Markus eventually attending an elite Comintern school. At the age of 19, he became a member of the KPD-in-Exile.

Catastrophe on Monday morning: the Stasi was dealt a severe blow when *Der Spiegel* revealed what Markus Wolf looked like in 1979.

This meant he was predestined to become a party official in a communist-dominated post-war Germany. He therefore returned to Germany at the end of May 1945, although it was not, despite rumours to the contrary that were encouraged even by Wolf himself, with the Ulbricht Group.[35] His role for the KPD at that time was as a journalist, with his reports from the Nuremburg trials being well-known not because of their quality but rather because of their author's reputation. But what the SED itself described as 'agitation and propaganda' proved to not be enough to satisfy Markus Wolf, and he was soon drawn towards another field in which the communist regime excelled. That field was espionage. In 1951, he transferred to the Institute for Economic Research, a front for the nucleus of the HVA. Within a few months, he had manoeuvred himself into the top position, and it was roughly at that time that the last photograph of him was published in the West prior to the one that appeared in 1979.

From 1952 to 1986, Wolf was in charge of East German foreign intelligence. He led the ultimately hopeless struggle of the Stasi against the Western, and especially the West German, system and used all the means at his disposal to do so without hesitation. These means included those that violated human rights: blackmail, abduction, and even the death penalty for renegade agents. One of the specialties of the HVA was the employment of Romeo agents. These were playboys in the service of the Stasi who would seduce and obtain information from lonely secretaries in Bonn ministries. Wolf and his case officers also offered a lot of money to those in

Until 1979, this was the only known photograph of Markus Wolf. He is shown attending a military parade, and he had by that time already manoeuvred himself to the top of the foreign intelligence service of the SED.

the West willing to commit treason or, as was often the case, those who had already persuaded themselves into thinking that the best socialist system was ultimately that which existed in East Germany. Under his leadership, the HVA, initially numbering only a few hundred men, grew into a formidable apparatus with more than 3,800 official employees, of which 1,369 worked full-time under false identities. The main task of the HVA was the coordination of its agents in the West. How many there were in total is unknown and probably never will be due to the destruction of files in 1989 and 1990. There were most likely tens of thousands in many different places. The security services of West Germany were infiltrated, as were the ministries in Bonn. There were also spies in the West German economy whose goal was to obtain information that could be used to modernise production in East Germany; there was some modest success in this regard. Another focus of the HVA was the Western media, with the ARD, the ZDF, Axel Springer Verlag, and *Der Spiegel* being the primary targets. Dietrich Staritz, who later worked in Mannheim as a researcher on the history of East Germany, acted as the unofficial collaborator 'Erich' during his time as an editor at *Der Spiegel*.[36]

The HVA invested a lot of energy into infiltrating the Bundestag. Although the Bundestag resisted an investigation for a long time, it eventually commissioned one in 2010. However, it was limited to members of parliament and therefore excluded the members of staff who would have been of far greater interest to an intelligence service like the Stasi. Even so, the Bundestag was clearly a major focus of espionage activity. There was at least one occasion on which the Stasi directly influenced West German politics. Specifically, it prevented the overthrow of SPD leader and chancellor Willy Brandt, who, by April 1972, had lost his already narrow majority in the Bundestag in the wake of his controversial efforts at rapprochement with East Germany and the Eastern Bloc. CDU leader Rainer Barzel was hoping to be elected as his successor in a constructive vote of no confidence that took place on 27 April 1972. At 1:22pm, Kai-Uwe von Hassel, the president of the Bundestag, announced the results of the secret ballot. Since the coalition factions of the SPD and FDP (Free Democratic Party) abstained almost unanimously, only 260 valid votes were cast. Barzel needed 249 votes to become chancellor, and he believed he could reach that number after so many former SPD and FDP parliamentarians had crossed the floor to join the CDU/CSU (the political alliance between the Christian Democratic Union and the Christian Social Union). However, he only received 247 votes, two short of what was required. The defeated Barzel went to the government bench and congratulated Brandt. It is noteworthy, though, that the Stasi had a hand in this vote. Two CDU/CSU members were bribed with money from East Berlin to abstain, which was in effect the same as voting against their leader. CDU politician Julius Steiner from Baden-Württemberg admitted as early as 1973 that he had sold his vote for 50,000 West German marks. This was confirmed after 1990 by former Stasi officers and contemporary Stasi documents. The second parliamentarian who sold his vote was most likely CSU politician Leo Wagner. Even though he vehemently denied this until his death, the surviving documents of the HVA indicate he had indeed been bribed. He had been experiencing financial difficulties and had been approached by a Western journalist close to the CSU who went by the name of Georg F. and who had been working for East Berlin since 1966 under the code name 'Dürer.' It later came to light that Wagner had received 50,000 West German marks from an unknown source shortly after the vote in the Bundestag. A fellow CSU politician claimed that he had lent Wagner this sum, but this was not convincing.[37] By manipulating the constructive vote of no confidence, the Stasi saved Brandt's chancellorship.

Yet conducting espionage in the West cost a lot of money. In a testimony to the investigation committee of the Bundestag on the activities of Alexander Schalck-Golodkowski in 1998, Markus Wolf's successor as head of the HVA, Werner Großmann, estimated the annual financial requirements 'for operational objectives' to be around 17.5 million East German marks and, more significantly, around 13.5 million West German marks.[38] It is open to question whether this money, from the point of view of the SED, was well-invested and whether, as a result, the activities of the HVA were successful. In any case, the clandestine effort to obtain Western industrial secrets and to influence the West German left did not significantly prolong the survival of the German Democratic Republic. Once the Soviet Union withdrew its guarantee to militarily support the East German dictatorship against any opposition, the ailing socialist state could no longer be saved, although this did nothing to alter the activities carried out by the 'pure Chekists'.

The Stasi in Berlin

Restricted areas and residential districts of the secret service

An apparatus with nearly 100,000 permanent employees requires extensive real estate in order to function. As the East German state was strictly centralised, the undisputed centre of the Stasi system lay in East Berlin, or more precisely in a

22-hectare restricted area in the Lichtenberg district. However, this large area represented only a small part of the real estate owned by the Stasi. There was a Stasi district department in every district capital of East Germany, often a hermetically sealed complex with its own remand centre for real or alleged opponents of the regime. In addition, the Stasi possessed office buildings in almost all district towns from where local surveillance operations were conducted. For Berlin, this meant that, aside from the complex in Normannenstraße, now known throughout Germany and beyond as the location of the headquarters of the Stasi, and aside from the large restricted area in Hohenschönhausen, where further central divisions of the Stasi were located, there was the similarly extensive district department that was initially located in several buildings in a former hospital complex in Prenzlauer Berg and subsequently, in the last years of the East German regime, in a newly built prefabricated building at the zoo in Friedrichsfelde. The Stasi also seized numerous smaller properties for its area precincts, and several thousand apartments were used for secret meetings with unofficial collaborators. Not to be forgotten are those rental apartment complexes that were almost exclusively used by Stasi employees, especially in Lichtenberg and Hohenschönhausen. Due to the protection of privacy, there exists no map of Berlin on which all or even most Stasi properties are marked. If there were such a map, it would surely illustrate the degree to which the Stasi octopus choked the East German capital.

The selection of Normannenstraße as the location for the headquarters of the Stasi is a demonstration of the importance of the role of Erich Mielke in the oppressive system of the SED regime. The Stasi was formed at the beginning of 1950 and was housed in the building of the former tax and revenue office in Lichtenberg, at the intersection of Magdalenenstraße and Normannenstraße and opposite Roedeliusplatz. It was in that very building that Mielke had commenced his service as head of the police station in Lichtenberg on 15 July 1945.[39] From April 1947, 32 rooms in the building were used by several departments of what was officially known as the Soviet Ministry of Information but was really the NKVD. Almost exactly opposite, on the southern side of Roedeliusplatz, lay the former district court of Lichtenberg in which Soviet Military Tribunal No. 48240, from June 1945, passed nearly all death sentences in the Soviet zone of occupation in Germany. The adjoining cell building had been built prior to the district court itself and was employed by Soviet authorities as the central, albeit not only, prison in East Berlin. Locked up there were mainly those political prisoners who were being subjected to show trials or who were earmarked for deportation to the Soviet Union.

When the Stasi was founded in 1950, it took possession of the building that had served as the headquarters for Mielke's police force in Lichtenberg. One advantage of this was that the Soviet advisors there would not be required to move; another was that the complex was already secure. This was not good enough for the Stasi though. It was only a short time before its employees complained that the residents of the apartment buildings on the opposite side of Normannenstraße (23 to 25d) could watch them while they worked. The result was that, regardless of the housing shortage at the time, the apartment buildings were vacated and taken over by the Stasi. Even that was not enough. In 1955, construction commenced on a large L-shaped building in neoclassical style. The six-storey building, later referred to within the Stasi as House 7, was completed within one year. It extended from a makeshift annexe to the original complex and was built on top of the old Helmutstraße, which soon disappeared from all city maps. According to the historian Christian Halbrock, Helmutstraße had in any case been more of a path than a road.[40] Some community gardens had to give way to the project. There could be no mistake that the Stasi intended to establish itself in Lichtenberg for the long term, with the low makeshift annexe between House 7 and the original complex being replaced by a new building in 1961 and 1962. The new building, named House 1, became Mielke's official headquarters. So great was Mielke's power within the Stasi that no one ever objected to the furnishings, opulent by East German standards, of his ministerial apartment. Until January 1990, it was in House 1 that the head of the Stasi, his most important deputies, the Executive Group of the Minister, the Bureau for Policies Implementation, and indeed all the central management divisions resided.

In the four decades of its existence, the Stasi continuously expanded its grounds in Lichtenberg. It gradually took over all the buildings on the block created by Frankfurter Allee, Ruschestraße, Magdalenenstraße, and Normannenstraße,

It was in the building of the former tax and revenue office near Roedeliusplatz that Erich Mielke commenced his rise in the SED regime. This building remained the location of the headquarters of the Stasi until 1990.

thereby forming a complete area that was off limits to those not employed by the Stasi. Old residential buildings in the area, especially along Frankfurter Allee and Magdalenenstraße, were converted into offices by the state-owned enterprise Spezialhochbau Berlin, a company given security clearance from, and assigned to, the Stasi. From the beginning of the 1970s, most new buildings were constructed using the WBS 70 prefabricated building system. It was not just the restricted area that came under Stasi control; it owned other properties nearby. The former district court and later Soviet secret service prison on Magdalenenstraße remained in use as a Stasi remand prison until 1989. It was there that political prisoners, if they were not East German citizens, could meet with their representatives, usually diplomats from foreign embassies or from the West German permanent mission. Such meetings were closely monitored by the Stasi. To the north of the main Stasi grounds, on the other side of the Hans Zschoke Stadium, the Stasi lay claim to an area whose size grew from the 1970s onwards. Where previously there had been a number of community gardens, there soon appeared half a dozen prefabricated buildings whose height ranged from six to 13 storeys. Also constructed were four other large buildings. This northern group of buildings made up a new restricted area, although it was not directly connected to that on Normannenstraße, for the small stadium of the Lichtenberg 47 football club lay in between. This bothered the Stasi planners at an early stage, who were of the view that the existence of a public sports field which hosted league games amidst its properties could not be justified.[41] Even so, the stadium was never moved and the two restricted areas were never linked. Nowadays, the history of the area on Gotlindestraße is largely forgotten, but that is

House 1 became the official headquarters for Mielke and his closest associates.

certainly not the case for the area between Frankfurter Allee and Normannenstraße. Located there today is not only the central archive of the Stasi Records Agency but also, in the extensively refurbished House 1, a number of exhibitions which include the preserved suite of rooms of the ministerial apartment.[42]

The second-largest piece of Stasi property lay in a former industrial area in Hohenschönhausen, on the north-eastern outskirts of Berlin. The NKVD had set up one of its 10 special camps in a large kitchen there in 1945, and it included two Nazi-era forced labour camps. In 1951, the Stasi assumed responsibility for the cells that had been built by the Soviets in the kitchen basement and used them as a central remand prison for 10 years. A new, modern cell building was then built by the inmates of the special camp, while the old prison continued to be operated as a penal labour camp. Aside from Bautzen II, the new building would be the most notorious Stasi prison in the decades that followed. The conditions in both prisons were atrocious: in the cellar prison, referred to by the detainees as the 'U-boat', physical torture continued to be used for some time; in the new prison building, the Stasi guards resorted to psychological methods, for example the total isolation of prisoners for months and sometimes even for years. Only in exceptional cases might an inmate have been allowed to see a lawyer. The guards consistently addressed the inmates by number only. A traffic light system was installed in the corridors so as to prevent any contact between inmates on the way to or from interrogation. If a prisoner, always under guard, came across a red light, he had to turn to face the wall at once. As a result, the inmates only ever saw the faces of guards and interrogators.

Yet the Stasi complex in Hohenschönhausen comprised many more facilities than just the prison. Housed in a residential and office building built in 1911 was the special archive of the Stasi for documents from the Nazi era. In 1954, the Stasi had commenced collecting and filing personal information. The 4.5 kilometres of files were inaccessible to the public and were generally thought to have been lost until the beginning of 1990. The purpose of this archive was to enable Stasi officers to defame Western politicians and to blackmail people of interest on either side of the inner German border. The prosecution of Nazi criminals mostly fell by the wayside. Although this archive had a historically and politically powerful impact, the largest Stasi facility in Hohenschönhausen was the Operational Technical Sector (OTS), which had a total of 1,085 full-time employees at the end of 1989. Its task was to develop special equipment for Stasi espionage operations. This included not only wiretapping systems and hidden cameras but also the tools with which Division M (Postal Control), with personnel in numerous post offices, opened tens of thousands of letters every day. This served to monitor private communications both within East Germany and with citizens in West Germany and abroad. Furthermore, cash and other valuables enclosed with letters were regularly confiscated. In this way, millions of West German marks flowed into the coffers of the Stasi and SED year after year. The OTS also developed and maintained the surveillance technology the Stasi used for listening to radio communications between West Berlin and West Germany and for recording telephone conversations within West Germany. The laboratories of the OTS in Hohenschönhausen, which predominantly lay within the restricted area, were probably the most modern part of the Stasi espionage juggernaut.

A third large Stasi complex was located in the district of Prenzlauer Berg in the East German capital from 1950 to 1985. The red brick buildings, originally erected as a hospital and infirmary on the corner of Prenzlauer Allee and Fröbelstraße, had housed the Prenzlauer Berg district office from 1934 to 1945 and had become available once the state institutions of the Nazi regime were dissolved at the end of the war. It was as early as 3 May 1945 that the Soviet headquarters in Prenzlauer Berg moved into the barely damaged buildings, and it was only shortly thereafter that the NKVD set up a prison in the basement of House 3. Many opponents of the forced union between the SPD and KPD were locked up there. They were often accused of 'espionage', although it was usually just the case that they were unwilling to support communist tyranny. Despite the claims made by the SED at the time, and by the Left Party today, very few of the prisoners were former Nazis. Both psychological and physical violence were extensively employed in the basement cells, all but one of which were windowless.

After the founding of the German Democratic Republic, the Soviet headquarters in Prenzlauer Berg was disbanded. The vacated area came under the control of a newly established Stasi district department for Greater Berlin. Although it had been clear since the end of the Berlin Blockade that the western part of the city was under the protection of the Western powers and that the Stasi had no authority there, the Stasi personnel in the former hospital were nonetheless greatly interested in West Berlin. Specifically, they planned various measures to be taken against West German critics of the East German regime. Bruno Beater worked there as the particularly brutal head of Main Division V, which was responsible for fighting opponents of the regime, and eventually became Erich Mielke's first deputy minister. The basement prison was used by the Stasi from January 1951, and it also served as an interrogation centre. Mielke, while still deputy head of the Stasi in September 1950, had issued 'guidelines on the registration of persons who carry out hostile activities'. An activity could be regarded as 'hostile' if it were 'intended to undermine the foundations of the German Democratic Republic'. Furthermore, 'active supporters of the former Hitler state' were to be apprehended. Considered as enemies were 'agents of foreign espionage organisations, terrorists, deviants, pests, saboteurs, participants in Schumacher's illegal work, Trotskyists', as well as 'members of religious sects and other people'. The 'participants in Schumacher's illegal work' meant social democrats in East Germany, while 'members of religious sects' were, among others, Jehovah's Witnesses.[43] Since the guards in the basement of House 3 had service dogs, the inmates called this prison the 'dog cellar'. Each cell came with no more than a plank bed and a bucket. Former prisoners like Hans-Eberhard Zahn told of how they had to stand still for hours on end during lengthy night-time interrogations. They were sometimes kicked in the hollows of their knees and were frequently pushed and shoved. Anyone who violated the strict prison rules could be locked in a standing cell, partially handcuffed against the wall, for several days. Such physical torture declined significantly after the death of Stalin in 1953. There are no reports from contemporary witnesses regarding how the standing cell in House 3 was used after 1954. The 'dog cellar' was closed two years later, and the inmates were transferred to a prison on Kissingenstraße in Pankow, Berlin.

Nevertheless, the building complex in Prenzlauer Berg remained the headquarters of the Stasi district department for Berlin. Up until 1985, it was there that numerous surveillance and decomposition measures were planned against political opponents. One of the most important targets of such measures was Friedrichshain pastor Rainer Eppelmann. Together with SED dissident Robert Havemann, Eppelmann had drawn up the Berlin Appeal in 1982 and put it into circulation. From that moment, Eppelmann was regarded as a dangerous enemy of the East German state, and the Stasi district department for Berlin even planned to assassinate him. In an undated report on 'operational work', the unofficial collaborator 'Hoffmann' wrote:

> Shortly after the death of Havemann, the plan was to exploit the fact that Eppelmann frequently drove back from Grünheide to Berlin late in the evening and at high speed. The objective was to bring about an accident in which Eppelmann would be injured or physically eliminated. Several possibilities were tested, like loosening the wheel nuts, destroying the discs in a curve, or setting up mirrors before a curve. But this plan was rejected by the divisional leadership, as the possibility could not be ruled out that bystanders would come to harm.[44]

Eppelmann was always accompanied by his wife on this trip. Although the Stasi wanted to bring the life of the pastor to an end, it was not prepared to do the same to his wife.

The inner-city grounds of the district department had in the meantime become too small, so relocation plans commenced in 1976. Career intelligence officer Wolfgang Schwanitz committed himself to this effort. He had started off as a case officer in the Lichtenberg area precinct in 1951 and rose to become the head of the Berlin district department from 1974 to 1986. Mielke was clearly so pleased with Schwanitz's performance that he appointed him deputy minister at the Stasi headquarters in Lichtenberg. Schwanitz even became Mielke's successor, albeit only for three weeks, as the head of the Stasi, which was renamed the Office for National Security. Since the reunification of Germany, Schwanitz has been one of the most vocal falsifiers of the history of the Stasi, which in his view has been 'legally rehabilitated'.[45] While planning for the relocation of the district department in the middle of the 1970s, he was keen to find a much larger property and set his sights on an area further to the east which lay on Straße der Befreiung in the vicinity of the zoo in Friedrichsfelde. The foundation stone was laid on 8 May 1978, 33 years after the end of the war in Europe, but the building project was soon held up due to a shortage of money and materials. Of the estimated 150 million East German marks required for the project, only 107 million were available. As a result, an office remained in Prenzlauer Berg even after the official relocation of the district department. A listening station had also been set up in the former basement cells for the purpose of monitoring East German telephone lines; it made no sense to move this station to Friedrichsfelde. Stasi officers therefore continued to work there well into the late autumn of 1989. The other divisions of the district department completed the move to Friedrichsfelde in October 1985. Despite cuts to the budget, an increase in the size of the complex there was intended.

In addition to the various service buildings, the Stasi in Berlin owned apartment dwellings almost exclusively inhabited by its employees. The isolation of those employees from the rest of the population was intentional: social cohesion could be better organised and controlled, while the privileges enjoyed by Stasi employees would attract less attention. The most important of these complexes lay near the restricted areas in Lichtenberg and Hohenschönhausen. The Stasi even set up its own housing administration. Opposite the headquarters of the Stasi, two high-rise buildings (Frankfurter Allee 172 and 174) were designated as 'residential properties of the Stasi', and the same was the case for the 11-storey apartment block at Frankfurter Allee 178–192. Also available to Stasi employees were the high-rise building at Harro-Schulze-Boysen-Straße 37 and that at Harnackstraße 24–28. The efforts of the Stasi to secure these particular buildings were justified, as it was easy to see inside the restricted area from the top floors. Just in case, a concrete cover was erected in front of the entrance of House 1 so Stasi leaders could get out of their chauffeured cars without risk of assassination. Even so, there is no known case of an assassination attempt by Western intelligence in the vicinity of the headquarters.

Two prefabricated apartment blocks were built in Hohenschönhausen for unmarried Stasi employees. These buildings now serve as hotels with fully refurbished rooms predominantly for conference guests. In addition, there were some complexes at the intersection of Freienwalder-Straße and Große-Leegen-Straße that were reserved for Stasi employees until 1990. The older houses in the surrounding area were mainly inhabited by the families of senior Stasi officers, some of whom still live there to this day. Even three decades after the Peaceful Revolution, the largest and still politically active group of former Stasi personnel probably lives in the vicinity of what is today the memorial for the victims of the Stasi in Hohenschönhausen. Most of them are former senior officers who were dismissed from the civil service in January 1990 and who were already too old to start anything new. They fought hard in court, with success, to receive generous pensions and were supported in this regard first by the PDS and then by the Left Party. Nevertheless, most of them resent their lost social status. It is no coincidence that election results for the Left Party tend to be above average in East Berlin and even particularly strong in Lichtenberg and Hohenschönhausen.

'Female unofficial collaborators on special operations'

Prostitution in the service of the Stasi

The question as to whether espionage or prostitution holds the dubious honour of being the oldest profession in the world might never be resolved. It can nevertheless be said that the two occupations have been interlinked for thousands of years, and the Stasi most certainly made use of sex to obtain secret information or to blackmail people of interest. This topic has always been accompanied by countless legends, and it is hard to distinguish between voyeuristic inventions or rumours on the one hand and the actual activities of sex spies on the other. An example of this phenomenon is the Salon Kitty brothel on Giesebrechtstraße in Charlottenburg, Berlin, which counted many foreign diplomats as well as political and military decision-makers among its clients during the Nazi era. In innumerable newspaper articles, a handful of films, and the sensationalist novel *Salon Kitty* by journalist Peter Norden, the salon has been stylised as a high-tech monitoring centre. In reality, from 1939 to 1942, the prostitutes at the salon sounded out their clients on behalf of the SS. The rooms were probably bugged, although the information obtained in this manner may have been limited due to technical difficulties. Not a single recording from the salon has emerged since the end of the war, and there is no known transcript of sex confessions. Even so, the spy brothel remains a source of fascination to this day.[46]

Sex is one of the most effective weapons in secret warfare. The Stasi systematically made use of prostitutes and even full-time female employees to obtain information.

Like the Gestapo, the Stasi employed prostitutes as spies. It probably began to do so from early 1954. Markus Wolf wrote in his memoirs that a Soviet advisor to the East German secret service at the time recommended a special establishment be set up on the occasion of the Berlin Conference of 1954: 'The idea was to create a fake brothel for the purpose of making contact with and obtaining information from conference participants.' However, this was easier said than done:

> We had no experience whatsoever in this type of espionage. With no time to lose, we prepared a small house in the Berlin suburb of Rauchfangswerder as a love nest. Downstairs, in the living room, where there was a good view of the lake, we had installed a listening device; upstairs, under the sloping ceiling, was a tiny bedroom with a camera built into the ceiling lighting together with a flashlight behind infrared panes.

The Stasi man who operated the apparatus had to 'squeeze himself into a narrow dungeon from a built-in cupboard' and then remain there until the prostitute and her client were finished. According to Wolf, even more difficult than setting up the equipment was finding women willing to participate. Prostitutes from the illegal red-light district in Scheunenviertel, Berlin, were out of the question, as they could hardly have met the presumably high demands of the international clientele. One of Wolf's employees therefore hired 'attractive and adventurous girls in a café who were not averse to doing the socialist fatherland a favour and earning a little extra money in the process'. Unofficial collaborators swarmed out to the location of the conference and sought to interest Western participants or at least well-networked

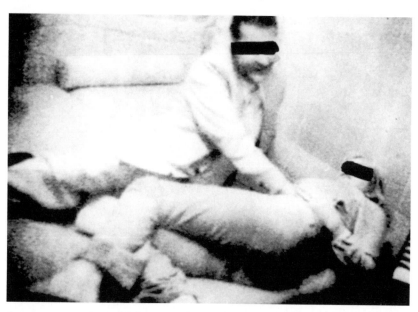

Sometimes, sex agents obtained information from their clients in bed; at other times, the men were photographed and subsequently blackmailed.

observers in an evening with East German women. According to Wolf, only one potential client—a reporter—accepted the offer. He was inadvertently given the wrong aperitif (i.e., without an aphrodisiac) with the result being that when he went to the kitchen for a chat with the housekeeper, he showed no interest at all in the ladies present.[47] It remains open to question whether Wolf's story is true. Deception, trickery, and lies had been second nature to the East German spy chief for decades by the time he wrote his memoirs in the 1990s. His memoirs should therefore be read with caution.

In any case, by the 1960s, sex had become a regular means by which the Stasi obtained information. Prostitutes—be they amateur hookers, unofficial collaborators, or even full-time Stasi employees—waited in East Berlin hotels for Western guests. Since prostitution was officially forbidden in East Germany, it was easy for the Stasi to persuade those it called 'loose women' to cooperate. A dissertation at the Law School in Potsdam, the intellectually modest elite training centre of the Stasi, dealt with the employment of 'female unofficial collaborators on special operations'. Its author was the Stasi officer Günther Harnisch, whose annual salary by 1989 was 21,911 East German marks, and he tried hard to avoid obvious facts. For the effective surveillance of 'privileged persons' from the West who were visiting East Berlin, it was necessary that 'constant observation' be guaranteed. 'Depending on the objective requirements of the specific conditions, the employment of female unofficial collaborators on special operations is particularly necessary, as their mode of behaviour fulfils the demands of heightened conspiracy.'[48]

Many politicians fell into the trap. It has been alleged, but never proven, that Uwe Barschel, the former minister-president of Schleswig-Holstein who died under mysterious circumstances, had been in contact with Stasi prostitutes. What is certain, however, is that the Stasi sought with success to entangle the West Berlin parliamentarian Heinrich Lummer in an affair. Lummer had just separated from his wife in 1973 when he started a relationship with 25-year-old East Berliner Susanne Rau. She told her lover, who was 15 years her senior and by that time head of the CDU parliamentary group in the Berlin House of Representatives, that she was unmarried and worked in the 'art trade of the East German state'. The affair lasted for about eight years, and it seems as if it was only in March 1981 that Lummer found out he had been a target of the Stasi. He had in the meantime become the president of the Berlin House of Representatives and was therefore worthwhile prey, so his girlfriend asked him over the phone to visit East Berlin. They arranged to meet at the Hotel Metropol, and, when they did meet, she was able to convince him to leave the hotel and accompany her to her apartment, which was in a prefabricated building in Marzahn. It was not long before their privacy was interrupted. Two men—'Wagner' and 'Lindner'—rang the doorbell, introduced themselves as representatives of the East German government, and requested that Lummer come with them for 'a political discussion'. Lummer accepted the proposal, whereupon they drove to Karl-Marx-Allee. They arrived not at a restaurant but rather at an apartment in which a meal had been prepared. Precisely what was discussed is not known, and although a follow-up meeting took place a few weeks later, Lummer, by then senator of the interior in the cabinet of Richard von Weizsäcker, then decided he would avoid East Berlin in future. The Stasi attempted discreetly, yet regularly, to blackmail him, and at the end of 1982, on the occasion of his 50th birthday, he received, among many other gifts, a bouquet of flowers from East Berlin with a greeting card from 'Susanne, Micha, and W. Lindner' attached. They hoped to see him again 'from near and afar' and wished for 'health and courage for our continued partnership'. Lummer alone knew what was really meant by these happy returns: they were intended to make it clear the East Germans had him in their grasp. While the details of the Lummer affair have never been fully clarified, there is no evidence this staunch right-wing politician ever worked for the Stasi.[49]

It is not known how many women were persuaded or forced by the Stasi to go into prostitution in the service of socialism. According to the perhaps voyeuristic magazine reports of the early 1990s, not only female unofficial collaborators, willing and unwilling, and professional prostitutes but also normal Stasi office workers were used for 'special operations'. There is indeed some evidence that Erich Mielke was the greatest pimp in German history. The East Berlin Palasthotel, which lay close to the Spree River, was one of the discreet meeting points for Western clients and East Berlin prostitutes. According to Barbara, a sex worker at the hotel, 'at least half of the women had intercourse on behalf of the Stasi', and it was perfectly clear to other employees at the hotel what was going on. 'We could not conduct business without contact with the Stasi,' recalled a bartender.[50]

CHAPTER SEVEN

In the 'jungle of espionage'

The SED image of the enemy

West Berlin in East German propaganda

For most people, there did not appear to be anything suspicious about the piece of news released by the General German News Service on the evening of 23 June 1948. The SED-controlled news agency reported: 'Due to technical difficulties, the transport department of the Soviet military administration has been forced to stop all freight and passenger trains to and from Berlin from six o'clock tomorrow morning.' This brief statement struck the American, British, and French military commands in West Germany and in the western sectors of the former capital of the Reich like a bombshell. The power supply to West Berlin was cut off that very night and it was the following morning that Soviet pioneers blocked the roads and railways connecting the western zones of occupation in Germany to the city in the middle of the Soviet zone. The three Western powers were faced with a simple question: should Berlin be held or given up? For Stalin and his German accomplices, the western sectors of the city were a major headache. According to the agreements made during the war against Hitler, the Western powers had the right to have troops stationed in Berlin. This had been intended to ensure joint control over the former enemy state, but it had become clear within a few months after the end of the war that West Berlin was turning into an outpost of democracy and freedom in the midst of the communist dictatorship being installed by Soviet authorities.

The Eastern Bloc twice risked major political crises to force the Western powers to withdraw from West Berlin: the first was the Berlin Blockade of 1948–1949, which the Americans and the British bypassed by supplying the city from the air; the second was the Khrushchev Ultimatum of 1958–1959, in which the Soviet leader demanded that the Western powers vacate West Berlin and conclude a peace treaty with both German states. In Moscow on 27 November 1958, the Kremlin chief announced:

> The Soviet government, in the course of the next six months, does not intend to make any change to the current arrangements for American, British, and French military movements from West Berlin to West Germany. We consider this period to be perfectly sufficient for finding a solution to the questions connected with the change of the situation in Berlin.[1]

If no understanding was reached in those six months, the Soviet Union would hand East Germany full control over access to West Berlin. The special rights of the Western powers in Berlin would then no longer be valid. This was a clear threat that could well have led to nuclear war, an indication of just how bothersome the existence of a free West Berlin was to the Eastern Bloc leadership.

It was during the six-month ultimatum period—in March 1959 to be precise—that the Committee for German Unity, a propaganda organisation of the SED, published a brochure titled *Spionage-Dschungel Westberlin* (The Espionage Jungle of West Berlin). Attention should be drawn to certain subtleties of terminology in the brochure, as it reveals the way in which divided Berlin was viewed by the SED. East German communists always distinguished between 'Berlin, the capital of the German Democratic Republic' and 'Westberlin', as if the latter were a separate political unit. West Germans, on the other hand, always referred to 'West-Berlin' and 'Ost-Berlin', using hyphens to emphasise the equality and togetherness of the two halves of the city. The intention of the brochure was to help shape public opinion:

> The several dozen espionage and sabotage organisations that conduct criminal activities from West Berlin pose a serious threat to peace. On behalf of the Western occupation forces and the militaristic Adenauer government, they wage the Cold War against the German Democratic Republic and the other socialist states and, in accordance with the NATO plan 'Outline', prepare for the war of revenge for German imperialism.[2]

Similar allegations were repeatedly published throughout the history of the SED regime. *Neues Deutschland* and *Berliner Zeitung* had been attacking the West since before the Berlin Blockade; the weekly newsreel *Der Augenzeuge* also resorted to aggressive tones. After the East German uprising of 17 June 1953, the chief commentator of the state radio broadcaster of East Germany, Karl-Eduard von Schnitzler, got carried away in his tirade of hate:

> It is not about norms, not about free elections, not about improving the standard of living, and not about freedom of any kind; instead, by abusing the good faith of some of the workers and employees of Berlin and by exploiting the improved working standards to carry out strikes and demonstrations, an attack was attempted by the paid provocateurs and scum of the West Berlin underworld on the freedom, on the existence, on the jobs, and on the families of our working population.

Schnitzler also named those allegedly responsible for the uprising:

> Prepared well in advance, evidently organised and led by the League of German Youth in West Berlin and by other fascist organisations in collaboration with Jakob Kaiser and his so-called departments, and with the intention of seeing this provocation to the end—that is to go for broke—the one-and-a-half-day adventure is the work of the so-called governing mayor of West Berlin, Ernst Reuter. He may attempt to create an alibi to explain his absence from West Berlin the moment the mines he laid were detonated, but the statements of witnesses and arrested provocateurs prove that he inspired and instigated this crime against the people of Berlin.[3]

Geheimdienst und Wühlorganisation

Rundfunkstation

Revanchistische bzw.
militärische Organisation

militärische Anlage der Westmächte

Flugplatz

Staatsgrenze

WEDDING Verwaltungsbezirk

Tegel Stadtteil

0 2 4 6 8 10 km

In this SED propaganda map from 1961, West Berlin appears to be filled with 'enemy strongpoints.'
Even Radio Free Berlin and Radio in the American Sector were regarded as espionage organisations.

It should be noted that the League of German Youth, a right-wing extremist organisation that was briefly supported by American intelligence, had nothing to do with the 1953 uprising. It had instead concerned itself with planning to assassinate West German SPD politicians and had therefore been outlawed as early as January 1953.

Schnitzler's attitude changed very little in the decades that followed, and the same was the case for SED agitation against West Berlin. Ulbricht's most prominent propagandist commented on the construction of the Berlin Wall in 1961 as follows:

> These are measures that, by virtue of our sovereignty, we have found necessary to take on our territory. … The bloodthirsty members of those spiffing organisations in West Berlin are now fenced in and are being prevented by the People's Police and the People's Army from carrying out their 'philanthropic' activities in the German Democratic Republic and the other socialist states. Enemy agents in our republic, suddenly unable to make it back to West Berlin, have been taken by surprise and are being tracked down. … And, of course, those politicians who have trap doors to West Berlin will find that they have now been closed shut. Their spearhead, which is aimed 'at the heart of the zone', has been blunted. Their 'thorn in the side' of the German Democratic Republic has been removed. They are now in a state of shock.[4]

At the end of September 1989, the television propaganda programme *Der Schwarze Kanal* sought to stir up hatred by claiming there were human trafficking organisations based in West Berlin that were bringing in and kidnapping East German citizens.[5] A few weeks later, during the Peaceful Revolution, the 'key witness' confessed that his story had been made up.

Karl-Eduard von Schnitzler was the chief propagandist of the East German media from 1948. In his television programme *Der Schwarze Kanal*, he commented polemically on excerpts from Western programmes.

East German publishers produced several versions of a map that was supposed to demonstrate the degree to which West Berlin was occupied by 'enemy strongpoints'. Marked on one version of this map that appeared shortly after, and that served to justify, the construction of the Wall in 1961 were 25 'secret service and subversive organisations,' 16 'revanchist or militaristic organisations', and 14 barracks or other installations belonging to the Western powers. The legend on the map added there were in reality many more facilities: 'more than 80 branches of espionage and terror organisations as well as 66 revanchist and militaristic associations'. Even though there is no known East German document that lists so many 'enemy strongpoints' in detail, the brochure *Spionage-Dschungel Westberlin* managed to provide the addresses of 26 organisations in West Berlin that, in the view of the SED, worked in secret against East Germany. Included were not only various branches of the intelligence agencies of the Western powers and of West Germany but also organisations like the Combat Group against Inhumanity, the Investigation Committee of Free Jurists, the East Offices of the major parties (CDU, SPD, and FDP), and several smaller groups. Another organisation that appeared in the brochure was Radio in the American Sector (RIAS), which was based in Schöneberg, Berlin.

Between enlightenment and terror

The Combat Group against Inhumanity

Mentioned in countless publications of SED propaganda as the main enemy of East Germany was the Combat Group against Inhumanity (KgU).[6] This group was a gift for the East German regime, as its actions helped to justify the severe criticism levelled at the 'enemy strongpoints' in West Berlin. Little was known about the KgU until a qualitatively questionable study by Enrico Heitzer, a fierce critic of the KgU, appeared in 2008. The East German researcher Jochen Staadt characterised this study as follows: 'Where the facts are insufficient, constructions have been used that even go beyond the SED propaganda of the time.'[7] The beginnings of the KgU would not have aroused suspicion. It was founded by Rainer Hildebrandt, more of an intellectual than the head of an espionage cell. He had been in contact with opponents of Hitler during World War II and had helped smuggle provisions into camps for Russian prisoners of war. He was arrested after the attempted assassination of Hitler on 20 July 1944, remained in prison until the end of the war, and thereafter wrote of his experiences in the Third Reich in a book titled *Wir sind die Letzten* (We are the Last). He soon became convinced there could be no excuse for remaining silent about certain events in the eastern zone. He pushed for demonstrations against the Soviet internment camps, which he termed the 'new concentration camps'.

It was in 1948 that Hildebrandt founded the KgU in collaboration with a number of acquaintances, including the chairman of the Berlin branch of the Young Union, Ernst Benda. The objective of the KgU was 'to investigate unlawful arrests and abductions in Berlin and in the eastern zone, to determine the whereabouts of those who were missing, and to notify their relatives'.[8] The files grew rapidly with information on missing persons, confidants, and potential SED henchmen. Also recorded were the names of NKVD officers as well as the plans of camps, torture chambers, and other detention centres. However, the information collected was often based on rumour and was therefore not particularly trustworthy. For example, despite all the crimes committed in the Soviet internment camp in Sachsenhausen, there was never an 'airtight death chamber' for murdering inmates by suffocation. Even so, the work of the KgU was a nuisance for the SED. The RIAS programme 'Wir warnen vor …' ('We warn against …') regularly broadcast the names of informers, be

Rainer Hildebrandt, the founder of the Combat Group against Inhumanity, had been put behind bars by the Nazis and was regarded by the SED as a deadly enemy.

they real or suspected, for the East German regime. These names were provided by Hildebrandt, whose group had established a large network that included numerous supporters at East German schools and universities. This group, with its effective network in East Germany and index of up to 380,000 names, drew the attention of Western agencies, and it was not long before it was being funded by the U.S. Army's Counter Intelligence Corps (CIC). The missing persons tracing service practically became a branch of an intelligence agency, and a special body was set up at the same time for questioning officers of the People's Police who had fled to the West. The KgU publicly denied that the information obtained from such questioning would be passed on to non-German organisations even though that was precisely what was happening.

In 1949 and 1950, the focus was very much on the documentation of the crimes of the SED and the enlightenment of the East German population. There were failures like the 'Days of Silence'. On two occasions, the KgU distributed leaflets urging East Germans to demonstrate their opposition to the Soviet occupation authorities by staying away from cinemas, theatres, and public events. The result was unsurprisingly counterproductive. All politically suspicious people were compelled to visit theatres and cinemas if they did not want to draw attention to themselves. Seldom had there been such well-attended events in East Germany as on those two occasions. In contrast, the 'F for Freedom' campaign was a success. Hundreds of thousands of leaflets displaying only a large letter 'F' were smuggled by the KgU into East Germany. They appeared in heavily frequented places, often being pasted on walls or thrown out the windows of moving trains. With RIAS frequently reporting on this campaign, the 'F' soon became a symbol of the resistance against the communist dictatorship, although the consequences could sometimes be fatal. For example, 18-year-old Ludwig Hayne was arrested on 20 July 1950 while distributing KgU and 'F' leaflets in Potsdamer Platz. Soviet Military Tribunal No. 48240 sentenced him to death for 'espionage' and, after the Presidium of the Supreme Soviet refused a pardon, he was shot dead in Moscow in late April 1951. A similar fate befell the somewhat older Günther Malkowski for distributing leaflets during the Leipzig Trade Fair in the spring of 1951. He was arrested by the People's Police and sentenced to death by Military Tribunal No. 48240 for 'espionage', 'anti-Soviet activities' and membership of a 'counterrevolutionary organisation'. He was then executed in July 1952 in the basement of Butyrka Prison in Moscow.[9] In the spring of 1951 alone, several hundred KgU informants fell into the clutches of Soviet and East German authorities, and up to 45 of them were executed.

Such excessive penalties led to the radicalisation of the KgU. The man who was primarily responsible for this radicalisation was Ernst Tillich who, like Hildebrandt, had been imprisoned during the Nazi era; it is probable he had joined the leadership of the KgU at the request of the CIC in early 1950. A member of the SPD, Tillich transformed the KgU into a militant organisation. He made use of a network of predominantly young, disillusioned, and sometimes angry East Germans to carry out minor acts of sabotage. Propaganda posters in East Berlin were set on fire with incendiary devices, and steel frameworks were rendered useless with acid. KgU supporters poured sugar into the tanks of SED and Stasi vehicles, thereby causing damage to their engines. At night, steel spikes were scattered—probably by those same supporters—on arterial roads around Berlin, the result being a number of flat tyres and even, on occasion, serious car accidents. Stink bombs were thrown at the World Festival of Youth and Students in 1951 and at other public events organised by the SED. Rather immoral was the targeting of the already extremely scarce food supplies in East Germany. For example, Tillich's people mixed soap into powdered milk in May and June 1951, while trains with perishable cargo were often sent in the wrong direction when the signs on the wagons were swapped around, which led to hundreds of tonnes of meat, fruit, and vegetables going bad. In September 1951, arson attacks were carried out at night—probably once more by KgU supporters—on grocery stores in the vicinity of Berlin. Large quantities of bread and many other foods were lost. Tillich fully supported these attacks despite the fact they harmed ordinary communities. Hildebrandt distanced himself from this approach and left the KgU in 1952.

Probably not directly on behalf of Tillich, but nonetheless with the support of the KgU, the former East German prisoner Johann Burianek carried out several attacks in 1951 and 1952. This was not enough to satisfy him. He wanted to establish his own secret organisation, the Partisans of Freedom, which he would lead himself under the direction of the KgU. Gerd Baitz, who under Tillich was responsible for such 'direct actions' against the East German regime, was not keen on this idea, but he nevertheless had no shortage of tasks to give to Burianek. One of those tasks was to steal the latest register of wanted people from a People's Police post on the outskirts of Berlin. It turned out that this could not be carried out at the planned time, as the police station was more heavily manned than anticipated. Burianek then decided he wanted to deal a crushing blow. He planned to blow up a railway bridge east of Berlin the moment the Blue Express, the train to Moscow, crossed it. While the KgU supplied the necessary explosives, it provided no further support to Burianek. It is unclear whether Tillich and Baitz knew precisely what Burianek planned to do. The Americans, who were interested in espionage but not sabotage, probably also declined to provide support. In early 1952, the KgU discovered

Burianek was being monitored. Instead of warning him and ordering him back to the safety of West Berlin, the KgU leadership decided it would just 'switch him off'. In other words, all contact with him would be broken off. Burianek nevertheless wanted to go ahead with his plan, yet his two attempts at the end of February 1952 failed. He and his group of saboteurs were arrested a few days later, and the East German authorities made short work of them. They were all tried on 23 May 1952, Burianek receiving the death penalty and his six friends being sentenced to between 10 years and life imprisonment. The way in which the trial was to unfold had been agreed on in advance between the judges and the SED apparatus.[10] Burianek was executed in early August 1952, but he was formally rehabilitated in 2005 on the grounds that he had been a victim of an unjust regime. A thorough investigation of his actions was conducted neither in 1952 nor in 2005. There has likewise been no serious investigation that demonstrates how the KgU hovered dangerously between enlightenment and terror.

Employment of clandestine methods

The Gehlen Organisation and the BND in West Berlin

Conducting espionage against the East German regime, and thereby providing the SED with some justification for its propaganda campaign against West Berlin, was the Gehlen Organisation, which was renamed the Federal Intelligence Service (BND) in 1956. Its chief, the former general staff officer Reinhard Gehlen, had made a career in the high command of the army and, as the head of Foreign Armies East during the Nazi era, had been one of the most important figures in military intelligence in Hitler's Wehrmacht. In the spring of 1945, he and his closest colleagues took themselves and their files to the safety of the Alps with the idea of offering their services to American military intelligence as experts on Soviet forces. It did not take long for the Americans to accept this offer, as they anticipated relations with Stalin were likely to deteriorate. Gehlen was permitted to establish a new secret service in Pullach, near Munich, on the site of what had once been a rarely used Führer headquarters. The primary task of this organisation was to maintain contact with former Wehrmacht soldiers who lived in the Soviet zone of occupation and obtain any information of military value from them. This network was operating very effectively by the time of the Berlin Blockade in 1948 and 1949.

West Berlin was an important base of operations for the BND. Several branches were located there, and they each managed their own contacts in East Germany. The information gathered, usually lists of the unit markings of Soviet and East German military vehicles or of the number plates of official cars, was generally unspectacular and in and of itself seemingly worthless, although careful analysis could reveal some details on the organisation and strength of troops in East Germany. Such analysis was usually not conducted in West Berlin. The city served rather as the most important meeting point for informants and secret service employees. According to two former Stasi officers, 'military spies in other locations in East Germany like Rostock, Erfurt, or Dresden would often catch early trains to go to rendezvous points in West Berlin'. The Stasi energetically sought to stop those spies: 'Observation personnel of the Stasi would travel on the trains going to West Berlin and would keep an eye on certain people who drew attention or who were pointed out by the transport police.' If a person under observation demonstrated the 'typical behaviour of a spy' upon arrival in the divided city, like making calls from a telephone booth or being picked up by a car, which 'in quite a few cases belonged to the American occupation forces', the counterintelligence division of the Stasi would begin a thorough investigation in the hometown of the person of interest.[11]

Soviet authorities and, before long, the Stasi, reported incredible numbers of allegedly exposed spies. In 1947 alone, Soviet military intelligence identified approximately 1,100 American and at least 703 British agents that it wanted to have arrested. In 1948, the number of reported arrests amounted to more than 3,000 and, in 1949, 1,607 of those arrested were said to have been informants paid by British intelligence. Between 1950 and 1955, Soviet and East German courts imposed the death penalty on 1,061 East German defendants for alleged acts of espionage. Most of those death penalties were carried out. It was in fact only rarely the case that any espionage had been involved, but finding a defendant guilty of espionage meant the most severe punishment could be handed out. Precisely how successful the BND was in conducting operations in East Germany from West Berlin is not known. It probably managed a network of approximately 4,000 contacts in the mid-1950s, although that was for the entire Eastern Bloc rather than for East Germany alone.[12] There are some tragic stories from the history of this network. Some BND contacts paid adolescent school children roughly 80 West German marks to monitor Soviet military convoys, the result being that an unknown number of teenagers were convicted and given long prison terms.

In addition to the drudgery of military surveillance, the Gehlen Organisation also achieved spectacular successes. One of those was the work of Helene 'Elli' Barczatis. Codenamed 'Gänseblümchen' and directed

'Elli' Barczatis, the secretary of the East German prime minister, was the most important BND agent in East Berlin. Shown here is the form for her committal to prison.

from West Berlin, she was the head secretary of the East German prime minister, Otto Grotewohl.[13] She had already been denounced and was already under surveillance before starting to work actively for West German intelligence. The Stasi observed her for more than four years, but with the help of a friend she was still able to smuggle confidential documents into West Berlin. It was only in March 1955 that the two were arrested. After months of interrogation that bordered on psychological and physical torture, and without any contact with the outside world or any support from lawyers, they were sentenced to death in a one-day trial. The BND was specifically mentioned in the reasons given for the judgement:

> In the interests of American imperialism and German monopoly capital, this organisation attempts to spy on every aspect of the political, economic, and cultural life of the German Democratic Republic. It passes on the information it gains to its American and West German clients, who then exploit this knowledge to unleash wild agitation against the German Democratic Republic, to exacerbate the occasional difficulties in supplying the population of our republic, and to take other measures against the building up of our economy. Their objective is to maintain capitalist conditions in West Germany and to bring the territory of our republic under the influence of monopoly capital. This organisation tries to thwart all efforts of the peace-loving people of the Soviet Union and of the German Democratic Republic to bring about an easing of tensions in the political situation and a peaceful coexistence between the countries of progress and those of capitalism.[14]

Gehlen's secret service employed many clandestine methods against East Germany, but it was not its goal to provoke a world war. There is no evidence that it made any attempts at assassination or sabotage, and it took no measures beyond the gathering of information, which was of course illegal and severely punished in East Germany. As a result, the public criticism of the BND by the SED was mostly made up. The smear brochure published by the Committee for German Unity in the spring of 1959, *Spionage-Dschungel Westberlin*, provided barely any concrete accusations against the BND. It made the claim that an agent named Weigel tried, 'on behalf of the Gehlen Organisation, to use explosive ampoules to destroy a steamship and to blow up an electricity pylon, the effect of which would have been the loss of power to the districts of Rostock and Schwerin'. There was no evidence to support this claim. It is sometimes possible to reconstruct the reasons, beyond general propaganda, for which the SED chose to report alleged misdeeds of Gehlen agents. For example, the allegation made in this brochure to the effect that West German spies had started fires in 'forests, barns, and grain fields' and had 'artificially caused' cases of livestock disease served the purpose of concealing from the East German population the inefficiency of East German agriculture.[15] The SED had already tried something similar in 1950 and 1951 by spreading rumours of American aircraft dropping Colorado beetles in large numbers over fields in East Germany. This image had taken hold in the minds of many East Germans.[16]

BND personnel in West Berlin constantly lived in the crosshairs of the Stasi. It was usually the aim of the Stasi to kidnap them or turn them into double agents in the

Reinhard Gehlen as a Wehrmacht officer and, in the 1950s, on a secret mission. He used the Cold War to his own advantage and created the BND.

service of East Germany. One of the greatest setbacks for the Gehlen Organisation was an affair involving a former Wehrmacht major, Wolfgang Höher. Released from Soviet captivity in 1949, Höher had gone to West Berlin and been hired as a case officer by the organisation. However, he worked in secret for the Stasi, betraying undercover informants by the dozen to East Berlin from 1951 onwards. It got worse, for he rose to become head of counterespionage in the Berlin office of the Gehlen Organisation. Unfortunately, Höher reported less about East German spies to Pullach and more about the organisation's employees to East Berlin. Information on the past lives of West German spies, especially during the Nazi era, was of particular interest to Markus Wolf for his counterespionage strategy. He would see to it that such information was disseminated, and a particularly noteworthy result of this appeared in the *Daily Express* in London on 17 March 1952. Under the heading 'Hitler General Now Spying For Dollars', the British star reporter Sefton Delmer wrote: 'Watch out for a name that promises bad things. ... It stands for what, in my opinion, is the most dangerous political explosive in Western Europe today. This name is Gehlen. ... Ten years ago, this was the name of one of Hitler's most capable staff officers. ... Today, Gehlen is the name of a secret organisation with great and ever-increasing power. ... As he built up his organisation, all sorts of former Nazis, men from the SS, and men from the SD (Himmler's secret service) crept in and gained full protection. Today, Gehlen is the head of an espionage organisation that has agents all over the world. ... The danger posed by this organisation lies in the future, as Gehlen's network of agents has already become an immense underground power in Germany.'[17] Much of this report was grossly exaggerated, but it drew the attention of the Western public to the organisation and thereby made its work more difficult. In early 1953, Höher began to sense he was under suspicion. He contacted Wolf in East Berlin and asked to be extracted. The Stasi granted his request, and a kidnapping was staged at Wittenbergplatz, Berlin, on 18 February 1953. So many false tracks were laid that even well-informed Western journalists like Wolfgang Zolling and Heinz Höhne still believed in 1971 that Höher had truly been kidnapped.[18] Höher provided the Stasi with a lot of information once he was under its protection, and he published a propaganda pamphlet titled *Agent 2996 enthüllt* (Agent 2996 Revealed) containing the wildest speculations about the work of the Gehlen Organisation against East Germany.

There was a second such successful coup for the Stasi when Hans-Joachim Geyer was turned, and it was not long afterwards that the Stasi abducted, though was unable to turn, two more organisation employees in West Berlin. Those two men, both of whom were rather important, were Werner Haase and Wilhelm van Ackern. Haase, a highly decorated Wehrmacht major, ran a branch of the Gehlen Organisation in West Berlin under the code name 'Heister'. In response to the fact that Geyer, after switching sides, betrayed numerous undercover informants and thereby caused a great deal of unease, Haase planned to do something innovative. He wanted to lay a telephone cable from the western sector of Berlin to the eastern sector so that it could be used as a secure connection between case officers and agents and as an alternative to the always risky meetings in person. This cable was supposed to go across the water ditch that marked the sector boundary between Treptow and Neukölln and connect a couple of summerhouses. However, the undercover agent who was to work on the connection on the East Berlin side had been exposed by Geyer and turned. When Haase arrived on the evening of 13 November 1953 to set up the connection on the west bank of the water ditch, for which purpose he tied the end of the cable to a toy boat and let it float to the east bank, the undercover agent, though on the east bank as agreed, had brought with him some Stasi men who had crossed to the west bank. They swiftly overpowered and abducted Haase. Although sentenced five weeks later to lifelong imprisonment for espionage, Haase was exchanged for an East German spy in 1956.

Wilhelm van Ackern, an employee of the Gehlen Organisation, was abducted by the Stasi and taken to East Germany in 1955. He remained behind bars for nine years, and most of that time was in the notorious Bautzen II.

Wilhelm van Ackern, who since 1952 had worked in West Berlin for the organisation in a role similar to that of Haase, also ended up being kidnapped by the Stasi. Van Ackern generally avoided East German territory. He stayed away from the sector boundary and always travelled between West Berlin and West Germany by air rather than by road or rail. This meant there would only be a chance to kidnap him in the middle of West Berlin. The Stasi made its preparations over the course of several months, coming up with and discarding several 'action plans'. Division II of the Stasi district department for Magdeburg drew up another 'arrest plan' on 22 March 1955, and Erich Mielke signed off on it on the evening of 23 March. Stasi Major Helmut Träger put the plan into effect the following day. Van Ackern was lured by the secret collaborator assigned to him, Fritz Weidemann (Stasi code name 'Schütte'), into an apartment at Gneisenaustraße 93 in Kreuzberg, Berlin. Weidemann had told van Ackern beforehand that he wanted to show him a reporting pouch, supposedly found at Rathenow Railway Station and now at the apartment, containing maps and documents belonging to a Soviet military officer. Van Ackern already knew of the apartment and therefore had no reason to be suspicious.

The plan was as follows: 'Since Wilhelm van Ackern speaks and can also read a little Russian, it can be expected that he will spend some time in the friend's apartment to examine the material in the reporting pouch. As in previous meetings, secret collaborator "Schütte" will offer alcohol to Wilhelm van Ackern and then some coffee afterwards for sobering up.' The duration of the meeting was set at 90 to 120 minutes: 'After drinking coffee, secret collaborator 'Schütte' will accompany Wilhelm van Ackern to his home. Once they reach the doorstep, van Ackern is to be taken by the operational group.'[19] Van Ackern had become drowsy within minutes of drinking the drug-infused coffee, so it was without difficulty that he was overpowered by the kidnapping squad and taken across the sector border to the Stasi prison in Hohenschönhausen. He was put on trial before the Supreme Court of East Germany, prior to which he was warned by Mielke to make no mention of being kidnapped if he wanted to avoid being sentenced to death. He ended up being sentenced to lifelong imprisonment and was taken to Bautzen II. Only in 1964 was he allowed to return to West Germany as one of the first prisoners whose release had been paid for. He then worked for the Senate of Berlin until his retirement in 1978.

Despite blows such as these, West Berlin remained an important base of operations for the BND. That even remained the case after the construction of the Wall in 1961. The BND had obtained and passed on pieces of information about this radical measure beforehand to the West German government, completing a report on 19 July 1961 that described the posting of new security units to East Berlin and the creation of emergency plans. Two weeks later, evidence emerged of the impending closure of the sector border, which included the cessation of suburban and underground railway traffic in the vicinity of that border. Neither Bonn nor anyone at Schöneberg Town Hall were convinced a wall would be built, especially given the Gehlen Organisation had previously reported in January 1953 that the cordoning off of West Berlin was imminent. The CIA had then raised similar concerns in 1957, and it was in view of such reports that CSU politician Franz Josef Strauß came to the conclusion that the building of a wall around West Berlin was 'only a possible development'.[20] While the construction of the Wall took place before the BND could do anything about it, this measure nevertheless failed to achieve its alleged primary purpose of making it more difficult for spies to enter East Germany. According to the BND experts Armin Wagner and Matthias Uhl: 'The continued flow of information to the BND after 13 August demonstrates that the connection to its sources was not broken off by the physical separation of Berlin.'[21]

Public 'espionage'

RIAS, the UfJ, and other organisations

While the KgU and the BND actively, and somewhat aggressively, carried out espionage against East Germany from West Berlin, there were a number of other organisations whose activities, even if less aggressive, were not appreciated by the SED regime and were therefore targeted by SED propaganda. It would be strange to say that espionage was conducted where everyone could see and hear it, but this was precisely what the Committee for German Unity accused the radio station RIAS of doing: 'RIAS is not only an instrument of agitation against the German Democratic Republic and the socialist countries but also an organisation that is directly involved in espionage activities against the republic.' According to the SED, this included 'on-air agent recruitment'. RIAS allegedly organised quiz games and manipulated the results so they were won by young East Germans. The winners would then have to go to the broadcasting centre in Schöneberg, in West Berlin, to collect their prizes. They would be 'sounded out by experienced agents, threatened and blackmailed into carrying out espionage, and, if ready to work as an agent, put in touch with the CIC'. RIAS journalists were paid 'bounties' for their assistance.[22] In addition, RIAS had supposedly instigated the uprising of 17 June 1953, which was always referred to by the SED as the 'fascist putsch'.

In fact, RIAS, which was run by Germans and funded by the U.S. State Department and, therefore, by American taxpayers, never made a secret of its disapproval of SED policies and never made use of secret service methods. It was the most important medium for independent information that could be accessed by East Germans. Not even a fraction of the conspiracy theories of the SED were true. This is demonstrated, for example, by the well-documented uprising of 1953. Although the construction brigades on Stalinallee in East Berlin had been making noise since Saturday 13 June and the first strikes occurred at the construction site of the hospital in Friedrichshain on the morning of 15 June, RIAS did not address the issue until 16 June at 4:30pm. By that time, the first anti-socialist mass demonstration in front of the House of Ministries, the former building of the Reich Ministry of Aviation, was over. RIAS reported:

Mit Rias hat es angefangen,
Und nun ist alles schief gegangen.
Statt frei das Leben zu genießen,
Muß er jetzt hinter Gittern büßen.

A drawing in an SED propaganda brochure from the early 1950s. The caption reads: 'it started with RIAS, and now everything's gone wrong; instead of enjoying life freely, he now has to atone behind bars.' The accusations against RIAS were largely made up by East German functionaries.

> Large mass demonstrations took place today in the Soviet sector of Berlin. Workers protested in front of the building of the zone government against the rise in work quotas, the conditions in the Soviet-occupied part of Germany, and the policies of the government itself. … The square before the government building was soon filled with people who chanted loudly: 'We demand higher wages and lower prices. We demand the removal of quotas. Down with the government. We want free elections!'[23]

This objective report did not amount to an open call for rebellion.

Rather than bringing about the events of 17 June, the German producers at RIAS, led by editor in chief Egon Bahr, and their American subsidisers sought to put on the brakes. Fifty years later, Bahr recounted a spontaneous visit by three young construction workers to the radio station on Kufsteiner Straße:

> I didn't expect that a delegation of those on strike would suddenly appear in front of my desk at RIAS. And, of course, I didn't expect that they'd ask RIAS to call for a general strike in the zone. They just said 'zone'. And obviously we couldn't. An American-controlled radio station couldn't call for a general strike in the Soviet-occupied zone, that is to say in the zone of another occupying power. I saw the glowing enthusiastic eyes of these people before me and their disappointment when I told them that it wasn't possible. To satisfy them to some degree, we asked: 'What are your demands?' They then listed them. And then we sat at the table and put them in plain German. We wrote down these five points and promised we'd broadcast them. And that's what we did. We only realised ten days later from the reports we received about what had happened here and there that things had flared up not only in Berlin and not only in Brandenburg but also practically in the entire zone and that the same points had been repeated everywhere in the same order and with the same wording. This meant that RIAS, without wanting or knowing it, had become the catalyst of the uprising.[24]

When, on the evening of 16 June 1953, RIAS broadcast what could have been understood as a call, complete with clauses, for participation in demonstrations, the Americans intervened at once. As Bahr recalled:

> I remember vividly that I received, for the first time in my days at RIAS, an instruction from our American controller, our director Gordon Ewing, a marvellous man. This happened when we began to broadcast the strikers' declaration that people should meet at seven o'clock the next morning, 17 June, at Strausberger Platz. We were worried that only a few people would turn up and that they'd be arrested. That's why we went ahead with the broadcast, so there'd be a bit more than just a few.

A mass demonstration in front of the House of Ministries in East Berlin on 16 June 1953. Despite what was widely believed, RIAS did not encourage the uprising.

Those in charge at the American embassy listened to and were alarmed by the broadcast, as Bahr soon found out:

> This American friend rushed into my office with a trembling beard and said that the high commissioner, Ambassador James B. Conant, had called and asked if RIAS wanted to start World War III. I said of course not. Yes, he said, but what if the Russians intervene? And what if the Russians keep marching or allow their tanks [to] roll straight to West Berlin? I said that that couldn't happen, but Ewing then asked whether I could guarantee that? Of course I couldn't, I said. There was no further discussion. Ewing told me to stop broadcasting the statement immediately.

Bahr was completely surprised by the American intervention and by the considerable alarm with which the matter was viewed. 'What we didn't realise was that the Americans were already being extremely cautious by then and the Russians even more so. Everyone was interested in maintaining the status quo. Nothing could be allowed to happen. There should be no war because of Berlin.'[25] With that, RIAS was kept on a much shorter leash than, for example, *Berliner Morgenpost*, which adopted a harsher tone in its issue of 17 June 1953. In any case, it no longer made a difference, for it had already been decided in Moscow that under no circumstances could the SED be permitted to be overthrown. It was therefore by noon that very Wednesday in June that Soviet tanks rolled into Berlin.

Just as much disliked by the authorities in East Berlin as RIAS was the Investigation Committee of Free Jurists (UfJ). The degree to which the work of this organisation irritated the SED is demonstrated by the severe criticism levelled by East German propaganda:

> The activities of this espionage organisation, officially disguised as a legal department and supported by the Senate of West Berlin, are particularly vile and outrageous. The Investigation

In contrast to RIAS, West Berlin newspapers clearly took a position in favour of the uprising in East Berlin. Shown here is the front page of the *Berliner Morgenpost* on 17 June 1953, the content of which is severely critical of the SED regime.

> Committee of Free Jurists lures citizens from the German Democratic Republic and from the democratic sector to West Berlin under the pretence of giving free legal advice so that it can then force these citizens to become agents.[26]

At the same time, the East Berlin publisher Kongress-Verlag released a 196-page inflammatory book about the UfJ titled ... *im Dienste der Unterwelt* (... in the Service of the Underworld). The blurb read in the style of a sensationalist novel:

> Well-dressed gentlemen with fine manners and with knowledge of legal vocabulary offer legal advice free of charge. Anyone who allows themselves to be deceived by their distinguished behaviour and to be lured into their trap inevitably walks along a criminal path. And the underhand human snatchers at Limastraße 29 in Zehlendorf have already been the undoing of a number of unwary people. Despite the extensive 'security' and 'protective' measures of the 'Free Jurists', the authors of this documentary report have succeeded in providing irrefutable evidence of the activities of the headquarters in Limastraße. Clearly revealed are the shady goings-on of the oh-so-respectable 'Jurists'. It is shown that these 'fighters for law and freedom' are nothing more than special troops who conduct acts of espionage and subversion so as to disrupt the building of our socialist state.[27]

Naturally, the UfJ saw itself quite differently. As stated in a brochure published in 1959:

> The recognition that the people of [East] Germany experience considerable material hardship and, even worse and more depressing, that they are defenceless against and at the mercy of a despotic dictatorship led to the formation of the Investigation Committee of Free Jurists in the

Soviet zone of Germany in 1949. The Bolshevik-Communist system of injustice should not be countered with terror but rather with the threat of the law and with the demand that the [East] German population no longer be deprived of general human rights, which are recognised by the Soviet Union, and that the fundamental rights guaranteed in the constitution of the 'German Democratic Republic' be respected.

The brochure also outlined the four main tasks of the UfJ: '1. Legal aid for the [East] German population in order to expand their sphere of freedom; 2. Legal education in order to keep alive a sense of universally applicable legal principles; 3. Informing the free world about the system of injustice in the Soviet zone; 4. Appraisal work for agencies in the Federal Republic of Germany and in West Berlin.'[28] A summary of the work carried out by the UfJ was later provided by one of its most important members, lawyer Siegfried Mampel, who was regarded by the SED as a 'top agent.'[29] 'In today's terminology, the UfJ was a human rights organisation rather like Amnesty International or the International Society for Human Rights, both of which were founded much later. What is now taken for granted was something fundamentally new back then.' Mampel justified the security measures adopted by the UfJ, something that may seem somewhat strange for a human rights organisation:

SED propaganda sought to discredit the UfJ by publishing defamatory books. Shown here is the front cover of such a book from 1959: ... *im Dienste der Unterwelt* (... in the Service of the Underworld).

The use of code names for employees and volunteers, the special security precautions for visitors who came from the Soviet-occupied part of Germany and who sought help and advice from the UfJ, and the compartmentalisation of different fields of activity meant that the UfJ bore some resemblance to a secret service. However, it was in fact nothing of the kind. It carried out its work in public and attached great importance to the fact that its activities and address were known far and wide, especially in the communist-dominated part of Germany. Its message was broadcast by RIAS on an almost daily basis.[30]

The UfJ also placed advertisements in newspapers to draw attention to its services—quite atypical for a secret service.

The UfJ was an organisation that only the Cold War could have produced. Its most important task was the documentation of injustice in East Germany and East Berlin. To this end, information was collected on a large scale from publicly available sources, leaked court judgements, and written and oral witness accounts. The existence of the SED very much justified the work of the UfJ. By 1962, four thick volumes with selected documents had been published under the title *Unrecht als System* (Injustice as a System). They dealt with the violation of human rights in all forms—politically motivated judgements against upstanding citizens who refused to conform to the SED line, infringements of civil rights, and expropriations or manipulations of fiscal law as a 'means of class struggle against the private economy'.[31] Another important task carried out by the UfJ was to provide East German citizens with the information they needed:

> The UfJ sought to reach a large audience to spread awareness of its legal services. It primarily did so through electronic mass media, especially with the broadcaster RIAS, but it also distributed flyers as widely as possible in East Germany. Individual advice was given at the head office in Zehlendorf, Berlin, as well as at a number of permanent and temporary branch offices. There were times when the UfJ was visited by around 150 people a day. In those years, it had, including technical staff, almost 80 full-time employees.[32]

The information gathered in Zehlendorf was naturally of interest to the intelligence community, although only to a limited degree. The UfJ barely had any information on military facilities, and it was only in exceptional cases that it was asked for material that might possibly have been of relevance to espionage assignments. Much more important for those at the UfJ was to make the western world aware of the conditions in East Germany and to support political prisoners and their families. A relief committee was specially set up by the UfJ so that, with the help of private donations, it could provide material aid to people forced to vacate their apartments or deprived of their jobs. A branch of the relief committee was located at the transit camp in Marienfelde, West Berlin, and it played an important role in admitting refugees there. Only those who had fled political persecution were eligible to receive state benefits, so it is perhaps not surprising that a large number of East German refugees claimed they belonged to this category. On behalf of the Senate of West Berlin, the UfJ, with the help of its card index, checked the information provided by applicants. Questions were asked, for example, about prison terms, interiors of prisons or police stations, and characteristics of interrogators. Only those who could convince UfJ members that they had indeed been persecuted received a certificate confirming this and thus the full support of the authorities in West Berlin. None of the remaining refugees were turned away, but they were given less material support and had to live on the fringes of West German society.[33]

The Stasi despised the UfJ and used every means at its disposal to combat it. Public defamation campaigns were a matter of course, and only on occasion did the Stasi base its statements on facts. One time it did so was with UfJ founder Horst Erdmann, a confidence trickster. Worse was the systematic psychological terror employed against important UfJ members or what the Stasi referred to as 'top agents'. In 1956, for example, a Stasi employee made the following note: 'Secret collaborator "Mücke" has been given the task of telephoning top agents on a regular basis. The objective of this is to put top agents and their wives in a state of horror and anxiety.' Wives received not only phone calls but also anonymous letters in which the work of their husbands was described as 'endangering peace'. A letter to the wife of Siegfried Mampel ended on a threatening note: 'Try to encourage your husband to pursue an honest job. Should you not succeed, I will approach the appropriate authorities to put a stop to the activities of your husband.' The private addresses of UfJ employees were made public with notices which stated that new advice centres for East German citizens had been set up at those addresses. The Stasi had special spies, or 'secret employees', who, posing as UfJ members, placed orders for goods or made demands on manpower. At the end of 1958, a party catering service was given the task of organising a celebration at the UfJ, even though such an event had not at all been planned. Carpooling agencies, pest controllers, heating engineers, and haulage companies arrived at the addresses they had been given to perform tasks that had been ordered but did not need to be done. Newspaper advertisements offered inexpensive office furniture that could be picked up at the UfJ, which of course led to a great deal of confusion. Deliveries that had not been requested regularly arrived from mail order companies. Offers to swap apartments were advertised in the names of UfJ employees. In one Stasi operation, removal services were ordered for several 'top agents' who were supposedly moving all at once from West Berlin to West Germany. A Stasi document clearly stated the aim of such measures:

> All these measures are intended to help put top agents and other UfJ members in a position where they have no idea what is going on. Furthermore, relatives who are affected by these measures will become frightened and terrified. The ultimate objective is obviously to paralyse the UfJ, for its members will have become too preoccupied with personal matters.[34]

That was only one level of the tactics of decomposition. More dangerous were the attacks planned against UfJ personnel. In one case, a departmental head was observed so that a favourable opportunity could be found to exploit his severe short-sightedness and stage an 'accident' while he was on his way to work. In another plan signed by a Stasi officer on 1 July 1961, it was intended that multiple 'top agents' would come to harm:

> Every morning, there are some employees of the UfJ headquarters who are picked up from their apartments by car. It will need to be clarified whether the route that we previously knew of is still being used. Once this has been checked, a suitable location will be chosen for throwing an object against the windscreen of the vehicle.[35]

Two leading members of the UfJ, Walter Linse and Erwin Neumann, were kidnapped by the Stasi and died in prison. Further kidnappings were planned but, it seems, not carried out. The mere risk of being abducted had an impact on the lives of all UfJ employees. They always had to be on the alert: any stranger, acquaintance, or even friend might very well have been a Stasi henchman. In the case of Linse, the Stasi relied not on its own personnel but rather on recruited criminals. By making use of the underworld, the Stasi was doing precisely what SED propaganda accused the UfJ of doing.

While the UfJ was severely disrupted by such decomposition tactics, it was not entirely tied down by them. It was a similar story for other 'enemy strongpoints' targeted by the Stasi. Among the organisations targeted were the East Offices of the democratic parties (CDU, SPD, and FDP), the Ministry of All-German Affairs, the Information Bureau West, the People's Commission for Peace and Freedom, and the Association of Victims of Stalinism. All these organisations documented the crimes and illegal measures of the SED while also smuggling flyers and similar material into East Germany. They rarely did anything beyond that. Even the propaganda brochure *Spionage-Dschungel Westberlin* could accuse them of no more than 'stirring things up against the German Democratic Republic'. Systematic attacks of the kind planned and implemented by the Stasi against the UfJ and other institutions were not carried out by any of these West German organisations. Not once in the propaganda book *Befehdet seit dem ersten Tag: Über drei Jahrzehnte Attentate gegen die DDR* (Under Assault from the First Day: More than Three Decades of Aggression against the German Democratic Republic), published in 1981, were there any specific allegations beyond those that had already been levelled at the KgU and the BND in 1959. This book could manage only vague and sweeping statements.[36] Rudolf Müller, who had dug a tunnel from Mitte to Kreuzberg to help East Germans escape to West Berlin and who had shot the East German border guard Reinhold Huhn in self-defence, was accused of all kinds of things. However, he had sought only to free his family and had done so with no support from the authorities and with only the willingness of the publisher Axel Springer to turn a blind eye.[37]

'Human trafficking'?

West Berlin—capital of escape aid

Despite the militarily secure border that ran through Berlin, the western part of the city remained a constant challenge for East German authorities. It was a showcase of the free world that reminded East Germans of the existence of an alternative to the SED regime and therefore prevented the full transition to some sort of conformity and sense of normality. The systematic destabilising effect of West Berlin itself had a greater impact on the dictatorship than any of the activities that were carried out from there. This is because West Berlin was a magnet for those who wished to flee from East Germany, and it was in West Berlin that almost all altruistic escape aid groups were based in the 1960s. There was the organisation around Detlev Girrmann, Bodo Köhler, and Dieter Thieme that had emerged from the Dahlem Student Union at the Free University of Berlin and became known as Unternehmen Reisebüro (Company Travel Bureau), and there was also the group around the doctor Burkhart Veigel that, by the end of the 1960s, had brought hundreds of East German citizens to freedom by creating false passports, bribing diplomats, and converting vehicles. Hasso Herschel, probably the most successful of those who helped escapees, also carried out his activities from West Berlin.

At the beginning of the 1970s, the focus of escape aid shifted from the border around the walled-in city to the highways between West Germany and West Berlin.

Thanks to the Transit Agreement of 1972, the passport controllers at border crossings, all of whom were Stasi members in the uniforms of the border troops, could no longer check vehicles arbitrarily. Nevertheless, the risk was still considerable. If there were reasonable grounds to suspect 'smuggling' was going on, the guards acted without mercy. In place of the mainly altruistically motivated escape aid in the years that immediately followed the construction of the Berlin Wall—when students helped fellow students, young men their girlfriends, and sons their parents to leave East Germany—there was now an increase in commercially motivated escape aid. Yet it should be emphasised that not all of those who were paid for their help were profiteers. Their efforts required time and money. Moreover, escape aid was not widespread. In the 1970s, roughly 200 to 300 East German citizens were successfully brought into West Germany each year. Only in 1973 was the number significantly greater, for the Transit Agreement had only just come into effect and, as a result, the Stasi checkpoints along the highways were not yet fully operational. The relatively low numbers after that are an indication of the immense effort the Stasi put into pursuing those who helped escapees.[38] The Stasi enjoyed a certain degree of success in this regard. By 1975, a good quarter of all those who tried to flee from East Germany were arrested along with their helpers. This rose to 50 per cent as transit routes began to be monitored more intensively and, according to Stasi files, peaked at 65 to 75 per cent. Escape aid thereby became a marginal phenomenon. With the emigration wave of the 1980s, and the departure of some political prisoners whose release had been paid for, there arose new ways of making it to West Germany that, although trying or unpleasant, were no longer life-threatening.[39]

As far as the SED was concerned, anyone who helped East Germans escape to West Germany, whether motivated by profit or altruism, was a member of a 'criminal gang of human traffickers'. An example of the way in which propaganda obscured reality and conspiracy theories replaced objective analysis can be seen in the polemical book *Bosse, Gangster, Kopfgeldjäger* (Bosses, Gangsters, Bounty Hunters), which was published in 1982: 'In reality, the branch of anti-state human trafficking directed against the socialist German Democratic Republic is a closely interconnected mix of political obscurity and underworld crime, a syndicate aiming for profit and subversive influence, a cooperative in which "serious" politicians work together with the most primitive of crooks.'[40]

On the contrary, there were many different types of people in West Berlin who helped escapees. Hartmut Richter, who left East Germany at the age of 18 in 1966 by swimming across the Teltow Canal, made use of the boot of his car to bring a total of 33 friends and relatives to freedom after the Transit Agreement had gone into effect. He worked alone rather than with an organisation. He was eventually caught in March 1975 when attempting to take his sister and her boyfriend to West Germany. Richter then remained in custody for a year before being sentenced to 15 years in prison for a proven 18 cases of 'smuggling'. As made clear in a Stasi memorandum, Richter's motive for becoming involved in the dangerous task of helping escapees was political: 'Richter is an enemy of the German Democratic Republic, and he openly expresses his hostile attitude.'[41]

Richter remained unshakable during his imprisonment. While in Rummelsburg Prison, he refused to inform on his fellow inmates despite being offered privileges and was therefore made to endure months of solitary confinement instead. He had to survive in prison against deliberately spread rumours that he was working for the Stasi. He went on a hunger strike three times, going without food for 21 days on one of those occasions. While this did not win him his freedom, his parents were eventually allowed to visit him. He justified the hunger strike in a number of flyers that he prepared for distribution in prison: 'To protest against the constant harassment by the henchmen of the regime, I am going on an indefinite hunger strike. Freedom for all those who help escapees. Freedom for all those willing to leave. Freedom for all political prisoners.' The flyers were found, and Richter was sent to Bautzen II for 'negatively influencing his fellow inmates'. Even there he defied the rules and continued to rebel. In October 1980, after Richter had spent five and a half years in prison, West German authorities paid for his release. He had been kept in solitary confinement for almost four of those years.

Rainer Schubert started to become involved in escape aid to bring acquaintances of his to the West. After some initial success, he professionalised this activity in cooperation with the shady Swiss escape helper Hans Ulrich Lenzlinger, who boasted of his wealth and success and conducted a rather aggressive public relations campaign. Schubert separated from him in 1974 and started his own escape aid organisation with 13 employees and several converted cars. His organisation brought almost a hundred East German citizens to freedom for up to 25,000 marks per escapee. The money was not his primary motive, as most of it was used for fees and expenses. According to his own account, Schubert brought some escapees out of East Germany without payment, and he repeatedly sought to outsmart the Stasi. In contrast to most other heads of escape aid organisations, he often travelled to East Berlin himself under a false name so he could meet his 'customers' in person. However, he fell into a trap in January 1975. An East German citizen by the name of Hans-Christian Sch., who supposedly wanted to flee to the West, contacted Schubert and arranged a meeting in East Berlin. This citizen had in fact spent two weeks in a Stasi prison and been persuaded to become an unofficial collaborator with the code name 'Fischer'. Schubert was arrested by the Stasi on the way to the rendezvous—a hotel on Alexanderplatz—and was kept in Hohenschönhausen Prison for more than a year. The Stasi attempted to turn him to their cause and even promised that his girlfriend from West Germany would be given safe-conduct to the Stasi headquarters on Normannenstraße. Schubert refused and was subjected to a show trial, being sentenced to 15 years in prison for 'criminal human trafficking'. The sentence had been decided on with the input of the leadership of the SED.

The public prosecutor demanded life imprisonment, but the less severe sentence was intended to demonstrate the alleged independence of the court. Schubert remained in prison for 106 months until West Germany bought his freedom at the end of 1983.

Kay Mierendorff, who used various methods to bring East German citizens to the West in the 1970s, avoided the clutches of the Stasi. One of those methods was to utilise trucks with hiding spots built into their cargo areas. He bribed Allied soldiers, usually Americans, and worked with diplomats from other countries who regularly drove from East to West Berlin via Checkpoint Charlie without being checked. Officially working as a property manager, Mierendorff also made use of escape routes through the other states of the Eastern Bloc. He moved from West Berlin to Schleswig-Holstein in 1974 and made escape aid his main business, and there were times when he had as many as 150 employees. The risk remained considerable, and the Stasi succeeded in arresting some escape helpers from Mierendorff's organisation. The arrestees were almost always sentenced to long prison terms. Mierendorff himself remained out of reach of Mielke's men for a long time, so the SED resorted to vitriolic propaganda to deter potential 'customers' in East Germany:

> As the well-appointed head of his company, Mierendorff has demonstrated what is understood in capitalism as private initiative. He has no scruples whatsoever. This is clear from the statements that have been made by those of his 'employees' who have been caught in the act and questioned by our investigative bodies. They report that 'the boss' tolerates no objections and that he sees to it that, as he puts it, 'cartridges are reserved' for accomplices who rebel. In the jargon of the Mierendorff clan, it is said that 'Kay has placed his bullet' whenever this procedure is followed. Mierendorff also encourages his gang members to 'place bullets' during their criminal undertakings in the German Democratic Republic. He not only makes an effort to equip them with firearms but also gives them instructions to open fire if the need arises and with the utmost ruthlessness, i.e., in situations where their human trafficking operations have been detected.[42]

This passage is almost entirely fictitious. There were never any escape helpers who wildly opened fire. Anyone who was caught, especially at the border crossings, was likely to be surrounded by men with automatic weapons at the ready. It would have been utter suicide to open fire in such a situation. When escape helpers were arrested, it was generally without resistance.

More effective than East German propaganda was the systematic defamation of Mierendorff in the Western media, especially in *Der Spiegel*. In response to a 1978 article, obviously inspired by murky East German sources, with the title 'Altes Schwein, wir knallen Dich ab' (We'll shoot you, old swine), Mierendorff arranged the printing of a reply with no fewer than 10 points. The editorial team chose to place the words 'Altes Schwein' above this reply.[43] The criticism of Mierendorff, which was very much based on the picture painted by the Stasi, did not abate. Even the Transit Commission, a body made up of traffic experts from both Germanies, served as an instrument in opposition to escape aid, and there were times when West

A doctored photograph, printed in an East German brochure, depicting escape helper Kay Mierendorff in front of the Berlin Wall. The Stasi sought to combat him with various means, eventually going as far as attempting to murder him.

German authorities gave serious consideration to the idea of drawing up legislation designed to put a stop to escape aid.[44]

When this was not accomplished, the Stasi opted for 'more effective' methods. It was only with great fortune that Mierendorff and his wife Antje survived the explosion of a letter bomb on 9 February 1981. His right hand was torn to pieces, his face was wounded, and his abdominal wall, liver, and bowels were ripped open. It is of no surprise that, in his last interview before he died of cancer at the age of 66, Mierendorff said: 'I have committed offences for political reasons. The help I offered to escapees was no adventure. It was often a life and death struggle.' Mierendorff made it clear that his work was never primarily about the money: 'We were only paid if an escape was successful.'[45]

While escape helpers had been in overwhelmingly bad repute in the left-wing liberal press since 1964, the commercial escape helpers of the 1970s onwards were virtually equated with criminals. Some of them were indeed criminals, like the Swiss pimp Hans Ulrich Lenzlinger, and, from 1976, only a small percentage of all escape aid efforts was altruistically or politically motivated. Nevertheless, escapees always needed help due to the existence of the criminal East German border regiments, which supported the SED dictatorship in withholding fundamental human rights from its citizens. Far from being 'human trafficking', escape aid was often, but not always, a form of resistance against the SED regime.[46]

Escape helpers worked covertly and frequently with methods borrowed from the world of espionage. However, by the end of the 1960s, they enjoyed almost no support from West German authorities. As early as New Year's Eve 1963/1964, the police in West Berlin had prevented a mass escape through a tunnel that had been dug under Bernauer Straße, as it did not want the Travel Permit Agreement of 17 December 1963 to be endangered. The tunnel had taken several months to complete, but only three girls managed to escape through it in the end.[47] Furthermore, to describe escape aid as 'secret service activity' is misleading. Although there may have been some shady characters among the escape helpers, it was the Stasi, in its effort to get the problem of alleged 'human traffickers' under control, that employed methods of the kind typical of a secret service. Such methods included assassination attempts. Escape helper Wolfgang Welsch was also a target. Within a period of 10 years, and with diplomatic help, Welsch had brought more than 220 people to freedom via other countries of the Eastern Bloc. This number included more than one hundred doctors, some with women and children. 'Enemy of the state no. 1', as Welsch described himself, only barely survived when an unofficial collaborator of the Stasi poisoned his meatballs.[48]

West Berlin might be regarded as having been a capital of escape aid, but this does not mean that the walled-in city was a 'jungle of espionage'.

CHAPTER EIGHT

The execution of espionage operations in Cold War Berlin

'Send all bandits to the devil'

The kidnapping of Walter Linse

The summer morning of Tuesday 8 July 1952 was perfectly normal until 7:22am. As usual, lawyer Walter Linse left his home in the quiet Gerichtsstraße at that time to go to the nearby Lichterfelde West Railway Station. A man approached Linse on the footpath and asked him for a light. The 49-year-old looked in his briefcase and was then punched multiple times. A second man grabbed Linse from behind and dragged him towards an Opel marked with a taxi sign. Linse resisted violently, so his kidnappers shot him in the leg before hurling him in the car and speeding off. Several of Linse's neighbours witnessed the kidnapping. A man taking his dachshund for a walk blew his whistle, women on either side of the street screamed, and the driver of a Volkswagen sounded his horn and tried to ram the getaway car. It was all to no avail. The Opel drove in excess of 120 kilometres per hour through the narrow border crossing that led to Teltow. Linse was taken to Hohenschönhausen, imprisoned in the Stasi detention centre, and immediately subjected to severe interrogation.[1]

As the head of the economic department of the Investigation Committee of Free Jurists (UfJ), Linse was a resolute anti-communist and greatly despised by the Stasi. Although Linse had played a role in the Aryanisation of Jewish property in Chemnitz between 1938 and 1945, this had nothing to do with the decision to kidnap him.[2] Rather, the reason was that the UfJ had begun preparations for an international legal conference in West Berlin which was to act as a tribunal against the illegitimate state that was the German Democratic Republic. The kidnapping was ordered by the Soviet secret service station in Karlshorst, East Berlin. While Linse's boss, Horst Erdmann, had been the original objective, the fact that a driver always took Erdmann from his home to the office meant that the thrifty Linse, who travelled by train, would be an easier target. A Stasi report dated 22 July 1952 described the preparations for the abduction in detail. The 'order for the arrest' had been issued on 14 June.[3] Just one day later, the kidnapping team, which consisted of several convicted criminals with no political background, drove to the intended

An arrest is made at the sector border in the 1950s. Brutal infringements of the rights of West Berliners by East German authorities were regularly the order of the day during that time.

crime scene 'to become acquainted with' the area. The first kidnapping attempt, made on 16 June, failed because the kidnappers were late and Linse was already on his way to the station. On the following day, and likewise on 20 and 24 June, Linse did not appear. The next attempt by the Stasi henchmen was undertaken on 4 July. This was also a failure, but success came four days later.

On 10 July 1952, the Soviet secret service reported Linse had been questioned by the Stasi and had confirmed 'the accounts of anti-Soviet activities by his organisation and the existence of espionage networks on the territory of the German Democratic Republic'.[4] This would hardly have come as a surprise, as it was clear the UfJ was an anti-communist, and therefore anti-Soviet, organisation with numerous informants in East Germany. Although the secret services of the Eastern Bloc announced they had immediately arrested 24 'agents' based on the information provided by Linse, it is more likely these suspects had been under observation for some time and the kidnapping served as an opportunity to arrest them. This is because the available evidence indicates Linse revealed nothing to his interrogators.

Walter Linse as a member of the UfJ and, a short time later, in Soviet captivity. He was the last German to be executed in Butyrka Prison in Moscow.

On that same 10 July, a large protest rally against the kidnapping of Linse took place on the square outside Schöneberg Town Hall. All political parties of West Berlin, the German Trade Union Confederation, and various anti-communist organisations had called for this rally, which between 20,000 and 30,000 people attended. Among them were informers, one of whom provided the Stasi with the following report:

> Four microphones on the lectern at the main entrance flanked by the flags of the various parties and organisations. On the balcony were the usual guests of honour (yesterday's enemies, today's allies), senior police officers with Dr Stumm at the front, and the remaining extras. Grim silence reigned over the crowd. The Freedom Bell rang across the square for several minutes. A spokesman opened the rally with a description of the kidnapping of Dr Linse. It immediately became apparent that not the speakers but rather the masses were the key players here. The crowd flared up with fanatical rage. The speakers were repeatedly interrupted by frenzied and wildly applauded hecklers who directed their fury against the SED.

The informer imaginatively described the reaction of the audience to the speech given by the governing mayor:

> Ernst Reuter was next. He started solidly, described his outrage, and declared that enough was enough. The masses clamoured. Much too late, they shouted. Reuter announced that measures would be taken: barriers, checkpoints, action against the SED in West Berlin, action against SED members, loss of jobs, suspension of support, and possibly arrest or deportation. The West Berlin judiciary will have to rethink how it reaches a verdict. The square turned into a cauldron of intense anger: 'Put them in prison. Put them in camps! Set fire to their lairs. Every SED man is an Eastern spy. Death to traitors!'[5]

Some supporters of the SED regime tried to disrupt the rally, which incurred the displeasure of the vast majority of the participants and led to the intervention of the police. As reported by *Der Spiegel*: 'The anger over the communist act of violence was taken out on the troublemakers with such intensity that the police had to take them into protective custody before they were lynched.'[6] Less than an hour later, the SED supporters were released. Even so, *Neues Deutschland* spun yarns the next day about 'fascist pogroms' taking place after the protest rally. An article on Linse cynically stated that West Berlin had 'lost an agent'. The sooner all 'gangsters' disappeared from the three western sectors of Berlin, the sooner 'normal conditions' would return there. It was in the interests of West Berliners 'to send all bandits, including Reuter, to the devil'.[7] According to Siegfried Mampel, this report in *Neues Deutschland* was 'the only time that the crime was mentioned in East Germany or anywhere in the Eastern Bloc'.[8] This was only partly true, as Stasi chief Wilhelm Zaisser admitted to the Central Committee of the SED, at the beginning of August 1952, that Linse was in the hands of East German authorities. However, the minister for state security claimed Linse had been 'recognised and arrested' by two officers of the People's Police 'on a train in the Soviet sector' and that he had with him his briefcase containing 'numerous documents about his espionage activities'.[9] The UfJ learnt of this statement made by Zaisser to the Central Committee and made it public. The SED responded with complete silence.

The large demonstration before Schöneberg Town Hall did just as little to help Linse as the telegram his wife sent to East German Prime Minister Otto Grotewohl: 'I expect my husband's immediate release if you don't want to be counted as a criminal yourself.'[10] Rather than replying, the SED head of government passed Helga Linse's message on to the Stasi, in whose files it reappeared four decades later. Even the Bundestag protested, and the International Commission of Jurists passed a resolution that condemned the kidnapping. Almost 150 jurists from 43 countries agreed the lack of response from East German authorities strongly indicated they were complicit in the crime. They called for 'appropriate measures' to be taken 'to bring about the immediate release of the victim of this kidnapping'.[11] It was, of course, of no use, as East German and Soviet authorities consistently evaded all queries in relation to Walter Linse. In West Berlin, Helga Linse subsequently received dozens of proposals for the rescue of her husband. The UfJ checked each proposal and found that most of them were attempts at fraud, especially as they tended to request four-figure advance payments. *Der Spiegel* reported: 'The Investigation Committee offered to deposit a large sum of money with a West Berlin notary as a reward for anyone who recommends a measure that leads to Dr Linse regaining his freedom. Nobody has taken up this offer so far.'[12]

Following the fall of the Wall and the opening of the Stasi archives, it has been possible to reconstruct what happened to Walter Linse after 8 July 1952. He remained imprisoned in Hohenschönhausen until December 1952. His conversations with himself and his prayers were recorded with hidden microphones, and informants were occasionally sent to his cell. Then the Stasi handed Linse over to the Soviets. Broken by months of interrogation, Linse confessed to espionage and subversion against East Germany and, in a secret trial in Lichtenberg on 23 September 1953, was sentenced to death by Soviet Military Tribunal No. 48240 for espionage, anti-Soviet propaganda, and the formation of an anti-Soviet organisation. He was taken to Moscow, where the Presidium of the Supreme Soviet denied his appeal for clemency on 2 December 1953. He was shot on 15 December 1953 in the basement of Butyrka Prison and then cremated and buried at Donskoy Monastery. He was the last of almost a thousand German victims executed in Moscow from 1950 to 1953. Only in 1996 did the Military Prosecutor's Office of the Russian Federation rehabilitate Walter Linse.[13]

BfV agent led astray

The mystery of Otto John

Chancellor Konrad Adenauer remained calm on the morning of 22 July 1954 when his secretary informed him of 'the most incredible piece of news since the founding of the Federal Republic'.[14] The president of the Federal Office for the Protection of the Constitution (BfV), Otto John, had disappeared from West Berlin without a trace. The chancellor was in his rose garden in Rhöndorf and was soon to set off for his summer holiday at Bühlerhöhe Palace Hotel in the Black Forest when he received the news. After thinking for a few moments, he approved the publication of a cautiously formulated announcement in the bulletin of the Press and Information Office. If someone like the top chief of domestic intelligence disappeared, all hell might very well break loose. Nevertheless, having approved the announcement, Adenauer proceeded to go on holiday.[15]

The 45-year-old John had flown to West Berlin with his wife to attend the memorial services for the victims of 20 July 1944. John had belonged to the wider circle of conspirators and had even been in the Bendlerblock on the day of the attempted coup against Hitler. He had been able to get away after its failure, but his brother Hans fell into the hands of the Gestapo and was executed. Otto John therefore had good reason to attend the ceremony, the first at which West German President Theodor Heuss would give an address. However, according to the recollection of some of those who travelled with him, Otto John had appeared to be in a somewhat nervous state on the flight to Berlin. Upon arrival at Tempelhof Airport, he let all the other passengers leave the aircraft first even though he sat near the door. He had his back turned to them as they passed him, which perhaps drew rather than deflected attention. After greeting his Berlin staff on the tarmac, John turned down all security measures. According to *Der Spiegel*, he had thought that he was 'man enough to take care of himself'.[16] He also drew attention at the reception, for the relatives of those who had been executed, held by the Senate of West Berlin on the eve of 20 July.

Good acquaintances of his found that he either did not greet them at all or, if he did, that he seemed to have a distant look in his eye. There was one colleague to whom he introduced his wife three times. The next morning, John, who was usually known for keeping his cool, was seen with red, tear-stained eyes at the prayer service for the victims of the conspiracy. He yet again attracted attention when he sobbed at the commemorative ceremony at the execution site in Plötzensee. 'Some of the women who sat behind him were of the impression that, after such a long time, the source of his mental anguish could not possibly be the death of his brother. They assumed that he might have been feigning sadness.'[17]

John left his hotel on 20 July 1954 at 7:40pm. He had with him a fake identity

Otto John's public appearance in East Berlin on 11 August 1954. His defection to East Germany was the largest political scandal of the 1950s for West Germany.

card and at least 750 marks in cash. To his wife, who was not quite feeling well, he said only that he was going to see some acquaintances. He had in fact arranged an appointment with two British intelligence officers, but he never turned up to the meeting. With growing concern, the two agents telephoned John's wife at the hotel. All she could tell them was that her husband had wanted to meet 'acquaintances from the Soviet zone'. It seems the head of the BfV had gone to Uhlandstraße to see his old friend Wolfgang Wohlgemuth, a gynaecologist and surgeon whom he almost always visited when he was in West Berlin. That evening, however, the two went on an unusual excursion. They reached the sector border on Invalidenstraße shortly after 9pm. Everything appeared to be in order to the West Berlin customs officer who was on duty at the checkpoint and who, as was his routine, informed the two men they were entering the Soviet sector. 'That's where we want to go,' was their response. 'We have to go to the Charité.' They then drove eastwards and disappeared.[18] The customs officer instinctively made note of the last three digits of the number plate. Wohlgemuth returned alone later that night, parked on Uhlandstraße at roughly midnight, and set off again at 5am. His receptionist found a puzzling note when she arrived at work that morning:

> A certain incident which might possibly raise false suspicions about me has compelled me to go to the Charité today. The lawyer Y. hereby receives the power of attorney over my property. Get in touch with Z. The situation here is that Herr John no longer wants to return to the western sector. He had a conversation with colleagues from East Berlin during his visit to the Charité. It might be suspected that I had influenced him. I will wait until this is clarified. Until we meet again, possibly at the Charité.[19]

Only a few hours had passed since the disappearance of John and, already, even though abductions were the order of the day for the Stasi in 1954, no one in the West Berlin Police seriously believed he had been kidnapped. The customs officer had identified John when shown photos of him and was firmly of the opinion the man had been sitting in the car of his own free will. John's pay was thereupon suspended on the evening of 21 July 1954, and the investigators informed the West German government of what had happened the next morning. But Interior Minister Gerhard Schröder had gone to the Bayreuth Festival, Secretary of State of the Chancellery Hans Globke was staying at a health resort in Bad Gastein, and the chancellor himself had decided to set off for the Bühlerhöhe Palace Hotel. Wild speculation reigned among journalists in Bonn, and fuel was added to the fire by an East German radio report:

> Following a speech given by Heuss on the occasion of the tenth anniversary of 20 July 1944, the president of the Federal Office for the Protection of the Constitution, Herr Dr Otto John, had a discussion in the democratic sector with leading figures of the German Democratic Republic. Herr Dr John decided on the basis of political considerations to place his services at the disposal of the authorities of the German Democratic Republic. The State Secretariat for State Security is currently investigating in more detail what has prompted Herr John to make contact with representatives of the state authorities of the German Democratic Republic. Dr Otto John was accompanied by Herr Dr Wolfgang Wohlgemuth, who lives in Charlottenburg in West Berlin.

The report went on to state that John was protesting against the reactivation of National Socialists in the West German public service and that he was now going over to East Germany in anticipation of the intensification of Adenauer's politics. There were, continued the report, opportunities for reunification, as shown by the Church Congress in Leipzig, but those opportunities were not being fully seized. Then came a statement that had supposedly been formulated by John himself:

> Germany is in danger of being torn apart forever by the conflict between East and West. A demonstrative act is required to encourage all Germans to demand reunification. That is why I took the step on the anniversary of 20 July of establishing contact with the Germans in the East.[20]

This news caused a sensation. One of the highest officials of West Germany—from the secret service milieu no less—had defected!

Not everyone was convinced, however. President Heuss had met John prior to 1945 in the house of Klaus Bonhoeffer, an opponent of Nazism, and he wrote the following to Adenauer two weeks after the disappearance of John:

> I am sorry that this unpleasant story of John, which in some respects is still a complete mystery to me, has disturbed you during your well-earned holiday. Assuming that his crossing over the border was voluntary, what at first came to mind was the affair involving Rudolf Hess, and then I thought of Günther Gereke, whose defection to East Germany ended up being of no consequence whatsoever, so I regard it as not unlikely that, in a few months from now, John will have become no more than an embarrassing anecdote. Even so, I cannot be entirely certain of this, for I am not blessed with the gift of foresight.

The chancellor replied two days later that he had, 'in response to multiple requests', made a radio address with regard to the John case. He added that 'the matter was packed in with a number of other remarks, as it does not seem right for a chancellor to speak only of this matter and nothing else'. He thought it a 'really annoying' and 'stupid matter' that involved endless telephone calls as well as visits from ministers and state secretaries.[21]

The hope of Heuss and Adenauer that the matter would go away was not fulfilled. On 11 August 1954, three weeks after his disappearance, Otto John appeared before the press in East Berlin and repeated roughly what had been stated in his name on 22 July:

> After very careful consideration, I decided to go to and remain in the German Democratic Republic. It is here that I see the best opportunities to work for the reunification of Germany and against the threat of a new war. Many bright and honest people in West Germany do not see the dangers that threaten us, as they are blinded by the propaganda of the West German government.[22]

John cited the plans for a European Defence Community (EDC) as the main reason for his decision to cross the border. He believed that Adenauer and his confidants would regard these plans as a means whereby the restoration of German militarism could be disguised and the recreation of a 'strong Wehrmacht' could be carried out. The other contingents of the EDC would be 'absorbed' sooner or later so that

Germany could dominate Europe once more.[23] When asked by journalists about the involvement of his friend Wolfgang Wohlgemuth in the crossing of the border, John answered that the doctor had played only a 'minor role'. After the press conference, John gave personal interviews to one British and two American correspondents. The West German Ministry of the Interior, which had in the meantime offered the astronomical sum of 500,000 West German marks as a reward for anyone who could resolve the John case, laconically announced after the press conference that the former head of the BfV had 'clearly placed his services at the disposal of communist propaganda and thus proved himself to be a traitor'.[24]

The John case was a significant victory for East Germany in its propaganda campaign against West Germany. Gerhard Schröder, the West German minister of the interior, regarded it as a 'serious setback in the Cold War'.[25] Some historians even speak of the 'greatest crisis in the first five years of the Federal Republic'.[26] Heuss was particularly critical of Schröder for offering so much money, opining this would 'not at all be understood by the people'. Schröder had to face a motion of no confidence in the Bundestag that had been tabled by Adenauer's coalition partner, the Free Democratic Party (FDP). Only thanks to the abstention of the Social Democratic Party (SPD) did Schröder, one of the most talented politicians of the Christian Democratic Union (CDU) despite being described by Adenauer as 'young, vain, and unpopular', survive the vote.[27]

The affair took an unexpected turn a year and a half later. On 11 December 1955 at 4:32pm, a Ford, coming from Unter den Linden, drove between the mighty

Otto John (centre) on the terrace of a restaurant on the corner of Stalinallee and Straße der Pariser Kommune. By not always doing what was expected of him, he ended up being a source of irritation for East German authorities.

pillars of the Brandenburg Gate and rolled towards the West Berlin checkpoint that stood a little to the west of the start of the Straße des 17. Juni. The customs officials recognised the car, with its Danish flag, as the vehicle of the correspondent Henrik Bonde-Henriksen, who regularly went back and forth between East and West Berlin. They gave him a friendly wave and let the car go through without being checked. At that moment, the Danish journalist, who was behind the wheel, glanced to his right and saw that the man who sat next to him was crying. After 510 days in East Berlin and the Soviet Union, Otto John had returned to the West. The two drove to Bonde-Henriksen's apartment in Lichterfelde, informed the West Berlin authorities of the news, and were flown to West Germany the next day at 6pm. John knew he was wanted for treason, and the West German government soon announced that he would indeed be questioned. Meanwhile, the General German News Service in East Berlin tersely reported that John had left East Germany in order to 'continue the fight against neofascism in West Germany'.[28]

What Otto John had to say when questioned came as a surprise. He claimed that he had been taken to East Berlin against his will. He had been anaesthetised in Wohlgemuth's apartment and whisked away to East Germany. It was only there, after being put under a great deal of pressure, that he decided to cooperate, although he always sought to find a way to return to the West. The Federal Court of Justice did not believe his statements and, in 1956, sentenced him to four years in prison. After serving two-thirds of his sentence, Heuss pardoned John at the end of July 1958. This decision had a side effect that had not been expected by the head of state: 'The consequences—for me!—were significant. I received telegrams and many, many letters asking for pardons for traffic offenders, pederasts, defrauders, and forgers, almost all of whom, naturally, had been convicted despite being innocent.' Adenauer, however, assured Heuss that 'things are forgotten very quickly in our era'.[29] John could not forget, and he stuck to his version of events until his death in 1997. Precisely what took place on the evening of 20 July 1954 remains a mystery to this day. However, with the opening of the Stasi archives and the statements made by the people involved, a third version of events has emerged that is probably closer to the truth than the theories of treason and kidnapping. John, who had felt increasingly isolated as an opponent of the policy of rearmament that had been pursued by Adenauer since the triumphant election victory in 1953, and who had felt he had been put under pressure by the federal chancellery as well as by his rival Reinhard Gehlen, had possibly been contacted by Soviet intelligence in late 1953 or early 1954 under a false flag. He may have been promised that he would be able to meet 'someone of political importance' in East Berlin to speak about 'the question of progressive groups in West Germany who might be capable of working in a unified Germany'. The head of the BfV may have agreed to this meeting and may have indicated he would be in Berlin on 20 July 1954. If this is what happened, the two parties evidently had different ideas. John probably wanted a secret conversation that would result in introductory steps towards reunification and would thereby considerably enhance his political influence. This

An undated photograph of Otto John after his return to West Germany.

would explain why John voluntarily went to East Berlin with Wohlgemuth. The KGB had other plans: 'We wanted to persuade him not to return to West Germany but rather to openly break with Adenauer and to deliver a corresponding political statement.'[30]

Once in East Berlin, it became clear to John that his plan had been an illusion. He refused to cooperate any further and was thereupon immobilised with pills in the villa he was staying at in Karlshorst. Wohlgemuth knew he would soon be sought after by investigators in West Berlin, which was why he drove back and left his receptionist his mysterious message. When John awoke, he realised he had been kept in East Germany against his will. According to his own account, John decided from that moment to put on an act and to make it look as if he was responding positively to the wishes of the Eastern intelligence services. While he made a number of statements on behalf of the East German regime, he was at the same time often seen throughout 1955 behaving in a manner that was rather unusual for a defector. He publicly criticised SED officials and sang American pop songs. After that, he returned to West Germany despite the fact that prison awaited him there.

Four years for the critic

The kidnapping of Karl Wilhelm Fricke

Karl Wilhelm Fricke, a young West Berlin journalist who was critical of the SED, was kidnapped by the Stasi on 1 April 1955. A contact by the name of 'Maurer' had called him and said he had been able to get hold of a much-awaited East German textbook. The contact wanted to know if Fricke could visit him. Fricke replied that he could and wrote in his calendar before leaving: 'Maurer 1500 hours / Geisbergstraße left / Post Office W 30'. From there, the journalist and his purported informant went to a nearby apartment, where Frau 'Maurer' was also waiting. The woman offered her guest cigarettes and a glass of brandy, and then the group talked for half an hour. Fricke soon became restless, as he had arranged to meet his fiancée that afternoon. Frau 'Maurer' handed him one last glass before he was to go, but this time the brandy tasted a little strange. When he became somewhat dizzy, he attributed it to the amount of alcohol he had consumed that early afternoon. Feeling nauseous, he levered himself up and made it to the bathroom. Once the nauseousness subsided, the journalist returned to his hosts, apologised, and asked them to call him a taxi. He then lost consciousness. It was shortly after 4pm.[31]

Herr and Frau Rittwangen, alias 'Maurer,' engineered the kidnapping of their acquaintance, Karl Wilhelm Fricke.

A mixture of atropine and scopolamine in the third glass of brandy had knocked Fricke out. Most likely packaged up in a sleeping bag, he was taken to East Berlin that evening without any fuss. Only seven hours later did he regain consciousness. He sat in a rather large room before a round table and was surrounded by four or five men, some of them in civilian clothing and others in uniform. One of the men hit him in the face. Fricke immediately recognised that he was in a dangerous situation and could only guess he had been taken to the Stasi prison in Hohenschönhausen. He staggered to the door and called for help, but he was pushed back and lost consciousness again after a short struggle. He awoke naked under a cold shower and was then allowed to sleep in a windowless cell on a cold, wooden plank bed. He was in slightly better shape the next morning and was shown into a dreary office. According to the records, the first interrogation of Fricke by the Stasi began at 7am on 2 April 1955. The interrogator repeatedly asked where Fricke obtained his information; Fricke replied each time that he had 'no connections of any criminal character whatsoever to people' in East Germany.[32] The days went by, but the tactic of deliberately exhausting the abductee did not have the desired effect. The Stasi, at a loss, concluded in its report: 'Fricke is strongly suspected of maintaining groups of agents in the German Democratic Republic on behalf of West Berlin espionage agencies. As a journalist, Fricke has been calling for war and inciting boycotts.' It is worth noting that Fricke's activities by no means resembled espionage as he had always published his criticism of the SED dictatorship openly and under his own name in the Western media.

The kidnapping and interrogation had not unfolded as planned. Fricke had not revealed any informants in the East, for he did not have any, and the effort to conceal the abduction itself had failed. Fricke's girlfriend, Friedelind Möhring, had been surprised to discover he had not arrived back home on the afternoon of 1 April, so she immediately raised the alarm. As Fricke was being questioned for the first time, West German officials searched his room in Friedenau and came across the note he had made in his calendar. That evening, Fricke's landlady received a telegram from Hanover: 'Had to go to an urgent meeting. Unfortunately, could not notify you beforehand. If Friedelind asks, tell her I will call her as soon as I get back. Maybe return tomorrow. Fricke.'[33] What was intended to be a diversion turned out to be ineffective. The criminal investigation department had found Fricke's identity papers in his apartment, but it was not possible to leave West Berlin in 1955 without such papers. It had become clear Fricke must have been kidnapped. 'Kurt Maurer' was soon questioned given that he was, according to the note in the calendar, the last person to see Fricke. He was provisionally detained a few hours later, but a West Berlin judge released him after another 24 hours. While Fricke was interrogated without access to a lawyer, his kidnapper was able to enjoy the blessings of a state under the rule of law. No sooner had 'Maurer' been released than he left for East Berlin.

Fricke remained steadfast while being subjected to psychological torture. Even after 19 weeks of interrogation, the Stasi knew no more than what its officers had

The Stasi intended to gain time with this fake telegram, but the West Berlin Police saw through the scheme.

persuaded themselves to believe at the beginning: 'Under the code name 'Student', the accused conducted extensive crimes against the German Democratic Republic.' Neither the interrogations nor any other investigations had produced any evidence of this, and the SED was certainly dissatisfied. The existing 'incriminating material' was of no use for a show trial, and discussions went back and forth between the East German public prosecutor's office, the Stasi and the SED headquarters as to how best to proceed. Officially, Fricke was still missing. The West German public did not know what had happened to him, and even his fiancée and editors received no news. He had not yet seen a lawyer, be it a freely chosen defence attorney from West Berlin or a court-appointed legal defender from East Germany. Only four days before the start of the trial did that change when Fricke was visited by Friedrich Wolff, a tame lawyer for the SED. Fricke asked him to file an application for the authorisation of West Berlin journalists to attend the proceedings. Wolff rejected this request on the grounds that it would be 'completely pointless'. He also refused to bring up the kidnapping of his client in court; a verdict was reached against the abductee after only five and a half hours—a prison sentence of four years. The basis of this judgement, 'crimes against Article 6 of the Constitution of the German Democratic Republic', corresponded exactly to the recommendation that had been made beforehand by the Central Committee of the SED to the public prosecutor.

Fricke was initially held in Brandenburg-Görden Prison and was then transferred to Bautzen II after a short time. He was kept in solitary confinement there for 963 days. At any rate, his relatives now knew he was alive. After serving two-thirds of his sentence, he requested the remaining time be suspended with probation. This was rejected by the East German judiciary. Although he displayed what the director of Bautzen II described on the third anniversary of the abduction as 'good behaviour towards supervisory officers', the problem was that 'his attitude towards the state of the workers and peasants, and towards the German Democratic Republic in general, is murky'.[34] It could have been said more clearly that, despite being kept in solitary

Karl Wilhelm Fricke imprisoned in Bautzen II and, 50 years later, in his house in Cologne. He remained a critic of the SED until the reunification of Germany in 1990.

confinement, Fricke uncompromisingly and resolutely remained a democrat and an opponent of the communist dictatorship. Only on 31 March 1959—three years and 364 days after his kidnapping—did Fricke receive his certificate of discharge. In a bureaucratically correct fashion, there was a note on the certificate to the effect that he was to return to his last official place of residence in Steglitz, West Berlin. The Stasi gave him a ticket, five East German marks, and some advice that he did not at all need: 'The bearer of this certificate of discharge has been advised that he has to leave the territory of the German Democratic Republic via the route prescribed for him in the shortest possible time.'[35] Waiting for him in West Berlin, as arranged by letter, were his fiancée and a friend. After four years, Fricke's odyssey through the horrors of East German socialism was at an end.

Warned and yet still caught off guard

The CIA, the NSA, the BND, and the building of the Berlin Wall

Everyone was wise after the event. From 13 August 1961, the people of Berlin, and of the rest of the world, knew that the SED was ready to set up a militarily secure frontier that ran through the centre of the four-power city. The lights around the Brandenburg Gate suddenly went out that night, East German uniformed men rolled out barbed wire along the sector border, and most trains came to a halt. Until that night, nobody had imagined—or wanted to imagine—that something of the kind might take place.

That was why the politicians in the capitals of the NATO countries as well as the people of West Berlin gave relatively little credence to the various signs that had appeared since the end of June 1961. Several intelligence agencies had reported fragments of information that, when considered carefully, pointed towards plans to seal off the three western sectors of Berlin. However, this was only recognised afterwards.

For example, the American National Security Agency (NSA) had obtained solid evidence four days before the commencement of the construction of the Berlin Wall that the border would be closed. A communications intelligence report on 9 August stated that the SED was planning 'to begin turning all foot traffic back at the sector border' and concluded 'that this might be the first step in a plan to close the border'.[36]

Communications intelligence refers to monitoring and obtaining information from the communications of potential enemies. Did the NSA overhear a telephone conversation between East German officials talking about the impending closure of the border in the first few days of August 1961? If so, did it know who those officials were? Or was the information second-hand, coming from a source that had to be concealed even from the government in Washington? This will most likely never be clarified with certainty, since it seems the original report has not been preserved. There exists only the summary provided in a formerly top-secret NSA report.

SED leader Walter Ulbricht knew in the summer of 1961 that he would have to block the reasonably safe escape route that led from East Germany to West Germany via West Berlin as soon as possible if he did not want his dictatorship to collapse. This would be the first time the inner-city sector border would be properly sealed off, and it would mean the admission of the greatest conceivable political defeat for the SED; specifically, the attempt to prove the superiority of a socialist alternative on the other side of an open border with West Germany will have failed. At the same time, the sealing off of West Berlin marked a temporary endpoint of years of political poker in which Soviet party and state leader Nikita Khrushchev had sought to force the Western powers to conclude a peace treaty and withdraw from West Berlin.

Any leaking of the plan to erect the Wall would have led to an immediate increase in the exodus of East German citizens and may have given rise to countermeasures by the Western powers. The SED therefore saw to it that preparations for carrying out the plan were made in the strictest secrecy. The person responsible for those preparations was the Secretary for Security of the Central Committee of the SED, Erich Honecker, who was regarded as Ulbricht's crown prince. Of course, dozens of other functionaries of the state party had to be informed of the plan in addition to hundreds of officers of the East German National People's Army, the East German Border Troops, and the Stasi. If the information obtained by the NSA on 9 August 1961 was in fact based on a bugged telephone conversation and not on the report of a spy, the two East Germans who were speaking with one another must have been in the know and must have, contrary to all instructions, been talking about the plan to close the border.

East German construction workers began to build the Berlin Wall out of prefabricated concrete elements from around 15 August 1961. The barrier had been made of barbed wire before then.

Indeed, it is true the NSA focused almost exclusively on electronic surveillance of this kind. Other methods of obtaining information, like human intelligence, were carried out by the Central Intelligence Agency (CIA). However, the CIA was completely caught off guard by the events of 13 August 1961.

Young CIA officer John Kenney was awake late that night when, at 3:24am, he heard breaking news on RIAS: 'Strong units of the communist People's Police sealed off the sector border between East and West Berlin overnight.' Kenney immediately went to his office in Dahlem, West Berlin, but he found that the CIA station there was perfectly quiet and that only the doorman and someone on night shift in the radio room were present. Neither of them had heard the radio report. The most important intelligence agency of the United States had no idea whatsoever of what was going on.[37]

This was not the case for all Western secret services. Aside from the NSA, the BND had its own information about unusual activity in East Germany. The BND headquarters in Pullach, near Munich, had already received some worrying news on 29 June 1961. Specifically, an agent had reported that units of the East German Border Troops were to be concentrated around Berlin: 'The 2nd Alert Unit of the People's Police, stationed in Rummelsburg in East Berlin and consisting of seven companies and one technical company, is soon to vacate its current quarters and will move into private accommodation. The vacated quarters will be occupied by the

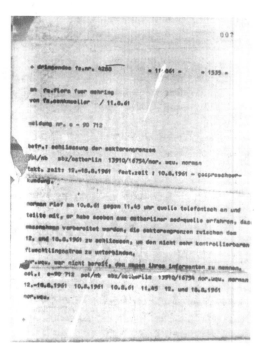

Two days before the border was closed, the BND in Pullach received this telex message from an agent in West Berlin.

alert unit from Basdorf.' According to the report, 'the government of the German Democratic Republic wants to have more personnel of the People's Police in Berlin'. The commander of the 2nd Alert Unit had made an announcement along these lines to his men during roll call, and this clearly proved to be a mistake: 'Many of the troops remarked that the commander ought not to have made this announcement, as the measures being taken were supposed to be top secret.'[38]

This, however, was only a small indication of what was about to take place. Only on 10 August 1961—one day after the NSA obtained its information and three days before the closing of the border—did the BND have a more concrete picture of the situation. At 11:45am that summer Thursday, a BND agent with the code name 'Norman' telephoned one of his sources, an SED functionary in East Berlin whose name is not known, and found out 'that preparations are being made to close the sector borders between 12 and 18 August 1961 in order to put a stop to what has become the uncontrollable flow of refugees'. Because 'Norman' was unwilling to reveal the identity of his source to the BND, the reliability of the information was not rated very highly to begin with. Although the information had been urgently telexed to Pullach, it was not passed on to the West German government in Bonn.[39]

Even those in charge at the NSA seemed to place little trust in the information that had come from SED circles. The news was certainly not passed on to the White House. President John F. Kennedy was furious later on that he had been too little informed about East German plans to seal off West Berlin. This was by no means the result of any conspiracy; rather, what was planned by East German authorities was beyond the imagination of American analysts. They could not believe the SED would go so far as to construct an inner-city death strip. The NSA information was therefore ignored for several days. By the early morning of 13 August 1961, it was too late.

It is possible West Berliners may have sensed what was in store for their city at least two days before the shock of the border closure. As the headline of *Berliner Morgenpost* on Friday 11 August read: 'SED wants to block escape routes. Lead-up to the height of terror?'[40] Yet this remained unthinkable until the moment units of the East German Border Troops, and of the Combat Groups of the Working Class, moved into position along the inner-city sector line.

Karl-Heinz Kurras

Betraying the West Berlin Police

Caution is the most important virtue for any spy. Dressed in clothes he had bought himself, including hat and glasses, Karl-Heinz Kurras boarded a train on 12 June 1964. The 37-year-old was the secret collaborator 'Otto Bohl' for the Stasi, and he did not want to be recognised. His destination was Friedrichstraße Railway Station, which, while located in East Berlin, served as a major border crossing between East and West. For a criminal investigation officer who sought to be transferred to the

Karl-Heinz Kurras at the opening of the first trial on 3 November 1967. He was considered to represent the 'ugly face of fascism,' although he was in fact a Stasi spy.

Department of State Protection of the West Berlin Police, such a journey, if noticed, would have demanded some sort of explanation. On the platform that Friday, shortly after 2pm, he established visual contact with his Stasi case officer, First Lieutenant Werner Eiserbeck, who led him to a door marked as a service entrance. The passage beyond bypassed the checkpoint that led to East Berlin and was usually used by East German railway employees who had to work on either side of the station.

Independently of each other, the two men went to the corner of Universitätsstraße and Unter den Linden where Eiserbeck had parked his car. Only once they were in the car and on their way to the safe house with the code name 'Kies' did they speak with one another. Kurras referred to Eiserbeck as 'Werner Beck' because he did not know his real name. The tenants of the safe house were also unknown to him. They were 'reliable unofficial collaborators' who had placed their home at the disposal of the Stasi when they had only a short time beforehand moved to North Vietnam, as representatives of East Germany, for the purpose of strengthening economic ties. Eiserbeck had set aside a considerable amount of time for the meeting. He gave Kurras a refresher course in encryption, provided him with new code documents to replace the previous and now damaged ones, and obtained from him a detailed report that covered the few months since their last meeting in East Berlin. Eiserbeck recorded the entire conversation and later prepared a number of written reports based on that recording.

It was important for Kurras that he be relieved from a special assignment he had been given. It had been his task to approach the secretary of the head of the Department of State Protection. He had made multiple attempts to do so, both in private and at police headquarters, and he was concerned further efforts to pursue her might raise suspicion. Eiserbeck agreed, writing in one of his reports that 'the request of the secret collaborator was granted'. After that, the Stasi officer initiated a 'detailed political discussion', and he noted with satisfaction that his spy 'pays attention to the current issues of the day and holds a positive opinion'. In this context, 'positive' would have meant along the lines of the SED. After more than seven hours, Eiserbeck brought Kurras back to the city centre and dropped him off near Friedrichstraße Railway Station. Kurras went to the 'Palace of Tears', as the border crossing at the station was known, and was cleared for departure. Eiserbeck had warned him to be careful, but everything went smoothly: 'No one was present while the secret collaborator went through the checkpoint. No incident of any kind took place.'[41]

The rendezvous between Kurras and Eiserbeck in East Berlin on 12 June 1964 was only one of many dozen such meetings. Even more frequent were meetings between Kurras and Stasi messengers in West Berlin, usually in the Schleusenkrug pub between the Berlin Zoological Garden and Großer Tiergarten park. From 1955 to 1967, Kurras handed over vast quantities of original material to the Stasi. He wrote or dictated at least 152 reports, and frequently consulted the register of residents in West Berlin as well as the card index of number plates. It seems he revealed everything to the Stasi that he could get his hands on. When he first started working as an agent, most of the information he provided was trivial—lists of police station units or reports of British and American military manoeuvres in Grunewald, West Berlin. During his time as a patrolman between 1955 and 1960, he started to provide more valuable material, like a copy of the code name directory used by the West Berlin Police for telephone communications. This enabled the Stasi not only to monitor telephone conversations but also to determine the identities of those who were speaking. Kurras also found out which of his colleagues were regarded as outstanding and earmarked for promotion so the Stasi could try to recruit or defame them. Kurras then became a top source for the Stasi when he was posted to the West Berlin Criminal Investigation Department in the middle of 1960. He reported on the internal matters of the State Office of Criminal Investigations, revealed the

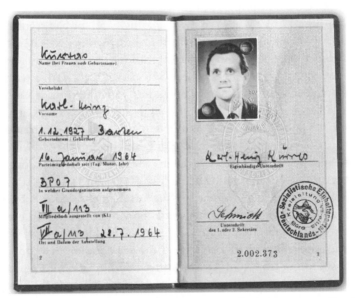

The original copy of Kurras's SED membership booklet is to be found in his Stasi files that came to light in May 2009. His Stasi case officer had supported his application for membership.

problems of his colleagues, and provided information on police measures along the Berlin Wall. Eventually, Kurras succeeded in his, and the Stasi's, goal of being transferred to the Department of State Protection. From the beginning of 1965, he delivered five ring binders with secret documents containing information on, among other things, unofficial collaborators of the Stasi who had been arrested, members of the Stasi who had deserted, and escape helpers.[42]

Such espionage activity was risky, as the West Berlin Police had its own counter-espionage unit. However, this unit was a part of the Department of State Protection and could therefore be easily observed by Kurras. He knew at an early stage if a police officer was under suspicion. Nevertheless, he only narrowly evaded exposure in 1965. 'We had concrete evidence that certain information was being leaked and that people we were about to arrest were being warned in advance', recalled Wilfried Kunoth, a colleague of Kurras's in the Department of State Protection, more than four decades later.[43] A special investigation under the code name 'Abendroth' was soon underway. Duty rosters and holiday plans were compared to begin with to determine which police officers might have knowledge of certain operations. After the group of suspects had been narrowed down, Kunoth and his colleagues employed the entire repertoire of intelligence methods they had at their disposal. This included tapping telephones, checking the odometer readings of private and official cars, and even surveillance. On 3 November 1965, the investigation had scored its first success. West Berlin detective sergeant Hans Weiß and his wife fell into the trap. Although the former revealed nothing, the latter started to talk and exposed one of the most important female Stasi informers at the West Berlin Police. The rather unpleasant code name of this informer was 'Pummel' (pudding), and she had regularly provided Kurras with any orders and information from East Berlin that Eiserbeck did not want to entrust to encoded radio messages. Kurras expressed his fury with Weiß's wife at his next meeting with Eiserbeck: 'I'd kill her myself, such a traitor she is!'[44]

The Stasi took this announcement by Kurras with the utmost seriousness, for they knew he had a particular passion for shooting. He went through up to 400 marks' worth of ammunition per month, a considerable sum given the average monthly wage for a West Berliner was 668 marks. The only way in which he could finance his expensive hobby was with the money he received from East Berlin. He received at least 4,500 marks from the Stasi in 1966, but this rose considerably in early 1967 to 1,000 marks per month.[45] Mielke's men ensured the loyalty of their top spy not only by paying him money but also by helping him acquire coveted or rare weapons for his collection. Kurras did not believe his behaviour would attract attention. He even commented to Eiserbeck on one occasion that the money from East Berlin would not lead to his exposure given that most of it disappeared in the expenditure of ammunition. The Stasi was somewhat concerned that his propensity for violence was a 'weakness of character'.[46] However, so long as Kurras continued to provide reliable information, the Stasi was happy to let him do what he wanted.

Yet it was not just for money that Karl-Heinz Kurras engaged in acts of espionage; he was fully committed to the communist cause. He had been drafted into the Wehrmacht as a 17-year-old in the autumn of 1944 and been fascinated with weapons and uniforms well before that. He therefore probably found a sense of fulfilment in the army. However, a passion for pistols could be dangerous in occupied post-war Germany, and he was arrested in December 1946 by the then Soviet secret service MGB for being in illegal possession of a weapon. Just four weeks later, Kurras stood before the military tribunal of the Soviet garrison in Berlin. Given the relatively short time that had elapsed between arrest and sentencing, it is likely Kurras had quickly signed the confession presented to him in Russian. He would have thereby been spared the almost endless questioning by the Soviet secret police, although the few accessible documents from the archives in Moscow do not reveal whether he had initially been subjected to harsh interrogation. What is certain is that the by then 19-year-old defendant was sentenced to 10 years in a prison camp for 'counterrevolutionary sabotage' under Article 58, Paragraph 14, of the Criminal Code of the Russian Socialist Federative Soviet Republic. He was sent to the former Nazi concentration camp in Sachsenhausen, which had been put back into operation by Soviet authorities on 16 August 1945 as Special Camp No. 7. Kurras was hardly unique among the prisoners there. Approximately 3,500 inmates had been detained in the camp for illegal possession of weapons. Conditions in the camp were such that one in five of the 60,000 prisoners who went there died.

Kurras, however, came out alive. He later remarked to Stasi officers that he had no complaints about the conditions of his imprisonment. This was probably because he was a 'helper' for the camp commandant, as he himself put it in a resume.[47] In addition, he had already become a communist prior to his arrest, or this is at least what is indicated by the files of the Soviet Ministry of Internal Affairs (MVD). In the autumn of 1949, the MVD, in preparation for closing the special camps, compiled lists of 'compromising material' against the Germans who were held in them. Kurras was the 976th name on 'List No. 4 of Germans sentenced by Soviet Military Tribunals who are to be released', and it is noted under his name that he had been a member of the SED since 1945, although this was somewhat imprecise given that the SED had only come into being in April 1946 through the forced merger of the KPD and SPD. It can therefore be understood that Kurras had become a KPD member in 1945, for had he originally been a member of the SPD, it is probable the Soviet authorities would have labelled this as 'compromising'. It is not known how Kurras came to appear on this list, but there are at least two possibilities. First, as early as 1948, SED chairman Wilhelm Pieck had approached Stalin with concerns that 'youths with socialist leanings' and even 'politically promising people of the SED' had been arrested. Kurras would have fit both categories. Second, Kurras might very well have spied on his fellow inmates in Sachsenhausen. Although there is no direct evidence of this, it is highly likely he had already been recruited by the Soviet secret

Berliner Morgenpost | Montag, 25. Mai 2009

THEMA | 3

Fall Ohnesorg Neue Details aus der IM-Akte zeigen, wie viele wichtige Informationen der ehemalige West-Berliner Polizist dem MfS lieferte

Während des Besuchs des iranischen Schahs und seiner Ehefrau 1967 in Berlin demonstrierten Studenten. Die Fotos zeigen, wie Polizisten auf Studenten einprügelten. Benno Ohnesorg wurde von dem Beamten Kurras erschossen (2. Foto v.l.)

Kurras war für die Stasi eine Top-Quelle

VON SVEN FELIX KELLERHOFF

Der frühere Stasi-Spitzel Karl-Heinz Kurras gestern auf dem Fahrrad in Spandau

Kurras bei seiner Aussage vor Gericht im November 1967

Wie das MfS die Bundesrepublik beeinflusste

Unterstützung auch für RAF-Terroristen

Forscher kritisieren die Birthler-Behörde

Weitere Aufklärung im Fall Benno Ohnesorg verlangt. Bundesbeauftragte weist Kritik zurück

The 17 volumes of the Kurras files amount to more than 5,000 pages. Kurras was an important source of information for the Stasi and his exposure received wide coverage in the German media.

service before 1950. This question might only be cleared up, if at all, by the files in Moscow which to this day remain classified. The card index of SED members will never be able to shed any light on the matter, as it was destroyed at the beginning of 1990 by the former state party, which by that time had been renamed the Party of Democratic Socialism (PDS).

In any case, Kurras was released from Sachsenhausen in February 1950, and he immediately applied for work with the People's Police in East Berlin. This was certainly a surprising decision for someone who had been in Soviet custody for more than four years. His application was unsuccessful, possibly because of his criminal record, but there was an alternative in the other police force of the divided city. Indeed, after his rejection by the People's Police, he went straight to the police headquarters on Friesenstraße in Tempelhof, West Berlin. It is open to question whether he informed the personnel there of his conviction and subsequent imprisonment in a Soviet internment camp. He is likely to have kept quiet about the real reason for his imprisonment and may have said he had been locked up for 'anti-Soviet propaganda'. That was at least what he argued in court in 1967. Either way, he had better success with the West Berlin Police: 'I went to Stumm's Police on 16 March 1950. I was employed and posted to Police Station 124. After a few weeks, I was transferred to the Charlottenburg operations area.'[48] Kurras seemed to fit the most important criteria for a police officer in the frontline city of the Cold War. He possessed a self-confident demeanour, valued order for its own sake, and presumably appeared anti-communist given his imprisonment in Sachsenhausen. It would never have occurred to the West Berlin Police that a young man who had spent three years in a Soviet camp could have been anything other than anti-communist. The senior personnel on Friesenstraße were probably happy to admit someone who said he wanted 'to choose the police service as a life career'.[49]

The next documented contact between Karl-Heinz Kurras and an Eastern secret service took place five years later. Having become a sergeant in the meantime, he suddenly appeared in the guardhouse of the building of the SED Central Committee in Mitte in April 1955 and requested to speak with someone from the Stasi. The officer summoned noted that Kurras wanted to move to East Germany, but he convinced him that he could better serve the cause of communism if he continued his career in the West Berlin Police while informing the Stasi of anything of importance that he learned. Kurras handwrote a declaration of commitment on 26 April 1955, and he still adhered to it 54 years later by denying, at least at first, that he had been an informer.

After the meeting in East Berlin on 12 June 1964, Kurras probably disposed of the clothes he had worn when crossing the border. He was generally very careful, but that changed when he shot and killed Benno Ohnesorg on 2 June 1967. The motive behind the shooting will probably remain a mystery. The historian Helmut Müller-Enbergs, who recognised the importance of the Kurras files and made them public in 2009, stated that the 17 volumes of those files had been 'well-maintained until the spring of 1967 and then significantly reduced in size after that'.[50] Before the shooting, Kurras had last met with Eiserbeck on 17 May 1967 and provided a detailed report on the plans of the West Berlin Police. It can only be speculated whether Eiserbeck had indicated to Kurras that some sort of escalation during the upcoming state visit of the Shah of Iran would be useful for the East German regime; there is no proof either way.

What is certain is that at 8:07pm on Friday 2 June 1967, police officers in the vicinity of the German Opera House in West Berlin were ordered to break up a violent and unannounced demonstration by several hundred opponents of the Shah. The officers wanted to make use of what was left of the daylight to avoid a state of panic at night. Some of the riot police officers, most of whom were relatively young, helped a pregnant woman make her way through the cordon, after which they started to push against the demonstrators. They sometimes used their truncheons without restraint, and plainclothes snatch squads were also employed to target and arrest ringleaders. Kurras was a part of one of those snatch squads, and the situation escalated dramatically. At 8:25pm, fleeing demonstrators were crowded together with some reporters and police officers in the courtyard of the house at Krumme Straße 66–67. Overzealous police officers, Kurras among them, thrashed the defenceless demonstrators there. Shortly after 8:30pm, a shot from Kurras's gun struck student Benno Ohnesorg in the back of the head. A uniformed officer immediately barked at Kurras: 'Are you crazy? Why are you shooting?' In a photograph that was taken only seconds later, Kurras looks completely surprised, although it is hard to know whether this was because of the shot or because of the reaction of his colleague. Several witnesses and police officers attended to the badly injured Ohnesorg at once. Four photographers took pictures, including Jürgen Henschel from the West Berlin SED newspaper *Wahrheit*, whose symbolic photograph was so dreadfully vivid that it became an icon of West German history.[51]

Alarmingly, Kurras received considerable support from his West Berlin colleagues, a consequence not only of a misplaced sense of solidarity but also of the left-wing propaganda, sometimes extreme, that arose in the immediate aftermath. The West Berlin Police, subjected to severe criticism, closed ranks. It can only be imagined what might have happened if Kurras's work as a top spy for the Stasi had become known at that time. In any case, the Stasi broke off its cooperation with 'Otto Bohl' at once. According to the records that have survived, there remained some tentative contact between Kurras and the Stasi, but this did not lead to anything discernible.[52] Nevertheless, the Kurras files continued to be an important source of information for the Stasi. Mielke's deputy, Gerhard Neiber, re-examined them in 1987. This re-examination was given the code name 'Vorstoß' and, although the details are unknown, the upshot was the decision taken in December 1989 to destroy the files right away. For some inexplicable reason, this did not happen.[53] The

Kurras affair surprisingly came up again in 2009 and led to weeks of public debate. In the middle of December 2014, Karl-Heinz Kurras died without having made any comment on his activities. He had always seemed bewildered whenever he was questioned. Whether such bewilderment had been feigned cannot be ascertained.

Firmly under control

80 per cent of the West Berlin Police under surveillance

The Stasi did not manage to install a second spy of the calibre of Karl-Heinz Kurras in the West Berlin Police. Nevertheless, more than half of the 190 or so Stasi informers in the Western security services up to 1972 were never identified. In that year, the Stasi division responsible for monitoring the West Berlin Police changed. Before then, Division VII of the Stasi district department for Berlin had been in overall control and had therefore been responsible for handling Kurras as well; after that, Main Division I added the West Berlin Police to its list of responsibilities, which included the East German People's Police and the East German National People's Army. Regardless of jurisdiction, though, the Stasi had the West Berlin Police firmly in its grasp.

Until 1972, there had always been between 10 and 20 different informers at any one time who reported from various areas within or close to the police apparatus. The duration for which an informer carried out their activities varied considerably—from a few months to, as in the case of Kurras, more than a decade. The primary interest of the Stasi at all times was the organisation and weaponry of the West Berlin Police as well as its level of preparedness for a possible military conflict over West Berlin. The total number of people in the West Berlin Police who worked for the Stasi up to 1972 has not yet been determined, as many code names were used at the time and many more remain unknown. On top of that, it cannot be ruled out that certain individuals used multiple code names.

To be found in the roughly 180 volumes of documents on the West Berlin Police produced by the Stasi district department for Berlin are telephone lists, floor plans of police stations, and payrolls of West Berlin police officers. The Stasi had even managed to obtain keys for some police stations in preparation for any eventual East German occupation of West Berlin. It is not entirely clear from the documents whether the Stasi truly expected an attack from West Berlin, something which, it should be noted, had never been up for discussion in the West. What can be said with certainty is that the Stasi prepared itself to take control of West Berlin. For this purpose, all police stations were photographed, number plates of police vehicles were noted down, and private apartments of police officers were sometimes observed. Werner Eiserbeck, who was Karl-Heinz Kurras's case officer until 1967, was to head a newly established Stasi area precinct for Schöneberg in the event of the occupation of the western sectors of Berlin. Some areas of the West Berlin Police were more extensively infiltrated than others. While there were large networks of informers in the districts of Spandau and Reinickendorf, the Stasi lacked worthwhile sources of information in the district of Kreuzberg.

The motives of informers changed significantly over time. Shortly after the split of the police force in Berlin between East and West, there remained many SED sympathisers in the West Berlin Police who secretly communicated confidential information to East Berlin. Later on, material incentives played a greater role. For example, there was one case where a policeman was building himself a house while his father, also a policeman, seemed to be able to pay for it without any concern. The father gradually made his son aware of the fact that the house had been paid for by East Berlin. The sums were substantial by the standards of the time, running into the hundreds of thousands of West German marks. This was a considerable expense for a nation lacking currency reserves like East Germany, which illustrates the great importance attached by the regime to monitoring the West Berlin Police.

In the 1970s, the nature of the war fought by the Stasi against the West Berlin Police changed in parallel to the transfer of divisional responsibility. There had been a decrease in the number of unofficial collaborators within the West Berlin Police, so the Stasi increased its efforts to recruit police officers via relatives and acquaintances. It sought to record the details of all active officers, and such details, if possible, would include photographs, names, addresses, and personal circumstances. Material for blackmail was collected and personal weaknesses were exploited. As early as 1972, a total of 7,209 West Berlin police officers were targeted by the Stasi; towards the end of the 1980s, this had risen to approximately 80 per cent of the 22,000 or so officers.

One of the few active informers in the police force in the 1980s was, it seems, a marksman who provided the Stasi with information on, among other things, the protection of West Berlin politicians. The code name of this unofficial collaborator was 'Opel', after his preferred make of car. Another unofficial collaborator was Hans H., code name 'Walter', who was paid a total of 229,190 marks for passing on reports from the police station at Tegel Airport. He was 'possibly the Stasi's most expensive police informant'.[54] Similarly expensive, yet presumably more profitable, was the electronic warfare conducted by the Stasi against the West Berlin Police. The Stasi monitored almost all the radio and telephone traffic of the West Berlin Police and even gained access to its internal investigation system. Information on 200,000 people, 30,000 vehicles, and 1,000 buildings and properties that were registered in connection to searches by the West Berlin Police found its way into the files of the Stasi. There was not a single search conducted by the West Berlin Police in the 1980s that the Stasi did not know about. Politicians and important senate employees in West Berlin were routinely monitored, and so too were journalists. The aim was always the same: to gather information surreptitiously and to obtain material that might be useful for blackmail.

Code name 'Dr Lutter'

A Stasi agent in the Marienfelde refugee camp

In October 1991, Federal President Richard von Weizsäcker awarded 83-year-old Götz Schlicht the Officer's Cross of the Order of Merit of the Federal Republic of Germany. This was the second medal for Schlicht, as he had already received the Cross of the Order of Merit in 1985, but these two decorations were not the only honours Schlicht could be proud of. On the orders of Erich Mielke, Schlicht had been secretly awarded the Medal of Merit of the German Democratic Republic on the occasion of his 80th birthday in March 1988. Before that, he had already been recognised as a Meritorious Member of State Security and had also been given the Combat Order of Merit for the People and the Fatherland in Gold. One of the reasons cited by the responsible Stasi colonel for the conferring of the Combat Order of Merit was as follows: 'He made a special contribution to the unmasking and liquidation of agents of the UfJ in the German Democratic Republic. In the 1960s and 1970s, he played a decisive role in the monitoring of the All-German Institute. The unofficial collaborator "Dr Lutter" was a loyal scout of the Stasi.'[55] Schlicht had obviously earnt the trust that the Stasi placed in him. Even as late as 8 November 1989, three weeks after Erich Honecker had been removed from power, Schlicht went to meet his case officer in order to hand over his latest report, just as he had been doing for more than three decades. Furthermore, he made arrangements for another meeting in February 1990. That meeting never came to pass, as East German citizens stormed the Stasi headquarters on Normannenstraße in Lichtenberg on 15 January 1990.

Schlicht was born in 1908 and studied law in Berlin. He was a junior lawyer at the Supreme Court from 1930 to 1933, but he had to leave the judicial service due to his allegedly non-Aryan descent and went to work for a publishing house instead. After managing to be Aryanised in some sort of bureaucratic process, he joined the police in 1940. Released from prison after the end of World War II, he served as a judge at Potsdam District Court from 1946 and as a member of the governing council in the Ministry of Justice of the State of Brandenburg. He was also a teacher at the Academy for Judges where he not only trained future East German judges but also met Walther Rosenthal, who would play an important role in shaping the course of his life. Rosenthal soon fled to West Berlin and worked there for the UfJ; it was via Rosenthal that Schlicht also came into contact with the UfJ. The UfJ entrusted him with disseminating information and provided him with pamphlets and flyers to hand out and to put in letterboxes in Potsdam.

The East German authorities arrested Schlicht and sentenced him to 10 years in prison for 'agitation against our order'. He served half a year of pre-trial detention in the Stasi prison on Lindenstraße in Potsdam (colloquially referred to as the 'Lindenhotel'), four years in Brandenburg-Görden Prison (one year of which was in solitary confinement) and then half a year in Bützow-Dreibergen Prison. A couple of Stasi officers then gave him the choice of serving the remaining five years, minus one day, of his sentence or of conducting counterespionage for the Stasi. These Stasi officers followed a clear mandate that was formulated in the 'Schedule of Activities for the First Quarter of 1957': 'Prisoners have been checked in association with Division VII to find out which ones are fully qualified lawyers. Close attention will be paid to such prisoners over an extended period so that they can be recruited and then sent to infiltrate the UfJ.' In anticipation of the recruitment of Schlicht, Hilde Benjamin, at that time the Minister of Justice, and before that a notoriously merciless judge referred to as 'The Red Guillotine', submitted a petition for clemency on behalf of Schlicht to East German President Wilhelm Pieck. 'Due to special circumstances,' she wrote, 'the convicted man should be given the opportunity to make up for some of the damage he tried to cause.'[56] Schlicht did not want to turn down this offer: 'I chose freedom over prison. I had a wife and six children. Of course, I signed. What else was I supposed to do?'[57] He added that the Stasi had warned him that 'unpleasant things' would happen if he were to break the agreement. Schlicht was aware of the kidnapping of Walter Linse in 1952 and had no desire to share his fate.

Released on 15 May 1957, Schlicht departed with his family for West Berlin on 11 June with the objective of finding Rosenthal and resuming work for the UfJ. He was given the Stasi code name 'Dr Luther', which was later changed to 'Dr Lutter', and it only took a few weeks before he was once again working for the UfJ. Rosenthal trusted Schlicht without question, for he regarded him as a close friend who had been punished so severely by the East German authorities. So far did this trust go that Rosenthal even ignored a warning from the East Office of the SPD. Schlicht did not rise to a position of leadership within the UfJ, but he nevertheless came into contact with a number of East German citizens who approached the organisation for advice. According to a Stasi file, at least 10 East Germans were arrested on the basis of his reports. This activity earnt Schlicht the derogatory nickname 'Judas' in 1993.[58] He also worked part-time at the Marienfelde refugee transit camp, where he questioned refugees who had arrived in West Berlin from East Germany. Siegfried Mampel, a colleague of Schlicht's at the UfJ who only learnt the truth about him in 1992 or 1993, wrote in retrospect:

> He caused a great deal of havoc with his activities at the refugee camp in Marienfelde. Those he questioned were in relative safety thanks to their arrival in West Berlin, but he routinely asked not only about their reasons for fleeing but also about the route they had taken and the people who had helped them. This traitor passed on to the Stasi entire pages of names and addresses of refugees. Because it was kept informed about escapees and escape routes, the Stasi could easily pester relatives and friends who had stayed behind and take possession of the assets of those who had fled. The information provided by the traitor therefore greatly aided the measures taken by the Stasi.[59]

In the summer of 1958, the head of the economic department of the UfJ, Erwin Neumann, was kidnapped by the Stasi while on a sailing excursion in Wannsee. It is not known whether Schlicht had something to do with this, but what was unusual even by East German standards was that Neumann was kept in solitary confinement until his death in 1967. Was Neumann denied contact with visitors and other inmates because he knew who had betrayed him? Whatever the case may be, Schlicht continued to work for the UfJ, which was integrated into the All-German Institute under the Ministry of Intra-German Relations in 1969. After his retirement, he edited the periodical *Recht in Ost und West* until 1990. He was paid for this and was able to continue using his office at the All-German Institute. Throughout that time, he delivered regular reports to the Stasi for 800 West German and 800 East German marks per month.

Before the construction of the Wall, Schlicht maintained contact with his case officer via a sophisticated mail drop system; they always met one another in the vicinity of Nöldnerplatz Railway Station in the eastern sector of Berlin. Schlicht travelled there by rail and changed trains several times to shake off pursuers. He was then picked up at the station by a Stasi car and taken to a safe house. However, the meetings became more complicated after 13 August 1961. Schlicht continued to visit East Berlin, which was quite atypical for a prominent member of the UfJ and later of the All-German Institute. Other visitors to East Germany from the West could not be allowed to see him under any circumstances. Schlicht therefore used either a special border crossing point inaccessible to most other people or a hidden location which required special arrangements to be made with the border troops, although these security measures were no longer necessary by the late 1980s. In coordination with the Stasi, Schlicht generally travelled to East Berlin, using his genuine personal documents, via Friedrichstraße Railway Station. The procedure for this was laid out in detail by the Stasi:

> The unofficial collaborator must apply for each entry separately as a way of sending a signal to the case officer. After crossing the border, the unofficial collaborator must independently make his way by rail to Nöldnerplatz Railway Station. Visual contact only is to be made at the foot of the stairs leading down from the platform to the tunnel underpass. The unofficial collaborator must appear at exactly the agreed time and must strive to avoid stopovers and waiting times. As a sign that the meeting can safely go ahead, the unofficial collaborator and the case officer must each carry in their right hand an agreed-upon object (bag, newspaper). Should the case officer at the visual meeting be someone other than the one the unofficial collaborator usually meets, the object carried by the case officer will be an important indicator for the unofficial collaborator that the meeting is still to take place. After visual contact has been made, the unofficial collaborator is to proceed safely from the station across Nöldnerplatz and along Lückstraße and Giselastraße to Leopoldstraße, where he is to get into the parked staff car. Up to that point, the surroundings are to be observed by the case officer. The unofficial collaborator will drive to begin with. The case officer is then to take over control of the vehicle and is to drive to the safe house ('Spree') of Main Division X. The security of the main meeting will be ensured by the property manager. After the meeting, the unofficial collaborator must be dropped off in

Ehrenfeldstraße in Karlshorst. From there, the unofficial collaborator must take care of himself and go to Karlshorst Railway Station. The unofficial collaborator is to take the train to the city centre and, possibly after some sightseeing, is to go to Friedrichstraße Railway Station, from where he will depart for West Berlin.[60]

Götz Schlicht was anything but contrite after being exposed. In response to a query from a reporter from the magazine *SuperIllu*, he said: 'When you work for a secret service, you feel no remorse.' When the reporter asked whether Schlicht did not at all feel bad about betraying people and working for an oppressive system, Schlicht replied: 'You can feel no such things when you work for a secret service.'[61] He even said proudly to a journalist from *Die Zeit*: 'I was in the secret service from the 1950s, so please don't underestimate me!'[62] Schlicht did not pay for his betrayal. Although the public prosecutor's office brought charges against him in November 1993, the case was soon dropped. It was determined he was unfit to stand trial due to his old age and, because of that, his physical and psychological frailty. It is questionable whether this was the right decision, for he lived for another dozen years and died in 2006.

A shabby joint for the Stasi

The Stasi hotel in Tempelhof

An overnight stay at the Luftbrücke Hotel at Tempelhof Airport cost exactly 27 marks per person, including breakfast and value-added tax, and it was not exactly one of the best places in West Berlin. With its 32 beds, the hotel at Dudenstraße 6 was little more than a dump with toilets off the hallway. Opened in 1976, its regular guests were assembly workers and various lower-ranking officials. Even the U.S. Air Force frequently reserved rooms there, as its largest base lay directly on the other side of the Tempelhofer Damm road. It could hardly have been guessed that this hotel would become an important base of operations for the Stasi. However, that was precisely what happened, and it was for that reason that the Stasi financed the running of the hotel.[63]

Assigned the Stasi code name 'Strongpoint Rhineland', the hotel served several purposes simultaneously. First, it gave the unofficial collaborator Heinrich Schneider, code name 'Rennfahrer' and officially the main tenant of the property and owner of the hotel, a comprehensible reason for his regular trips from his hometown of Trebur, Hesse, to West Berlin.[64] The real objective was the journey itself. He usually met with senior Stasi officers to report on his work for them, namely heading a network of agents in West Germany. This network sometimes consisted of as many as 18 informers. Schneider, who had spent several years in prison, could procure almost anything the Stasi needed, be it West German number plates, police identity cards, modern bulletproof vests, or new weapons. He could even fulfil unusual requests most of the time. On one occasion, he smuggled three boxes of wigs into

East Germany. To ensure Schneider's group could protect itself, the Stasi trained many of its members in the use of weapons.[65]

Schneider also took on classic espionage assignments. For example, his network investigated the activities of a Greek interpreter in West Berlin and also kept an eye on a cell of the anti-Soviet Ukrainian Revolutionary Democratic Party in Neu-Ulm. One of his greatest achievements was the recruitment of a chemical engineer who had expressed an interest in additional income. Under the code name 'Berliner', this chemical engineer proved to be a valuable source of information, although he was under the mistaken impression that he was working for the CIA the entire time. In return for information relating to the chemical industry, 'Berliner' received around 20,000 marks per year. Such information was evidently of great importance for the East German economy. Markus Wolf certainly stressed on several occasions that it was 'considerably beneficial from an economic point of view'.[66]

Furthermore, Schneider was prepared to carry out the 'dirty work' of kidnappings and contract killings. When the Olympic Games were taking place in Munich in 1972, he had special boxes built in which members of the East German team harbouring thoughts of fleeing could, if necessary, be forcibly returned to their homeland. He made similar preparations for the 1974 World Cup, although it turned out that they were unnecessary.[67] He was eager to commit murder on the night of 16/17 February 1975. With his accomplice Josef Tuszynski, whose code name was 'Karate', he attacked 33-year-old Siegfried Schulze, an anti-communist activist who repeatedly provoked the SED with detonations at the Berlin Wall, demonstrations at border crossings, and hunger strikes for political prisoners. The 'objective', who was assigned the code name 'Fürst' by the Stasi, was to be 'liquidated'. The task was given to Schneider and, a short time later, he and the small yet well-trained and unscrupulous Tuszynski lay in wait for their victim. They took Schulze by surprise in the entrance hall at Kurfürstenstraße 25. Tuszynski struck Schulze's neck with a karate chop so powerful it could have been fatal, but Schulze, staggering somewhat, remained on his feet. Tuszynski grabbed him and hit him hard again, while Schneider rammed the now dazed victim three times in the head with his pistol. There was so much blood Schneider later bragged he had either smashed the victim's skull or had burst the artery in his temple. Schulze continued to resist. Schneider became impatient and wanted to shoot his victim in the mouth. However, the magazine had slipped out of his pistol while he had been using it as a hammer. The noise in the hall had in the meantime attracted the attention of the neighbours, so the Stasi killers had to flee before they could finish the job. Schulze managed to reach his apartment via the back entrance of the hall and barricaded himself inside.[68]

For Tuszynski, a hardened criminal who travelled with forged papers and was wanted by the police, the Luftbrücke Hotel served as safe accommodation. This was the second purpose of the hotel.[69] When the hotel came under the surveillance of the West Berlin Police in 1977, the experienced Tuszynski was fully aware of it, but it turned out the police only had it in for a few dealers who were staying there at the time. In 1979, the Stasi files on 'Strongpoint Rhineland' concluded that 'there are no indications whatsoever that the enemy intends to target the property'.

The hotel was managed by Anna-Margareta Brandt, an unofficial collaborator with the Stasi code name 'Janett'.[70] She was Tuszynski's partner and employed him as the caretaker of the hotel. After two years, they decided to live on the premises so they would not have to drive to and from work every day; they could thereby gain more time for surveillance and other Stasi assignments. The Stasi paid them 40,000 marks for this and also paid for their accumulated losses of the first two years. In return, they both had to pledge in writing that they would not violate West Berlin laws while they were living in the hotel. The Stasi wanted neither a stir to be caused nor the money they had invested to be wasted.

A third purpose of the hotel unexpectedly arose in 1979. The U.S. Air Force signed a lump-sum contract with the hotel, the value of which was at least 10,000 marks. Brandt promptly passed on the details of American personnel to East Berlin, where they were carefully registered and kept ready for future evaluation. In addition to the hotel guest lists, she passed on the names and vehicle number plates of two men who, in her presence, had discussed plans for the evacuation of an East German citizen.[71] Nevertheless, the benefits of the dump could not last. An increasing number of guests wanted toilets and showers in their rooms, but the Stasi was of the view that the hotel was of limited value and the costs required for renovating it could not be justified. A decision was therefore made at the end of 1979: 'Given the extent of return on investment, it does not seem advisable to extend the lease, which will expire in the summer of 1981.' When Brandt fell seriously ill a little later and her relationship with Tuszynski came to an end, the closure of the hotel was brought forward to January 1981. It was sold to businessmen who wanted to use the 20 rooms to house asylum seekers.

With an international warrant out for his arrest and the search effort by the police intensifying, Tuszynski withdrew to East Berlin in October 1983 and, with the help of the Stasi, went into hiding under another name. He was given an apartment in a prefabricated building and received a monthly pension of 1,200 East German marks, 50 per cent greater than the average income. Schneider, on the other hand, continued to carry out assignments for the Stasi even after his time as a hotelier ended. He took on various tasks in West Berlin and West Germany and was paid almost 400,000 West German marks in total.[72] Markus Wolf wrote to him on numerous occasions to thank him for his services, and one Stasi officer had formed the opinion that Schneider was a 'steadfast and honest patriot who is always ready for action'. Schneider received the commemorative badge for the 35th anniversary of the formation of the Stasi; he had already been awarded the Patriotic Order of Merit in Bronze and the Medal for Faithful Service in the National People's Army. He was arrested in 1992 and sentenced to four and a half years in prison for the attempted murder of Schulze. In contrast, Tuszynski managed to avoid punishment. When he and Brandt were tried in 1996, he claimed he had only pretended to accept assignments from the Stasi and that it had never been his intention to murder Schulze. Since it was not possible to prove the opposite was the case, the accused could only be charged with causing grievous bodily harm. This was already barred by the statute of limitations, as the crime had been committed in West Berlin. This meant there could be no suspension of the statute of limitations of the kind that applied to crimes that had occurred in East Germany.

The enemy of my enemy

Stasi support for terrorism

'Thank goodness it was just the East German state security.'[73] This was what Inge Viett remembered of the reaction of her friends when she once turned up late for a meeting in West Berlin. After all, she and her comrades always travelled under false names, and any delay could have been an indication their freedom had come to an end. It was 1978, and Viett wanted to meet with other left-wing terrorists in order to plan the liberation of her comrade Till Meyer from Moabit Prison in West Berlin. She had arrived at Schönefeld Airport from Prague and then gone to the border crossing point at Friedrichstraße Railway Station; it was there she was brought to a halt. 'Please wait,' the passport inspector told her. Was something wrong with her forged papers? 'I can't believe it,' she said. 'I've already gone through several borders and airports. All the details can be verified.' The East German border guard officer led the 34-year-old into a small, bare room, and she had to wait there for a while before the door flew open and a fat, rough-looking man entered. 'Good afternoon, comrade!' he said. Viett recalled her thoughts at that moment: 'Comrade? Well, maybe things aren't so bad.' The man introduced himself as 'Harry', which was in fact his real first name (his full name was Harry Dahl), and he addressed the woman by her real name. 'I was trembling all over,' remembered Viett, 'but he assured me straightaway that I had nothing to fear. While the East German authorities did not agree with our practice of terrorism, it would not correspond to their communist ideals to betray us to their opponents.' The terrorist and the Stasi officer in charge of Main Division XXII (Counter-Terrorism) spoke with one another for two hours. He then made her an offer. The terrorists could make their movements under false names known to the Stasi in advance so that 'no unforeseeable things' would happen at the border crossings. Viett rejected the offer. Dahl regarded this to be perfectly fine and asked if she had anything planned in West Berlin in the near future that might lead to major investigations. She vaguely confirmed that this might be the case and 'seized the opportunity with both hands' to ensure 'the neutrality of the German Democratic Republic' should she and her comrades 'have to flee the city across the border'. The Stasi colonel promised there would be no cooperation with the West German Police. After that, he allowed Viett to leave. When she eventually met with her friends, she was able to reassure them: 'We can now plan a safe escape route by rail to Friedrichstrasse.'[74]

Viett took advantage of this new opportunity on 27 May 1978. Alongside another terrorist, she snuck into the visiting area of Moabit Prison that day. The two-armed women succeeded in freeing Meyer, who was one of the founders of the terrorist group 2 June Movement. The three of them hopped into a VW van and drove straight to Lehrter Railway Station. A sympathiser was waiting for them with tickets bought in advance, and from there it was only one station away to Friedrichstraße. Upon entering East Berlin, however, one of the terrorists 'got stuck'. The border guard had noticed her hidden pistol. Viett reacted quickly:

> I stayed with her, thinking very quickly. We could not be held up by the customs officials. We had to stick to the plan. They searched me as well and took away my gun. I asked for the officer in charge, mentioned Harry, and asked that we be allowed to continue our journey quickly and discreetly. And that was what happened. The officer soon came back, handed us our pistols and documents, and wished us a safe journey.[75]

From the beginning of the wave of terrorism in West Germany, the Stasi offered protection for the enemies of their enemy. As early as August 1970, at which point the only serious crime of the newly formed Red Army Faction (also known as the Baader-Meinhof Group) was its engineering of the escape of Andreas Baader from prison, the left-wing extremist Hans-Jürgen Bäcker fell into the clutches of the Stasi at Schönefeld Airport. He had in his possession a pistol and a forged Arab passport. The East German customs officials alerted their Stasi colleagues who took Bäcker to a safe house in Karlshorst in East Berlin. The interrogation lasted 24 hours, and Bäcker was amazed at how much the Stasi already knew about the Baader-Meinhof Group. It was a pleasant conversation. Bäcker was given roast chicken, Coca-Cola, and West German Roth-Händle cigarettes. He wrote down a summary of his career and activities and was then allowed to enter West Berlin a day later via Friedrichstraße Railway Station. The Stasi men even gave him his pistol back.[76] A short time later, journalist Ulrike Meinhof, who was wanted for attempted murder, met with Stasi representatives in East Berlin. She wanted to clarify whether East Germany would support the West German terrorists in their activities by granting them safe-conduct. Although the Stasi representatives could not guarantee this, they were nevertheless prepared to offer her asylum. Meinhof refused the offer.[77]

Ten years later, after the failure of the major offensive of the Red Army Faction on West German democracy in the German Autumn of 1977 and the subsequent success of the West German Police in apprehending the criminals, Viett, who by 1980 was working closely with the Stasi, organised the disappearance of eight terrorists who were willing to go into hiding in East Germany. They were given new identities and, with considerable effort, were settled in East Germany. They were soon followed by another member of the Red Army Faction and then by Viett herself after an attempted murder of a French police officer in Paris. When the Red Army Faction assassin Susanne Albrecht, married under the name 'Ingrid Jäger' and in hiding in East Germany, was discovered by accident in 1986, the Stasi helped once again. She and her son were immediately given new identities and a new apartment in an anonymous estate of prefabricated buildings in Marzahn in East Berlin. A new job was organised for her husband in a nuclear research institute near Moscow, and, in February 1988, the family was reunited in the Soviet Union. Only in the summer of 1990 were Albrecht, Viett, and eight other former members of the Red Army Faction arrested. Main Division XXII of the Stasi, until its dissolution, had proven effective in protecting these terrorists.

Palestinian terrorists could also count on the support of the Stasi. Main Division XXII knew at least six days in advance of the bomb attack that was planned, and carried out, on the La Belle discotheque, predominantly frequented by American soldiers, on Hauptstraße in Schöneberg, West Berlin, on the night of 4/5 April 1986. This was because there were one or two Stasi informers among or near the perpetrators who had been hired by Libyan intelligence. East German authorities turned a blind eye to the smuggling of arms via the foreigner and diplomatic crossing at Friedrichstraße, and this was how, at the end of March 1986, Libyan agents were able to bring explosives and submachine guns into Kreuzberg, West Berlin, and store them in the apartment of 31-year-old Palestinian Imad Salim Mahmoud. When, coincidentally, the car of one of the Libyan agents was checked in West Berlin shortly afterwards, Mahmoud successfully insisted the material should be sent back to East Berlin immediately.

In making the arrangements to do this, an unknown Stasi officer made a handwritten note next to Mahmoud's name: 'unofficial collaborator of XXII'. The Palestinian, who simply appeared to be a student at the Technical University in the western district of Charlottenburg, also worked as an informer for the main division of the Stasi responsible for counterterrorism. In addition, he was one of the four men behind the bomb attack that killed two American soldiers and a Turkish woman. Another 28 people were seriously wounded by the nail bomb, while almost everyone else who had been in La Belle would have suffered from damaged eardrums as a result of the detonation. For the actual act of planting the bomb, Mahmoud and his accomplices had selected three Arabs and two German sisters. At least two of these five terrorists were registered as unofficial collaborators of the Stasi.[78]

Without the support of the Stasi, the Red Army Faction and other terrorist organisations would have been unable to continue their rampage against West German democracy for so long and to such a murderous extent. For the many former Stasi members who had built up an effective network in reunified Germany for the purposes of manipulating history, this fact proved to be somewhat problematic. They therefore arranged the publication of a book in which 'fact and fiction' were seemingly separated when it came to the question of cooperation between terrorists and the Stasi. However, the book, largely written by Mielke's former deputy General Gerhard Neiber (whose salary in 1989 had been 62,250 East German marks) and his colleague Lieutenant-Colonel Gerhard Plomann (37,500 East German marks), had almost nothing to do with reality:

> In fulfilling the tasks assigned to it, the Stasi fought against terrorism with all suitable and legitimate means and methods. It restricted the reach of terrorism, pushed it back, and generally kept it away from the German Democratic Republic and its allies. The resources and methods of intelligence were applied correctly and expediently. ... Any attempt to criminalise the Stasi by insinuating that the main division responsible for counterterrorism supported or even organised terrorism is unconvincing.[79]

Unfaithful spy

The defection of Werner Stiller

It was a cold winter day on 18 January 1979. Darkness had long descended on central Berlin that evening when Werner Stiller, a Stasi lieutenant, went to Friedrichstraße Railway Station. The 31-year-old ignored the red and white striped gate on Georgenstraße, which for East German citizens represented the furthermost boundary. Anyone who was spotted beyond that boundary could at best expect a sharp warning from the border troops and at worst an accusation of 'attempted flight from the German Democratic Republic'. This did not concern Stiller. He quietly walked to an inconspicuous grey steel door which served as an entrance for railway personnel only.[80] He had in his possession his Stasi identity card, his passport, and, most importantly, service assignment documents and special border permit documents. These documents were indispensable for anyone, even a Stasi officer, who wanted to cross the death strip in the direction of West Berlin. Stiller stepped through the door into an empty, pale yellow anteroom; in the opposite wall was a door not with a handle but rather a small window with a curtain. Stiller rang a bell next to the door, whereupon the curtain was pushed aside and a head in an officer's cap appeared. Stiller held his identity card against the glass. There was a hum, the door lock sprang open, and Stiller went through.

The length of the next room was separated by a counter. Behind it sat the officer in the uniform of a captain of the East German Border Troops, although he was in fact a comrade of Stiller's from Main Division VI of the Stasi. 'For me, he was at that moment the most important person in the world. Everything depended on him. Stocky and somewhat corpulent, but with a pleasant face, he sat behind the counter and looked at me questioningly.' The lock of the door through which Stiller had entered clicked into place. There was no going back. 'Bloody awful weather out there,' Stiller grumbled. 'I'll have to transfer to this place before long. All day in a warm room. I wouldn't mind something like that.' His comrade grinned and replied: 'If you work hard and reach my age, maybe then you can try to apply for a transfer.'

Stiller presented his papers. The captain examined them carefully and asked suddenly: 'Do you mean to say that these service assignment documents have been filled out properly?' The lieutenant caught his breath for a moment and then answered quickly: 'How should I know? The secretary filled it out and my superior officer signed it. Everything ought to be in order!' But it was not. Since 1 January 1979, the actual purpose of the assignment had to be stated. The captain glanced at the suitcase in Stiller's possession, but assumed it was to be handed over to a contact in West Berlin. 'A note must be made here that it is "operational work" and, in brackets, "baggage"!'

Stiller had not been aware of this when he had filled out the documents only a short time before and had forged the signature of his superior. He slowly reached for the pistol in his coat pocket, knowing he would be in trouble if the captain were to telephone the officer on duty at Stasi headquarters. Fortunately, the captain could not be bothered to do so: 'All right. I'll let you through this time. But let your division know. Where would we be if service regulations were no longer observed!' He pressed a hidden button, and the next door hummed and opened. Stiller took his suitcase, said thank you, and entered the part of the station that, although still in East German territory, provided access to West Berlin. He was headed for line 6 of the underground railway, which was operated by the Berlin Transport Company of West Berlin and was to some degree less well-monitored than the surface-running lines, for which, according to the Four Power Agreement on Berlin, East German railway authorities were responsible. This meant camera surveillance in the above-ground station concourse was extensive while that underground was not. Stiller navigated the labyrinth of corridors that had been constructed as a result of the placement of a border crossing in what had previously been an ordinary interchange station. He checked the time. It was 8:38pm. He went past the ticket machine, not wanting to miss the next train, but he was a slow runner and did not reach the train before it departed at 8:41pm. He glanced at the timetable. The next train was six minutes away. Those were the longest minutes in his life. He stood by a steel girder, trying not to be noticed. Although much of the underground railway was not monitored, he knew the Stasi did have cameras pointing towards the platform. His escape attempt might still fail if someone were to recognise his face on one of the monitors. Nothing happened. The train arrived on time and Stiller got on without hindrance. He went right to the front so he could take the driver hostage in the event of anything going wrong. There were a few nerve-racking moments when the train slowed and drove at a snail's pace through Oranienburger Straße Railway Station. Would everything go wrong at the last moment? But then the train picked up speed. It decelerated a couple more times and passed slowly through deserted stations and then at one point it came to a stop. Stiller looked out the window. The train had arrived at Reinickendorfer Straße Railway Station. His flight to the West, together with a suitcase full of secret documents, had been successful. He got in a taxi and set off for Tegel Airport.

Ministerrat der Deutschen Demokratischen Republik
Ministerium für Staatssicherheit

A 077205

Werner Stiller's official identity card. His defection was a major victory for West German intelligence and a severe blow for the Stasi.

While Stiller waited in the police station at the airport to be flown out to West Germany, the Stasi personnel at Friedrichstraße Railway Station noticed he had been gone for longer than expected. Even if the handover to a contact in West Berlin had not worked out, there was no reason for a Stasi officer to spend more than an hour in the western part of the station. The report of Stiller's disappearance soon reached the Main Directorate for Reconnaissance (HVA), for it was there, in the Sector for Science and Technology, that Stiller had worked. The news spoiled the 56th birthday of the head of the HVA, Markus Wolf, which was the day after Stiller had fled. In his memoirs two decades later, Wolf downplayed the impact of the event on the Stasi and referred to Stiller as 'small fry'.[81] In reality, the consequences went far beyond the loss of a promising employee. Stiller betrayed more than 50 Stasi spies in West Germany, Austria, France, and the United States. At least nine were arrested; the rest were able to make it back to East Germany. What was worse was that Stiller had been regarded as an almost ideal Chekist right up to the moment he had fled. If such a man could succumb to the temptations of the West, who in the security apparatus could the SED truly trust? Stiller, born in 1947, came from a poor background. He profited from the social upheavals in East Germany that had resulted from many of the educated elite escaping to the West, attended secondary school, and, from 1966, studied physics in Leipzig. Heavily involved in the Free German Youth, he joined the SED in 1967, and it was only logical that the Stasi began to show an interest in the young scientist in March 1970. Stiller fully expected he would be recruited, and it was during his first meeting with a Stasi representative that he declared: 'I will go wherever the party sends me.'[82] He acquitted himself well first as an unofficial collaborator and then, from 1972, as a full-time employee. He had even risen to become an honorary party secretary shortly before his flight. The Stasi expert Jens Gieseke assesses the significance of Stiller's escape as follows:

> Hundreds, perhaps thousands, of Stasi employees had careers like that of Stiller. It was precisely this that made his defection so alarming. Despite all the checks that were in place, and despite a career that met official standards through and through, here was a Stasi officer who had made his way to the West.[83]

Stiller was thoroughly questioned by the West German Federal Intelligence Service (BND), after which he was given a new identity ('Klaus-Peter Fischer'). He was an investment banker for several years in the United States, and later in London, and then returned to reunified Germany in 1991 where he worked as a stock market trader in Frankfurt. In the late 1990s, he moved to Budapest and was active as a businessman until his death in 2016. A detailed description of his life was published in 1986. Although Stiller's name was on the cover, it was largely produced by the BND as an exercise in disinformation, portraying Stiller's contact with the BND prior to his defection as more extensive than it had been in reality. The book served as an opportunity for Stiller and the BND to exacerbate the blow that had been dealt to Mielke's organisation by the defection. It is therefore of little surprise that the Stasi put a great deal of effort into trying to find and then kidnap or kill Stiller. Indeed, at the beginning of the 1980s, Mielke offered a reward of one million West German marks for anyone who killed the fugitive agent or who brought him back to East Germany. The head of the Stasi set up a commission that answered directly to him and whose purpose was to see to the capture of Stiller: 'Dead or alive—but alive is better.'[84] A Stasi colonel is even said to have boasted that he was in contact with West German criminals who were willing to kill Stiller for the money. The urgency Mielke attached to the matter is demonstrated by an outburst of his before the policy board of the Ministry for State Security three years after the defection of Stiller: 'Unfortunately, we are not immune to the possibility that there might still be a traitor among us. We are not immune to this, comrades! If I knew for certain, I'd want the traitor dead tomorrow. But because I'm a humanist, he should get a short trial.'[85] Mielke's 'humanism' took some getting used to. Stiller had long since been sentenced to death in absentia, but he managed to evade Mielke's henchmen.

Finale

The biggest coup

The Rosenholz data files

The clandestine war in Berlin lasted for a good 45 years. It began with the entry of Allied troops into what became the three western sectors of the ruined former capital of the Reich on 4 July 1945 and ended with the reunification of Germany on 3 October 1990, before the Two Plus Four Agreement came into effect and all remaining special rights of the four nations of the anti-Hitler coalition were renounced. Countless millions of dollars, rubles, and marks flowed into the numerous intelligence agencies and related organisations on both sides during that period, but the climax had not yet been reached. Only after the reunification of Germany, probably in 1992, did the greatest coup take place. It was of the kind that secret agents would not normally dare to dream of. The CIA somehow came into possession of several Stasi microfilms with highly sensitive material. Recorded on those microfilms was the card index of at least several hundred thousand, or possibly more, people who had been in contact with the Main Directorate for Reconnaissance (HVA), the foreign espionage wing of the Stasi. The level-headed American national security journalist Walter Pincus was in full agreement with the opinion expressed by one of his sources, a former intelligence official who had probably been involved in the operation that led to the acquisition of the microfilms: 'When the complete history of the closing days of the Cold War is written, this will be one of CIA's greatest triumphs.'[1]

On its own initiative from the end of October 1989 and with the cunningly obtained consent of East German civil rights activists at the Central Round Table two months later, the HVA destroyed its own archive to the greatest possible extent. Around half a million index cards were chopped up into small pieces. This measure was supposed to ensure that Stasi spies—who were euphemistically referred to as 'scouts for peace' and who, in many cases, had been betraying the secrets of their Western employers to East Berlin for decades—were protected from exposure and conviction as far as possible. All incriminating documents were therefore destroyed, the HVA was dissolved, and its former employees were sworn to absolute secrecy. In the months of the Peaceful Revolution, Stasi defectors were lured by Western secret

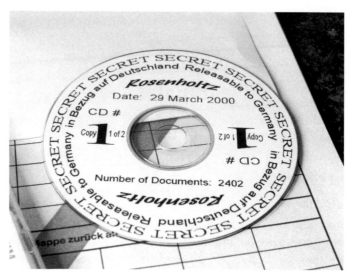

One of the CD-ROMs containing the 'Rosenholz' files. Whoever at the CIA came up with the name did not know how to spell 'rosewood' in German.

services with a lot of money. The CIA allegedly offered one million marks in cash to one particular HVA officer who was of interest should he be willing to reveal all. At the headquarters of the Stasi on Normannenstraße in East Berlin, almost all documents that would have been indispensable for the exposure of traitors in West Germany and West Berlin were lost as a result of the act of destruction. Only in exceptional cases—mainly in regional Stasi precinct offices—were remnants of HVA files preserved. In Leipzig, the Citizens' Committee for the Dissolution of the State Security Service refused the demand made by the last minister of the interior of East Germany, Peter-Michael Diestel, to the effect that it hand over, presumably for destruction, the documents of Division XV, the local branch of the HVA. It was thanks to the preservation of this mountain of paper—several kilometres of files that were partly torn and partly prepared for removal—that many former unofficial collaborators could be revealed. In 2007, for example, the ARD journalist Hagen Boßdorf was convicted on account of having been an unofficial collaborator.[2]

As befits a real intelligence coup, there are many different accounts as to how the CIA came into possession of the microfilms. What is certain is that these microfilms were created as backup files by the HVA in 1988 and were subject to the highest level of secrecy. By the end of that year, it had become standard practice for microfilm copies of documents to be made. However, so sensitive were the documents considered that not even the trustworthy Photo Office of the HVA was entrusted with microfilming. The task was instead carried out by the Registration Office of the HVA with a camera specially installed in its workspace. It was intended that the microfilms be destroyed along with all other documents during the period of sociopolitical change in late 1989 and early 1990, and, according to an official record that has been preserved, most of those microfilms were indeed disposed of between 6 and 8 April 1990.

According to the most frequently told version of the story, a Stasi lieutenant-colonel by the name of Rainer Hemmann received the order to take the microfilms to the East Berlin headquarters of the KGB and hand them over there to the Soviet liaison officer to the HVA, a certain Sascha Prinzipalov: 'In December 1989, my superior officer ordered me to move the microfilms of the material from Unit 7 to Karlshorst.' The 42-year-old Hemmann was given a black courier bag, and he drove his Stasi vehicle, a Lada, to what was the largest residency of the KGB outside the Soviet Union. He met Prinzipalov at the entrance: 'The bag was like a pilot's case, and I placed it in Sascha's hands.' Hemmann never found out what happened next. Speaking of the event 10 years later, he conjectured the material had been couriered to Moscow. The microfilms then, according to this version of the story, made their way into the hands of the CIA via Prinzipalov and KGB Colonel Alexander Siubenko. Allegedly, Siubenko made contact with Lieutenant-Colonel James Atwood, an agent at the CIA branch in Berlin. Atwood went to Moscow in 1992 and received the material from one of these two KGB officers for the modest sum of $75,000. However, this story cannot be verified, for the three people involved had died by the time journalists and historians tried to contact them. In addition, the last head of the HVA, Colonel-General Werner Großmann, claimed that 'we did not give anything to the Russians'.[3]

How then did the microfilms wind up in the hands of the CIA? Were there senior HVA officers who themselves sold the material to the Americans? This is what former officers like Klaus Eichner and Andreas Dobbert believe, and they regard it as 'one of our greatest defeats'. While they cannot be entirely sure this is what happened, they did, as former subdivisional and unit heads in Stasi counterintelligence, know about the background of the microfilming process:

> Our bureaucracy of petty pen pushers obviously ignored the basic rules of intelligence work. To compile so much paperwork and, on top of that, to make microfilm copies of them was a massive violation of the protection of our sources of information. In the turmoil brought about by the liquidation of the Stasi and the dissolution of the HVA, this highly explosive material was by no means secure enough to prevent someone from earning a few silver coins from it. Was Judas amongst those in charge?[4]

If an HVA officer did indeed sell the microfilms, he would be well-advised to keep quiet. 'Hopefully, I will find out who did this to us,' said Großmann threateningly in 2005.[5]

It is possible both versions of events are the product of disinformation and that it may never come to light how the CIA got hold of the microfilms. Whatever the case may be, the microfilms were being analysed by the CIA from the end of 1992. Proof of this can be found in the fact that one of the most important HVA spies, the unofficial collaborator Rainer Rupp (alias 'Topas') at NATO headquarters in Brussels, was unmasked at the beginning of 1993. At approximately the same time, the head of the CIA station in Bonn, Milton Bearden, informed the German Chancellery of the material in their possession. The German government insisted that employees of the Federal Office for the Protection of the Constitution (BfV) be allowed to evaluate the documents themselves in Washington. In the end, 1553 suspected cases of breaches of secrecy were reported to the public prosecutor's office, and a wave of preliminary investigations followed. The BND probably learnt about the microfilms from former Stasi officers, but it alleged it had been told about them by the KGB in return for loans of billions of marks to Boris Yeltsin's Russia. This enabled the German government to exert pressure on the United States for access to the microfilms that the CIA had supposedly bought from the KGB, to create doubts in the CIA about the reliability of the microfilms, and to undermine the credibility of the CIA agents who bought them. The suggestion the KGB had sold information to the CIA and had then told the BND about it raised the ire of former Soviet intelligence officers, many of whom had continued to work in the successor agency to the KGB, the Federal Security Service.

The microfilms are known in Germany today as the 'Rosenholz' files, a term that must somehow describe the understanding of the BfV of the content of the secret material. Helmut Müller-Enbergs, an expert on the partial copies of the material that was given to the Stasi Records Agency from 2003, wrote:

> The name chosen by the CIA for the operation itself remains unknown. ... The media to this day almost always associates the word 'Rosenholz' with the CIA operation. As can be seen from the illustration of one of the CDs that appeared in *Der Spiegel* in April 2000, the Americans used the imaginary word 'Rosenholtz'.[6]

Because the CIA only passed on copies of index cards that dealt with West German unofficial collaborators, rumours spread that other agents listed in the microfilms had been turned by the CIA and had therefore been compelled to continue to engage in espionage.

Three decades after the fall of the Berlin Wall and the events of the Peaceful Revolution in East Germany, foreign secret services are still infiltrating the seat of government in Berlin. The United States, Russia, and a number of medium-sized states have agents stationed in the German capital. They sit in their embassies, where listening antennas rotate on the roofs, and collect information both legally and illegally. These states exert their influence through unofficial contacts with decision-makers in politics, through dirty means like blackmail, or through the dissemination of disinformation to journalists or lobbyists.

Sources and literature

Archival sources

Bundesarchiv Koblenz
B141 (Bundesministerium der Justiz): 11815, 11816, 11817.

Landesarchiv Berlin
C Rep. 124, No. 400.

Archive of the Stasi Records Agency (BStU) in Berlin
MfS AIM, no. 4902: 88.
MfS AIM, no. 9229: 87.
MfS AIM, no. A 593: 79.
MfS BV Berlin, KD Lichtenberg: 13088.
MfS BV Halle, KD Halle: XV 748/75 vol. 2.
MfS GH 2: 70, vols 1, 2, 9, 17.
MfS GH 105: 57, vol. 5.
MfS HA I: 4289.
MfS HA III: 490, 6329, 6710, 6875, 10822, 10795, 11371, 11682, 11793, 14455.
MfS HA VIII: 1525, 7123.
MfS HVA, Abteilung IX.
MfS Teilablage A, no. 156: 85.
MfS XV/2704/72.
MfS ZA: 1405.
MfS ZA AU 104: 90.
Stasi Mediathek.

Public Record Office, Kew, London
British Embassy in Bonn on LIVE OAK, 7 April 1966.
'Draft Charter to the Chief BRIXMIS from the UK High Commissioner,' Appendix B to JIC (GERMANY) (52) 17.
FO 1042/227.
Letter from the British military government in Berlin to the British high commissioner in Bonn, Sir Frank Roberts, on 22 April 1966.
'Notes of the use of Soviet troops in aid of the civil power 16 June–10 July 1953' (BRX/405/29).
'Report on RAF BRIXMIS activities in connection with the crash of a Red Air Force Firebar Aircraft in West Berlin on 6 April 1966' (BRX/5600/1/AIR).
Soviet Aircraft Crash in the Havel, 6 April 1966 (BRX/600/3).

Collection of the Allied Museum in Berlin

Bowman, Steve, *Teufelsberg, Berlin and the Cold War*, unpublished manuscript, June 1997.
USMLM Unit History, 1964–1988.
Video interview with Col. (ret.) Carol Hemphill on 29 April 1997.
Video interview with Sergei Kondrashov and David Murpy in September 1997.

Newspapers and periodicals

Der Abend
Aus Politik und Zeitgeschichte
Berliner Kurier
Berliner Morgenpost
Berliner Zeitung
Bild (Berlin)
Bulletin des Presse- und Informationsamtes der Bundesregierung
B.Z.
B.Z. am Abend
The Daily Telegraph
Le Figaro
Frankfurter Allgemeine Zeitung
Gesetzblatt der Deutschen Demokratischen Republik
Hamburger Abendblatt
Horch & Guck
Illustrierte Berliner Zeitschrift
The Independent
Märkische Allgemeine Zeitung
Die Neue Zeitung
Neues Deutschland
Neue Zürcher Zeitung
New York Harold Tribune
New York Times
SBZ-Archiv
Der Spiegel
Stenografische Berichte des Deutschen Bundestages
Der Stern
Süddeutsche Zeitung
SuperIllu
Der Tagesspiegel
Telegraf
The Times
The Washington Post
The Washington Times
Die Welt
Welt am Sonntag
Westdeutsche Allgemeine Zeitung
Die Zeit

Published primary sources

Adenauer, Konrad, & Heuss, Theodor, *Unter vier Augen: Gespräche aus den Gründerjahren 1949–1959*, Berlin: Siedler, 1999.

Allertz, Robert, *Die RAF und das MfS: Fakten und Fiktionen*, Berlin: Edition Ost, 2008.

Bahr, Egon, 'Tag der gesamtdeutschen Geschichte,' *Aus Politik und Zeitgeschichte*, no. 23, 2003, pp. 3–4.

Berlin, 9 vols, Berlin: Senat von Berlin, 1961–1978.

Blake, George, *Keine andere Wahl: Die Autobiographie des wichtigsten Doppelagenten aus der Ära des kalten Krieges*, Berlin: Ed. q, 1995.

Carney, Jeffrey M., *Against All Enemies: An American's Cold War Journey*, published through Amazon, 2013.

Charisius, Albrecht, & Mader, Julius, *Nicht länger geheim: Entwicklung, System und Arbeitsweise des imperialistischen deutschen Geheimdienstes*, East Berlin: Deutscher Militärverlag, 1975.

Clandestine Services History: The Berlin Tunnel Operation 1952–1956, ed. CIA (at https://fas.org/irp/cia/product/tunnel-200702.pdf, accessed 20 August 2008).

Denkschrift Östliche Untergrundarbeit gegen West-Berlin—Stand: 15. April 1959, Berlin: Senator für Inneres, 1959.

Deutsche flüchten zu Deutschen: Der Flüchtlingsstrom aus dem sowjetisch besetzten Gebiet nach Berlin, Berlin: Senator für Arbeit und Sozialwesen, 1956.

Dowe, Dieter (ed.), *Kurt Müller (1903–1990) zum Gedenken*, Bonn: Friedrich-Ebert-Stiftung, 1991.

Eichner, Klaus & Dobbert, Andreas, *Headquarters Germany: Die US-Geheimdienste in Deutschland*, 3rd edition, Berlin: Edition Ost, 2008.

Eichner, Klaus & Schramm, Gotthold (eds), *Angriff und Abwehr: Die deutschen Geheimdienste nach 1945*, Berlin: Edition Ost, 2007.

Eppelmann, Rainer, *Fremd im eigenen Haus: Mein Leben im anderen Deutschland*, Cologne: Kiepenheuer und Witsch, 1993.

Fricke, Karl-Wilhelm, *Menschenraub in Berlin: Karl-Wilhelm Fricke über seine Erlebnisse*, Bonn: Rheinischer Merkur, 1960.

Fricke, Karl-Wilhelm, *Akten-Einsicht: Rekonstruktion einer politischen Verfolgung*, 3rd edition, Berlin: Ch. Links, 1996.

Fricke, Karl-Wilhelm, & Klewin, Silke, *Bautzen II: Sonderhaftanstalt unter MfS-Kontrolle 1956 bis 1989—Bericht und Dokumentation*, Leipzig: Kiepenheuer, 2001.

Friedensburg, Ferdinand, *Es ging um Deutschlands Einheit: Rückschau eines Berliners auf die Jahre nach 1945*, Berlin: Haude und Spener, 1971.

Gehlen, Reinhard, *Der Dienst: Erinnerungen 1942–1971*, Mainz: v. Hase & Koehler, 1971.

Grimmer, Reinhard, et al. (eds), *Die Sicherheit: Zur Abwehrarbeit des MfS, Bd. 1*, Berlin: Edition Ost, 2003.

Hechelhammer, Bodo (ed.), *Berlinkrise 1958 und Schließung der Sektorengrenzen in Berlin am 13. August 1961 in den Akten des Bundesnachrichtendienstes*, Berlin: Bundesnachrichtendienst Mitteilung der Forschungs- und Arbeitsgruppe Geschichte des BND, 2011.

Heiliger, Hartmut, *Die Feindpotenzen der funkelektronischen Aufklärung des Gegners in Westberlin*, dissertation at the Law School in Potsdam, 1985 (BStU MfS-HA III, No. 14455).

Heinrich, Eberhard, & Ullrich, Klaus, *Befehdet seit dem ersten Tag: Über drei Jahrzehnte Attentate gegen die DDR*, East Berlin: Dietz, 1981.

Heller, Friedrich, & Maurer, Hans-Joachim, *Unrecht als System, Teil 3: 1954–1958*, Bonn: Bundesministerium für gesamtdeutsche Fragen, 1958.

Herz, Peter, *Berlin-Lichtenberg, Normannenstraße 22: Agentenzentrale SSD*, Berlin: Untersuchungsausschuss Freiheitlicher Juristen, 1960.

Heuss, Theodor, & Adenauer, Konrad, *Unserem Vaterland zugute: Der Briefwechsel 1948–1963*, Munich: Siedler, 1989.

Hiecke, Hanfried, *Deckname Walter: Enthüllungen des ehemaligen Mitarbeiters der sogenannten 'Kampfgruppe gegen Unmenschlichkeit' Hanfried Hiecke*, East Berlin: Kongress-Verlag, 1953.

Hiecke, Hanfried, *im Dienste der Unterwelt: Dokumentarbericht über den 'Untersuchungsauschuss freiheitlicher Juristen,'* East Berlin: Kongress-Verlag, 1959.

Internationaler Juristen-Kongress: West-Berlin 1952: Gesamtbericht—Referate und Protokolle, The Hague: Internationaler Juristenausschuss, 1953.

John, Otto, *Ich wählte Deutschland*, East Berlin: Ausschuss für Deutsche Einheit, 1954.

John, Otto, *Zweimal kam ich heim*, Düsseldorf: Econ Verlag, 1969.

Katalog des Unrechts, Berlin: Untersuchungsausschuss freiheitlicher Juristen, 1956.

Keiderling, Gerhard (eds), *'Gruppe Ulbricht' in Berlin April bis Juni 1945: Von den Vorbereitungen im Sommer 1944 bis zur Wiedergründung der KPD im Juni 1945*, Berlin: Berlin Verlag Arno Spitz, 1993.

Kierstein, Herbert (ed.), *Heiße Schlachten im Kalten Krieg: Unbekannte Fälle und Fakten*, Berlin: Edition Ost, 2007.

Leonhard, Wolfgang, *Die Revolution entlässt ihre Kinder*, 22nd ed., Cologne: Kiepenheuer & Witsch, 2005.

Pragal, Peter, *Der geduldete Klassenfeind: Als Westkorrespondent in der DDR*, Berlin: Osburg, 2008.

Rosenthal, Walther (ed.), *Untersuchungsausschuss Freiheitlicher Juristen: Zielsetzung und Arbeitsweise*, Berlin: Untersuchungsausschuss Freiheitlicher Juristen, 1959.

Schütt, Hans-Dieter, *Markus Wolf: Letzte Gespräche*, Berlin: Das Neue Berlin, 2007.

Spionage-Dschungel Westberlin: Eine Dokumentation über die westdeutschen und Westberliner Sabotage- und Spionageorganisationen und über die Geheimagenturen der imperialistischen Westmächte, East Berlin: Ausschuss für Deutsche Einheit, 1959.

Stacy, William E., *The Nicholson Incident: A Case Study of US-Soviet Negotiations*, Heidelberg, 1988 (declassified October 2004).

Stejskal, James, *Special Forces Berlin: Clandestine Cold War Operations of the US Army's Elite, 1956–1990*, Havertown PA: Casemate, 2017.

Steury, Donald P. (ed.), *On the Front Lines of the Cold War: Documents on the Intelligence War in Berlin, 1946 to 1961*, Washington DC: CIA History Staff, Center for the Study of Intelligence, 1999.

Stiller, Werner, *Im Zentrum der Spionage*, 5th edition, Mainz: v. Hase und Köhler, 1986.

Strauß, Franz Josef, *Die Erinnerungen*, Munich: Pantheon, 2015.

Suckut, Siegfried (ed.), *Das Wörterbuch der Staatssicherheit: Definition zur 'politisch-operativen Arbeit,'* 3rd edition, Berlin: Ch. Links, 1996.

Thaysen, Uwe (ed.), *Der zentrale Runde Tisch der DDR—Wortprotokoll und Dokumente, Bd. 2: Umbruch*, Opladen: Westdeutscher Verlag, 2000.

Unmenschlichkeit als System: Dokumentarbericht über die 'Kampfgruppen gegen Unmenschlichkeit e.V.,' Berlin: Kongress-Verlag, 1957.

Video 'Sowjetischer Flugzeugabsturz über dem Stößensee,' at *Die Berliner Mauer: Geschichte in Bildern* (https://www.berlin-mauer.de/videos/sowjetischer-flugzeugabsturz-im-stoessensee-568/).

Viett, Inge, *Nie war ich furchtloser: Autobiographie*, Hamburg: Nautilus, 1997.

Wagner, Helmut, *Schöne Grüße aus Pullach: Operationen des BND gegen die DDR*, 4th edtion, Berlin: Edition Ost, 2006.

Wolf, Claus, *Bosse, Gangster, Kopfgeldjäger: Flüchtlingskampagnen und Menschenhandel— Motive und Methoden*, East Berlin: Verlag Neues Leben, 1982.

Wolf, Markus, *Spionagechef im geheimen Krieg: Erinnerungen*, Munich: List, 1997.

Wolf, Markus, 'Ten Years of German Unification,' *National Security and the Future*, vol. 1 (2000), no. 2 (at https://hrcak.srce.hr/index.php?show=clanak&id_clanak_jezik=28773).

Secondary literature

Agarew, A. F., Kobbe, K.-P., Großer, R., Sisowa, I. W., *Im Himmel über Berlin: Eine tragische Seite der Epoche des Kalten Krieges*, Ryazan: Das russische Wort, 2012.

Alexander, Peter, & Milwoky, Francis, *Hobbynutten, Fremdgeher, Bettspitzel … und die Stasi war immer mit dabei*, Berlin: Hussock, 2005.

Arnold, Dietmar, & Kellerhoff, Sven Felix, *Die Fluchttunnel von Berlin*, Berlin: Propyläen, 2008.

Aust, Stefan, *Der Baader-Meinhof-Komplex*, Hamburg: Hoffmann und Campe, 2008.

Bailey, George, & Kondraschow, Sergej A., & Murphy, David E., *Die unsichtbare Front: Der Krieg der Geheimdienste im geteilten Berlin*, Berlin: Ullstein, 2000.

Barnekow, Rolf, 'Das Anzapfen der sowjetischen Militärkommunikation,' in *'Ist ja fantastisch!' Die Geschichte des Berliner Spionagetunnels*, Berlin: AlliiertenMuseum, 2006.

Bästlein, Klaus, *Der Fall Mielke: Die Ermittlungen gegen den Minister für Staatssicherheit der DDR*, Baden-Baden: Nomos Verlagsgesellschaft, 2002.

Bästlein, Klaus, *Vom NS-Täter zum Opfer des Stalinismus: Dr. Walter Linse—ein deutscher Jurist im 20. Jahrhundert*, Berlin: Landesbeauftragten für die Unterlagen des Staatssicherheitsdienstes der ehemaligen DDR, 2008.

Baumgartner, Gabriel, & Hebig, Dieter, *Biographisches Handbuch der SBZ/DDR 1945–1990*, Munich: De Gruyter, 1996.

Beer, Siegfried, 'Rund um den 'Dritten Mann': Amerikanische Geheimdienste in Österreich 1945–1955,' in Erwin A. Schmidl (ed.), *Österreich im frühen Kalten Krieg 1945–1958: Spione, Partisanen, Kriegspläne*, Vienna: Böhlau Verlag, 2000.

Behling, Klaus, *Berlin im Kalten Krieg: Schauplätze und Ereignisse*, Berlin: Homilius, 2008.

Behling, Klaus, & Eik, Jan, *Vertuschte Verbrechen: Kriminalität in der Stasi*, Leipzig: Militzke, 2007.

Behling, Klaus, & Eik, Jan, *Transit in den Tod: Kriminalität in der Stasi*, Leipzig: Militzke, 2008.

Behling, Klaus, & Eik, Jan, *Lautloser Terror: Kriminalität in der Stasi*, Leipzig: Militzke, 2009.

Behrend, Hans-Dieter, *Die alliierten Militärverbindungsmissionen im Kalten Krieg auf deutschem Boden*, Berlin: Helle Panke, 2002.

Bourke, Sean, *Der Ausbruch*, Hamburg: Hoffmann und Campe, 1972.

Detjen, Marion, *Ein Loch in der Mauer: Die Geschichte der Fluchthilfe im geteilten Deutschland 1961–1989*, Munich: Siedler, 2005.

Diedrich, Torsten, & Ehlert, Hans, & Wenzke, Rüdiger (eds), *Im Dienste der Partei: Handbuch der bewaffneten Organe der DDR*, Berlin: Ch. Links, 1998.

Effner, Bettina, & Heidemeyer, Helge (eds), *Flucht im geteilten Deutschland: Erinnerungsstätte Notaufnahmelager Marienfelde*, Berlin: be.bra verlag, 2005.

Elliot, Geoffrey, & Shukman, Harold, *Secret Classrooms: An Untold Story of the Cold War*, London: St Ermin's, 2002.

ENIGMA 2000 Newsletter, issue 5, July 2001, p. 1 (at http://www.signalshed.com/nletter01.html).

Erler, Peter, *Polizeimajor Karl Heinrich: NS-Gegner und Antikommunist—Eine biographische Skizze*, Berlin: Jaron, 2007.

Erler, Peter, & Knabe, Hubertus, *Der verbotene Stadtteil: Stasi-Sperrbezirk Berlin-Hohenschönhausen*, Berlin: Jaron, 2005.

Falck, Uta, *VEB Bordell: Geschichte der Prostitution in der DDR*, Berlin: Ch. Links, 1998.

Feick, Dagmar, 'Der Tunnel und die Folgen im sowjetischen Sektor,' in *'Ist ja fantastisch!' Die Geschichte des Berliner Spionagetunnels*, Berlin: AlliiertenMuseum, 2006.

Finn, Gerhard, *Nichtstun ist Mord: Die Kampfgruppe gegen Unmenschlichkeit—KgU*, Bad Münstereifel: Westkreuz-Verlag, 2000.

Flemming, Thomas, *Berlin im Kalten Krieg: Der Kampf um die geteilte Stadt*, Berlin: Berlin Edition, 2008.

Flemming, Thomas, *Kein Tag der deutschen Einheit: 17. Juni 1953*, Berlin: bre.bra verlag, 2003.

Frank, Mario, *Walter Ulbricht: Eine deutsche Biografie*, Berlin: Siedler, 2001.

Fricke, Karl-Wilhelm, *MfS intern: Macht, Strukturen, Auflösung der DDR-Staatssicherheit—Analyse und Dokumentation*, Cologne: Verlag Wissenschaft und Politik, 1991.

Fricke, Karl-Wilhelm, & Engelmann, Roger, *Konzentrierte Schläge: Staatssicherheitsaktionen und politische Prozesse in der DDR 1953–1956*, Berlin: Ch. Links, 1998.

Gaddis, John Lewis, *Der Kalte Krieg: Eine neue Geschichte*, Munich: Siedler, 2007.

Geraghty, Tony, *Brixmis: The Untold Exploits of Britain's Most Daring Cold War Spy Mission*, London: HarperCollins, 1996.

Gieseke, Jens, *Die hauptamtlichen Mitarbeiter der Staatssicherheit: Personalstruktur und Lebenswelt 1950–1989/90*, Berlin: Ch. Links, 2000.

Gieseke, Jens, *Der Mielke-Konzern: Die Geschichte der Stasi 1945–1990*, Munich: Deutsche Verlags-Anstalt, 2006.

Hagemann, Frank, *Der Untersuchungsausschuss freiheitlicher Juristen 1949 bis 1969*, Frankfurt am Main: Lang, 1994.

Halbrock, Christian, *Stasi-Stadt: Die MfS-Zentrale in Berlin-Lichtenberg*, Berlin: Ch. Links, 2009.

Harrington, Stuart A., *Traitors Among Us: Inside the Spy Catcher's World*, Novato CA: Presidio Press, 1999.

Heimann, Siegfried, *Karl Heinrich und die Berliner SPD, die sowjetische Militäradministration und die SED: Ein Fallbeispiel*, Bonn: Historisches Forschungszentrum, 2007.

Heisig, Matthias, 'Gefährliche Begegnung: Autos, "Blockierung" und der Tod von Philippe Mariotti,' in *Mission erfüllt: Die militärischen Verbindungsmissionen der Westmächte 1946–1990*, Berlin: AlliiertenMuseum, 2004.

Heitzer, Enrico, *Affäre Walter: Die vergessene Verhaftungswelle*, Berlin: Metropol, 2008.

Herbstritt, Georg, & Müller-Enbergs, Helmut (eds), *Das Gesicht dem Westen zu: DDR-Spionage gegen die Bundesrepublik Deutschland*, Bremen: Edition Temmen, 2003.

Hoffmann, Constantin, *Ich musste raus: 13 Wege aus der DDR*, Halle (Saale): Mitteldeutscher Verlag, 2009.

Jander, Martin, 'Differenzen im antiimperialistischen Kampf,' in Wolfgang Kraushaar (ed.), *Die RAF und der linke Terrorismus, Band 1*, Hamburg: Hamburger Edition, 2006.

Jardin, Pierre, 'Französischer Nachrichtendienst in Deutschland in den ersten Jahren des Kalten Krieges,' in Wolfgang Krieger & Jürgen Weber (eds), *Spionage für den Frieden?: Nachrichtendienste in Deutschland während des Kalten Krieges*, Munich: Olzog, 1997.

Keil, Lars-Broder, & Kellerhoff, Sven Felix, *Gerüchte machen Geschichte: Folgenreiche Falschmeldungen im 20. Jahrhundert*, Berlin: Ch. Links, 2006.

Kirsch, Benno, *Walter Linse 1903–1953–1996*, Dresden: Stiftung Sächsische Gedenkstätten zur Erinnerung an die Opfer Politischer Gewaltherrschaft, 2007.

Klambauer, Otto, *Der Kalte Krieg in Österreich: Vom Dritten Mann zum Fall des Eisernen Vorhangs*, Vienna: Ueberreuter, 2000.

Knabe, Hubertus, *Die unterwanderte Republik: Stasi im Westen*, Berlin: Propyläen, 1999.

Knabe, Hubertus, *Der diskrete Charme der DDR: Stasi und Westmedien*, Berlin: Propyläen, 2001.

Knabe, Hubertus, *Die Täter sind unter uns: Über das Schönreden der SED-Diktatur*, Berlin: Propyläen, 2007.

König, Horst, *Militärstandort Storkow: Märkisch-Oderland Werkstätten*, Strausberg: Stadt, 2008.

Koop, Volker, *Besetzt: Sowjetische Besatzungspolitik in Deutschland*, Berlin: be.bra verlag, 2008.

Kostka, Bernd von, 'Die Berliner Luftbrücke 1948/49,' in Michael C. Bienert (ed.), *Die Vier Mächte in Berlin: Beiträge zur Politik der Alliierten in der besetzten Stadt*, Berlin: Landesarchiv Berlin, 2007.

Krieger, Wolfgang & Weber, Jürgen (eds), *Spionage für den Frieden?: Nachrichtendienste in Deutschland während des Kalten Krieges*, Munich: Olzog, 1997.

Krüger, Dieter, & Wagner, Armin (eds), *Konspiration als Beruf: Deutsche Geheimdienstchefs im Kalten Krieg*, Berlin: Ch. Links, 2003.

Maddrell, Paul, *Spying on Science: Western Intelligence in Divided Germany 1945–1961*, Oxford: Oxford University Press, 2006.

Mahnke, Dieter, 'Das Berlin-Problem: Die Berlin-Krise 1958–1961/62,' in *Materialien der Enquete-Kommission 'Aufarbeitung von Geschichte und Folgen der SED-Diktatur in Deutschland,'* vol. V/2, Baden-Baden: Nomos Verlagsgesellschaft, 1995, pp. 1766–1821.

Mampel, Siegfried, *Die Verfassung der Sowjetischen Besatzungszone Deutschlands: Text und Kommentar*, 2nd edition, Frankfurt am Main: Metzner, 1966.

Mampel, Siegfried, *Entführungsfall Dr. Walter Linse: Menschenraub und Justizmord als Mittel des Staatsterrors*, 3rd edition, Berlin: Landesbeauftragten für die Unterlagen des Staatssicherheitsdienstes der ehemaligen DDR, 2006.

Mampel, Siegfried, *Der Untergrundkampf des Ministeriums für Staatssicherheit gegen den Untersuchungsausschuß Freiheitlicher Juristen in West-Berlin*, 4th edition, Berlin: Landesbeauftragten für die Unterlagen des Staatssicherheitsdienstes der ehemaligen DDR, 1999.

Manificat, Patrick, *Propousk! Missions derrière le rideau de fer 1947–1989*, Limoges: Lavauzelle Editions, 2008.

Meineke, Annett (ed.), *Duell im Dunkel: Spionage im geteilten Deutschland*, Vienna: Böhlau, 2002.

Merz, Kai-Uwe, *Kalter Krieg als antikommunistischer Widerstand: Die Kampfgruppe gegen Unmenschlichkeit 1948–1959*, Munich: Oldenbourg, 1987.

Montgomery, Hugh, 'Herausforderung Berliner Tunnel,' in *'Ist ja fantastisch!' Die Geschichte des Berliner Spionagetunnels*, Berlin: AlliiertenMuseum, 2006.

Mueller, Michael, & Kanonenberg, Andreas, *Die RAF-Stasi-Connection*, Berlin: Rowohlt, 1992.

Müller, Peter F., & Mueller, Michael, *Gegen Freund und Feind: Der BND—Geheime Politik und schmutzige Geschäfte*, Reinbek: Rowohlt, 2002.

Müller-Enbergs, Helmut, *Rosenholz: Eine Quellenkritik*, Berlin: Landesbeauftragten für die Unterlagen des Staatssicherheitsdienstes der ehemaligen DDR, 2007.

Müller-Enbergs, Helmut, & Jabs, Cornelia, 'Der 2. Juni 1967 und die Staatssicherheit,' *Deutschland Archiv*, vol. 42 (2009), no. 3, pp. 395–400.

Mußgnug, Dorothee, *Alliierte Militärmissionen in Deutschland 1946–1990*, Berlin: Duncker & Humblot, 2001.

Norden, Peter, *Salon Kitty: Ein Report*, Munich: Südwest Verlag, 1970.

Offizielle Homesite des 6941st Guard Battalion (www.guardbattalion.de).

Otto, Wilfriede, *Erich Mielke: Biographie*, Berlin: Dietz, 2000.

Peters, Butz, *Tödlicher Irrtum: Die Geschichte der RAF*, Frankfurt am Main: Fischer, 2007.

Prenzlauer, Ecke Fröbelstraße: Hospital der Reichshauptstadt, Haftort der Geheimdienste, Bezirksamt Prenzlauer Berg—1889–1989, ed. Berlin-Brandenburgische Geschichtswerkstatt, Berlin: Lukas Verlag, 2006.

Randle, Michael, & Pottle, Pat, *The Blake Escape: How We Freed George Blake—and Why*, London: Harrap, 1989.

Reese, Mary Ellen, *Organisation Gehlen: Der kalte Krieg und der Aufbau des deutschen Geheimdienstes*, Berlin: Rowohlt, 1992.

Roewer, Helmut, *Im Visier der Geheimdienste: Deutschland und Russland im Kalten Krieg*, Bergisch Gladbach: Lübbe, 2008.

Roewer, Helmut, & Schäfer, Stefan, & Uhl, Matthias, *Lexikon der Geheimdienste im 20. Jahrhundert*, Munich: Herbig, 2003.

Roginskij, Arsenij, & Drauschke, Frank, & Kaminsky, Anna, *Erschossen in Moskau: Die deutschen Opfer des Stalinismus auf dem Moskauer Friedhof Donskoje 1950–1953*, Berlin: Metropol, 2005.

Schlegelmilch, Arthur, *Hauptstadt im Zonendeutschland: Die Entstehung der Berliner Nachkriegsdemokratie 1945–1949*, Berlin: Haude und Spener, 1993.

Schroeder, Klaus, & Staadt, Jochen (eds), *Feindwärts der Mauer: Das Ministerium für Staatssicherheit und die West-Berliner Polizei*, Frankfurt am Main: Peter Lang Edition, 2014.

Schulzki-Haddouti, Christiane, 'Abhör-Dschungel: Geheimdienste lessen ungeniert mit,' *c't*, 1998, no. 5 (at https://www.heise.de/ct/artikel/Abhoer-Dschungel-286194.html).

Shell, Kurt L., *Bedrohung und Bewährung: Führung und Bevölkerung in der Berlin-Krise*, Opladen: Westdeutscher Verlag, 1965.

Smith, Arthur L., *Kidnap City: Cold War Berlin*, London: Greenwood Press, 2002.

Staadt, Jochen, & Voigt, Tobias, & Wolle, Stefan, *Operation Fernsehen: Die Stasi und die Medien in Ost und West*, Göttingen: Vandenhoeck & Ruprecht, 2008.

Stafford, David, *Berlin underground: Wie der KGB und die westlichen Geheimdienste Weltpolitik machten*, Hamburg: Europäische Verlagsanstalt, 2003.

Stasi Museum website (https://www.stasimuseum.de/en/enindex.htm).

Stockton, Bayard, *Flawed Patriot: The Rise and Fall of CIA Legend Bill Harvey*, Dulles: Potomac Books, 2006.

Stöver, Bernd, 'Der Fall Otto John,' *Vierteljahrshefte für Zeitgeschichte*, vol. 47 (1999), no. 1, pp. 103–136.

Stöver, Bernd, *Der Kalte Krieg: Geschichte eines radikalen Zeitalters 1947–1991*, Munich: Beck, 2007.

Streckel, Söhnke, *Lizensierte Spionage: Die alliierten Militärverbindungsmissionen und das MfS*, Magdeburg: Landesbeauftragten für die Unterlagen des Staatssicherheitsdienstes der ehemaligen DDR, 2008.

Trotnow, Helmut, 'Schüsse in Techentin,' in *Mission erfüllt: Die militärischen Verbindungsmissionen der Westmächte 1946–1990*, Berlin: AlliiertenMuseum, 2004.

Trotnow, Helmut, & Kostka, Bernd von, *'Ist ja fantastisch!' Die Geschichte des Berliner Spionagetunnels*, Berlin: AlliiertenMuseum, 2006.

Vogel, Steve, *Betrayal in Berlin: George Blake, the Berlin Tunnel and the Greatest Conspiracy of the Cold War*, New York: John Murray, 2019.

Wagner, Armin, & Uhl, Matthias, *BND contra Sowjetarmee: Westdeutsche Militärspionage in der DDR*, Berlin: Ch. Links, 2007.

Wegmann, Bodo, *Entstehung und Vorläufer des Staatssicherheitsdienstes der DDR: Strukturanalytische Aspekte*, Berlin: Helle Panke, 1997.

Wegmann, Bodo, *Zwischen Normannenstraße und Camp Nikolaus: Die Entstehung deutscher Nachrichtendienste nach 1945*, Berlin: B. Wegmann, 1999.

Weiner, Tim, *CIA: Die ganze Geschichte*, Frankfurt am Main: S. Fischer, 2008.

Welsch, Wolfgang, *Der verklärte Diktatur: Der verdrängte Widerstand gegen den SED-Staat*, Aachen: Helios, 2009.

Werkentin, Falco, *Politische Strafjustiz in der Ära Ulbricht*, Berlin: Ch. Links, 1995.

Wettig, Gerhard, *Chruschtschows Berlin-Krise 1958–1963: Drohpolitik und Mauerbau*, Munich: Oldenbourg, 2006.

Williams, Peter, *Brixmis in the 1980s: The Cold War's 'Great Game,'* Parallel History Project on Cooperative Security, 2007 (at www.php.ethz.ch).

Winkler, Christopher, 'Die U.S. Military Liaison Mission im Vorfeld der 2. Berliner Krise: Der Hubschraubezwischenfall von 1958,' in Michael Lemke (ed.), *Schaufenster der Systemkonkurrenz: Die Region Berlin-Brandenburg im Kalten Krieg*, Vienna: Böhlau Verlag, 2006.

Woodhead, Leslie, *My Life as a Spy*, London: Pan Macmillan, 2005.

Wylde, Nigel, 'Mit der Brixmis jenseits des Eisernen Vorhangs,' in *Mission erfüllt: Die militärischen Verbindungsmissionen der Westmächte 1946–1990*, Berlin: AlliiertenMuseum, 2004.

Television documentaries and radio podcasts

'Confrontation at the Stößensee,' *Cold War Conversations Podcast*, April 2021 (at https://coldwarconversations.com/episode171/).

Dornblüth, Gesine, & Franke, Thomas, 'Flugzeugabsturz über West-Berlin: Die vergessenen Helden vom Stößensee,' *Deutschlandfunk Kultur*, 20 March 2019 (podcast at https://srv.deutschlandradio.de/themes/dradio/script/aod/index.html?audioMode=3&audioID=885649&state=).

Jan, Yves, *Au Coeur de la Guerre Froide: Les Missions de Potsdam*, 2007.

Klemke, Christian, & Lorenzen, Jan N., *Alltag einer Behörde: Das Ministerium für Staatssicherheit*, 2006.

Kloss, Harriet, & Thöß, Markus, *Deckname Blitz: Der Spion vom Teufelsberg*, 2004.

'Wolfgang Leonhard,' *Mein Kriegsende*, WDR Fernsehen, 2 May 2005.

Picture credits

• Allied Museum / Archiv: pp. 4, 5, 6, 9, 10, 14, 27, 30 (2), 40, 41, 49.
• Allied Museum / Brixmis: pp. 65, 68, 72, 75, 77.
• Allied Museum / CIA: pp. 45 (2).
• Allied Museum / Chodan: pp. 32, 43, 51, 54, 58, 71.
• Allied Museum / MMFL: pp. 64, 74, 80, 83, back cover.
• Allied Museum / USMLM: pp. 66, 84, 86.
• Allied Museum / US Air Force: pp. 11, 20 top, 22, 34.
• Allied Museum / US Army: pp. 17, 33.
• ARD: p. 143 (2).
• Axel Springer Company Archive: pp. 149, 180.
• Bautzen Memorial: p. 144.
• Berlin-Hohenschönhausen Memorial: p. 160 (2).
• Bundesnachrichtendienst (BND): p. 174.
• Dušan Martinček/Odeon Fiction GmbH, Magenta TV, ZDF, Seven Stories LTD, Wilma Film s.r.o., 2020, Foreword ix
• Karl-Wilhelm Fricke: pp. 169, 170, 171 (2).
• INSCOM Command History Office File: p. 20 below.
• Horst König: pp. 60, 61.
• Bernd von Kostka: pp. 15, 29, 46, 53, 55, 59, 67, 69, 78.
• Police Historical Collection Berlin: p. 106.
• Stasi Records Agency (BStU): pp. 82, 107, 108, 111, 120, 123, 124, 129, 130, 148, 157, 176, 187, 196, 200.
• All remaining photographs: archive of Sven Felix Kellerhoff.

Please notify the publisher if, despite our best efforts, any image rights have not been acknowledged.

Endnotes

Foreword to the English edition

1   *Die Welt*, 3 November 2013.
2   *Die Welt*, 27 October 2013.
3   Steve Vogel, *Betrayal in Berlin: George Blake, the Berlin Tunnel and the Greatest Conspiracy of the Cold War*, New York: John Murray, 2019.

Foreword to the first edition

1   *Westdeutsche Allgemeine Zeitung*, 29 January 1965.
2   George Blake, *Keine andere Wahl: Die Autobiographie des wichtigsten Doppelagenten aus der Ära des kalten Krieges*, Berlin: Ed. q, 1995, p. 228.
3   Cf. Steven Aftergood, 'CIA Bungles Declassification of Official Histories', *Federation of American Scientists*, 6 December 2007, at https://fas.org/blogs/secrecy/2007/12/cia_bungles_declassification_o/.
4   Armin Wagner & Matthias Uhl, *BND contra Sowjetarmee: Westdeutsche Militärspionage in der DDR*, Berlin: Ch. Links, 2007.

Chapter 1. Espionage hub of Berlin

1   Siegfried Beer, 'Rund um den "Dritten Mann": Amerikanische Geheimdienste in Österreich 1945–1955', in Erwin A. Schmidl (ed.), *Österreich im frühen Kalten Krieg 1945–1958: Spione, Partisanen, Kriegspläne*, Vienna: Böhlau Verlag, 2000, pp. 89–90.
2   Otto Klambauer, *Der Kalte Krieg in Österreich: Vom Dritten Mann zum Fall des Eisernen Vorhangs*, Vienna: Ueberreuter, 2000, p. 127.
3   Tim Weiner, *CIA: Die ganze Geschichte*, Frankfurt am Main: S. Fischer, 2008, p. 20.
4   Quoted in ibid., p. 34.
5   Quoted in ibid., p. 44.
6   Donald P. Steury (ed.), *On the Front Lines of the Cold War: Documents on the Intelligence War in Berlin, 1946 to 1961*, Washington DC: CIA History Staff, Center for the Study of Intelligence, 1999, p. 3.
7   George Bailey & Sergej A. Kondraschow & David E. Murphy, *Die unsichtbare Front: Der Krieg der Geheimdienste im geteilten Berlin*, Berlin: Ullstein, 2000, p. 64.
8   Ibid., p. 77.
9   Bodo Wegmann, *Zwischen Normannenstraße und Camp Nikolaus: Die Entstehung deutscher Nachrichtendienste nach 1945*, Berlin: B. Wegmann, 1999, p. 10.
10 Bailey et al., *Die unsichtbare Front*, pp. 76–79.

11   An example from the time of the Berlin Blockade can be found in ibid., p. 95. Further examples were presented at the 1996 conference Kalten Krieg auf dem Teufelsberg.

12   Memorandum for the President, 22 December 1947, in Steury (ed.), *On the Front Lines of the Cold War*, p. 144.

13   Bailey et al., *Die unsichtbare Front*, p. 20.

14   Steury (ed.), *On the Front Lines of the Cold War*, pp. 131–132.

15   Ibid., pp. 132, 141, 149–156.

16   Bernd von Kostka, 'Die Berliner Luftbrücke 1948/49', in Michael C. Bienert (ed.), *Die Vier Mächte in Berlin: Beiträge zur Politik der Alliierten in der besetzten Stadt*, Berlin: Landesarchiv Berlin, 2007, pp. 82–83.

17   So Bessette in his lecture, 'Looking through the Iron Curtain: Cold War Aerial Reconnaissance in the Berlin Air Corridors and Beyond'.

18   Pierre Jardin, 'Französischer Nachrichtendienst in Deutschland in den ersten Jahren des Kalten Krieges', in Wolfgang Krieger & Jürgen Weber (eds), *Spionage für den Frieden?: Nachrichtendienste in Deutschland während des Kalten Krieges*, Munich: Olzog, 1997, pp. 103–104.

19   Ibid., p. 109.

20   Paul Maddrell, *Spying on Science: Western Intelligence in Divided Germany 1945–1961*, Oxford: Oxford University Press, 2006, p. 27.

21   Ibid., p. 35.

22   *Deutsche flüchten zu Deutschen: Der Flüchtlingsstrom aus dem sowjetisch besetzten Gebiet nach Berlin*, Berlin: Senator für Arbeit und Sozialwesen, 1956, p. 15.

23   Maddrell, *Spying on Science*, p. 47.

24   Ibid., pp. 56–57.

25   Ibid., p. 58.

26   Bailey et al., *Die unsichtbare Front*, pp. 301–314.

27   Steury (ed.), *On the Front Lines of the Cold War*, pp. 536–537.

28   Ibid., pp. 604–605.

29   Maddrell, *Spying on Science*, pp. 254–260.

30   Steury (ed.), *On the Front Lines of the Cold War*, p. 609.

Chapter 2. Rising from the ruins

1   Steve Bowman, *Teufelsberg, Berlin and the Cold War*, unpublished manuscript, June 1997, p. 5.

2   Ibid.

3   Horst Ulrich (ed.), *Berlin Handbuch: Das Lexikon der Bundeshauptstadt*, Berlin: FAB Verlag, 1993, p. 1227.

4   Ibid., p. 1228.

5   Bowman, *Teufelsberg, Berlin and the Cold War*, p. 20.

6   Ibid.

7   Hartmut Heiliger, *Die Feindpotenzen der funkelektronischen Aufklärung des Gegners in Westberlin*, dissertation at the Law School in Potsdam, 1985 (BStU MfS HA III, No. 14455), p. 8.

8   Homepage of the 6941st Guard Battalion on the topic of Marienfelde (www.guardbattalion.de).

9   Ibid.

10   Heiliger, *Die Feindpotenzen der funkelektronischen Aufklärung des Gegners in Westberlin*, p. 5.

11   Ibid., p. 6.

12   Ibid., p. 10.

13 Leslie Woodhead, *My Life as a Spy*, London: Pan Macmillan, 2005, p. 56; see also Geoffrey Elliot & Harold Shukman, *Secret Classrooms: An Untold Story of the Cold War*, London: St Ermin's, 2002.

14 Heiliger, *Die Feindpotenzen der funkelektronischen Aufklärung des Gegners in Westberlin*, p. 13.

15 Christiane Schulzki-Haddouti, 'Abhör-Dschungel: Geheimdienste lessen ungeniert mit', *c't*, 1998, no. 5, p. 3 (at https://www.heise.de/ct/artikel/Abhoer-Dschungel-286194.html).

16 Ibid., p. 4.

17 Ibid., p. 5.

18 Bowman, *Teufelsberg, Berlin and the Cold War*, p. 37.

19 Video interview with Col. (ret.) Carol Hemphill on 29 April 1997.

20 '34 Verletzte nach Explosion eines Dokumentenvernichters', *Der Tagesspiegel*, 6 September 1986.

21 Video interview with Col. Hemphill.

22 Bowman, *Teufelsberg, Berlin and the Cold War*, p. 41.

23 Ibid., p. 52.

24 Kraft, 'Einschätzung des Standes und der Wirksamkeit durchgeführter luftgestützter Aufklärungshandlungen gegen das Operationsgebiet Westberlin', p. 1 (BStU MfS HA III 6875).

25 'Sachstandsbericht zum ELOKA-Objekt "Teufelsberg" in West-Berlin', p. 8 (BStU MfS HA III 6329). See also 'Zur Struktur und Tätigkeit der Dienststelle der Fernmelde/Elektronischen Spionage des Geheimdienstes der USA-Landstreitkräfte INSCOM: US Army Field Station Berlin—USAFSB' (BStU MfS HVA, Abteilung IX, at https://www.stasi-mediathek.de/medien/analyse-der-struktur-und-taetigkeit-derus-army-field-station-berlin-usafsb-teufelsberg/blatt/1/). The authors of these Stasi documents are not known.

26 'Sachstandsbericht zum ELOKA-Objekt "Teufelsberg" in West-Berlin', p. 9.

27 *ENIGMA 2000 Newsletter*, issue 5, July 2001, p. 1 (at http://www.signalshed.com/nletter01.html).

28 Ibid., p. 3.

29 'Prime released after 19 years in jail for spying', *The Independent*, 14 March 2001.

30 Stuart A. Harrington, *Traitors Among Us: Inside the Spy Catcher's World*, Novato CA: Presidio Press, 1999, p. 319.

31 See the documentary film by Harriet Kloss & Markus Thöß, *Deckname Blitz: Der Spion vom Teufelsberg*, 2004.

32 Ibid.

33 Harrington, *Traitors Among Us*, pp. 339–340.

34 Quoted in Kloss & Thöß, *Deckname Blitz*.

35 Harrington, *Traitors Among Us*, p. 57ff.

36 Markus Wolf, 'Ten Years of German Unification', *National Security and the Future*, vol. 1 (2000), no. 2, p. 6 (at https://hrcak.srce.hr/index.php?show=clanak&id_clanak_jezik=28773).

37 Video interview with Col. Hemphill.

38 See Karin Assmann, 'Jagd nach dem "Stasi Superstar"', *Der Spiegel*, 20 January 2014, at www.spiegel.de/einestages/stasispion-james-hall-er-stahl-streng-geheime-nsa-akten-a-953290.html, accessed February 2016.

39 Jeffrey M. Carney, *Against All Enemies: An American's Cold War Journey*, published through Amazon, 2013, p. 151.

40 Ibid., p. 189.

41 Ibid., p. 668.

42 *The Washington Times*, 21 July 2003.

43 *Berliner Morgenpost*, 18 June 2021, p. 17.

Chapter 3. Digging for gold

1 *Clandestine Services History: The Berlin Tunnel Operation 1952–1956*, ed. CIA, at https://fas.org/irp/cia/product/tunnel-200702.pdf, accessed 20 August 2008. This report was prepared by the CIA in August 1967 and declassified in February 2007. Several names and passages have been redacted.

2 The 'PB' part of this code name is an encryption whose meaning is not entirely clear. 'JOINTLY' is a code word that was selected by those involved in the operation. It may have been chosen as an allusion to Anglo-American cooperation.

3 See the article by Steve Aftergood on the website of the Federation of American Scientists (FAS): 'CIA Bungles Declassification of Official Histories,' at http://www.fas.org/blog/secrecy/2007/page/3, accessed 20 August 2008.

4 Beer, 'Rund um den "Dritten Mann"', pp. 73–100.

5 David Stafford, *Berlin underground: Wie der KGB und die westlichen Geheimdienste Weltpolitik machten*, Hamburg: Europäische Verlagsanstalt, 2003, pp. 52–59, 102–110.

6 Ibid., pp. 69–74.

7 Ibid., pp. 76–79.

8 'Turning a Cold War Scheme into Reality: Engineering the Berlin Tunnel', p. 4. This redacted article was first published in 2004. The declassified version appeared on the CIA website four years later. The author of the article, a former member of the CIA, was not named.

9 In addition, 3100 tonnes of soil had been moved. See 'Turning a Cold War Scheme into Reality,' p. 1.

10 Stafford, *Berlin underground*, pp. 139–143.

11 Rolf Barnekow, 'Das Anzapfen der sowjetischen Militärkommunikation', in *'Ist ja fantastisch!' Die Geschichte des Berliner Spionagetunnels*, Berlin: AlliiertenMuseum, 2006, pp. 58–66.

12 Landesarchiv Berlin, C Rep. 124, No. 400: 'Gutachten über die fernmeldetechnischen Anlagen des Anschaltepunktes für Mithörleitungen', pp. 2–3. This report was produced in East Germany and used in the legal proceedings in West Berlin in 1957 and 1958 that resulted from the complaint of an East German farmer, Paul Noack, whose orchard had been largely destroyed by the removal of the tunnel.

13 George Blake, *Keine andere Wahl: Die Autobiographie des wichtigsten Doppelagenten aus der Ära des kalten Krieges*, Berlin: Ed. q, 1995, p. 187ff.

14 This is according to a statement made by Sergei Kondrashov in an interview at the Allied Museum in Berlin in September 1997.

15 Bailey et al., *Die unsichtbare Front*, p. 281ff.

16 Kondrashov, interview, Berlin, 1997.

17 *Clandestine Services History*, p. 21.

18 Hugh Montgomery, 'Herausforderung Berliner Tunnel', in *'Ist ja fantastisch!' Die Geschichte des Berliner Spionagetunnels*, Berlin: AlliiertenMuseum, 2006, pp. 54–55.

19 Cited in Steury (ed.), *On the Front Lines of the Cold War*, pp. 372, 378.

20 Kondrashov, interview, Berlin, 1997.

21 As related by Lothar Löwe in his opening speech for the exhibition *Ist ja fantastisch!* at the Allied Museum in Berlin in April 2006.

22 Conversation between the author and Heinz Junge in the spring of 2006.

23 *Clandestine Services History*, appendices C-2, C-3, and C-5.

24 Dagmar Feick, 'Der Tunnel und die Folgen im sowjetischen Sektor', in *'Ist ja fantastisch!' Die Geschichte des Berliner Spionagetunnels*, Berlin: AlliiertenMuseum, 2006, pp. 68–76.

25 *Clandestine Services History*, p. 26.

26   Ibid., appendix B, pp. 1–6; Bailey et al., *Die unsichtbare Front*, pp. 292–300.

27   Blake, *Keine andere Wahl*, pp. 209–227.

28   The inmates who helped Blake escape wrote books on what took place: Sean Bourke, *Der Ausbruch*, Hamburg: Hoffmann und Campe, 1972; Michael Randle & Pat Pottle, *The Blake Escape: How We Freed George Blake—and Why*, London: Harrap, 1989.

29   Vogel, *Betrayal in Berlin*, p. 229.

30   See BStU MfS HA I 4289, pp. 1–6, for the plan of 8 July 1967 for Operation *Radar*. A geological survey from 1993 confirms that there no longer existed a continuous tunnel. No geomagnetic anomalies down to a depth of 20 metres were to be found in the area that used to lie within East Berlin. See 'Gradienten-Fluxgate-Gradiometer Untersuchung auf dem Gelände der Radarstation in Neukölln-Rudow', a copy of which is in the archive of the Allied Museum in Berlin.

31   See BStU MfS HA I 4289 for the report on the measures taken to drill into the old tunnel of the US radar station in Rudow.

32   See the files of the legal proceedings between Massante and the building and housing inspectorate of Neukölln from the years 1985 to 1987.

33   Harald Freitag interviewed by Bernd von Kostka on 12 September 2012.

Chapter 4. Licence to spy

1   Hans-Dieter Behrend, *Die alliierten Militärverbindungsmissionen im Kalten Krieg auf deutschem Boden*, Berlin: Helle Panke, 2002, p. 31.

2   Interview on *Tagesthemen*, ARD, on 16 November 2007.

3   Article 2 of the agreement stated: 'Each Commander-in-Chief in his zone of occupation will have attached to him military, naval and air representatives of the other two Commanders-in-Chief for liaison duties.' Cited in Dorothee Mußgnug, *Alliierte Militärmissionen in Deutschland 1946–1990*, Berlin: Duncker & Humblot, 2001, p. 17, n. 40.

4   All three agreements are quoted in full in ibid., pp. 230–235.

5   The residence of the British mission, a villa on Heiliger See at Seestraße 35–37, was acquired after the mission was disbanded by the designer Wolfgang Joop, who still lives there today.

6   Christopher Winkler, 'Die U.S. Military Liaison Mission im Vorfeld der 2. Berliner Krise: Der Hubschrauberzwischenfall von 1958', in Michael Lemke (ed.), *Schaufenster der Systemkonkurrenz: Die Region Berlin-Brandenburg im Kalten Krieg*, Vienna: Böhlau Verlag, 2006, p. 72.

7   Nigel Wylde, 'Mit der Brixmis jenseits des Eisernen Vorhangs', in *Mission erfüllt: Die militärischen Verbindungsmissionen der Westmächte 1946–1990*, Berlin: AlliiertenMuseum, 2004, pp. 36–40.

8   'Draft Charter to the Chief BRIXMIS from the UK High Commissioner', Appendix B to JIC (GERMANY) (52) 17.

9   'Experience has proven that intelligence developed by our military mission is the most reliable and dependable source available to this command in order to insure warning of indications of Soviet intention to initiate a surprise land invasion of Western Europe.' From a telegram sent by the commander in chief of the US armed forces in Europe to the US secretary of state on 20 June 1958, cited in Winkler, 'Die U.S. Military Liaison Mission im Vorfeld der 2. Berliner Krise', p. 78.

10   Wylde, 'Mit der Brixmis jenseits des Eisernen Vorhangs', p. 43.

11   Peter Williams, *Brixmis in the 1980s: The Cold War's 'Great Game,'* Parallel History Project on Cooperative Security, 2007, p. 32 (at www.php.ethz.ch).

12   At the beginning of the 1980s, PRAs covered almost 40 percent of East German territory. See ibid., p. 34.

13   See information labels about the mission vehicles in the special exhibition *Mission erfüllt* at the Allied Museum in Berlin in 2004.

14 Söhnke Streckel, *Lizensierte Spionage: Die alliierten Militärverbindungsmissionen und das MfS*, Magdeburg: Landesbeauftragten für die Unterlagen des Staatssicherheitsdienstes der ehemaligen DDR, 2008, p. 27, n. 1.

15 Williams, *Brixmis in the 1980s*, pp. 22–24.

16 'Notes of the use of Soviet troops in aid of the civil power 16 June–10 July 1953' (BRX/405/29).

17 The BRIXMIS Monthly Report for June 1953, p. 2, states: '… this particular move must have created almost a world's record in the huge number of tanks left crashed, bogged or just plain broken-down along the various axes of movement.'

18 'Notes of the use of Soviet troops in aid of the civil power', point 8.

19 Patrick Manificat, *Propousk! Missions derrière le rideau de fer 1947–1989*, Limoges: Lavauzelle Editions, 2008, pp. 340–349.

20 Ibid.

21 Ibid.

22 Tony Geraghty, *Brixmis: The Untold Exploits of Britain's Most Daring Cold War Spy Mission*, London: HarperCollins, 1996, pp. 123–124.

23 'Report on RAF BRIXMIS activities in connection with the crash of a Red Air Force Firebar Aircraft in West Berlin on 6 April 1966' (BRX/5600/1/AIR).

24 Ibid.

25 A. F. Agarew, K.-P. Kobbe, R. Großer, I. W. Sisowa, *Im Himmel über Berlin: Eine tragische Seite der Epoche des Kalten Krieges*, Ryazan: Das russische Wort, 2012, p. 99.

26 British Embassy in Bonn on LIVE OAK, 7 April 1966. Public Record Office, Kew, London.

27 'Confrontation at the Stößensee', *Cold War Conversations Podcast*, April 2021 (at https://coldwarconversations.com/episode171/).

28 Agarew et al., *Im Himmel über Berlin*, p. 106.

29 Letter from the British military government in Berlin to the British high commissioner in Bonn, Sir Frank Roberts, on 22 April 1966. Public Record Office, Kew, London.

30 See video 'Sowjetischer Flugzeugabsturz über dem Stößensee', at *Die Berliner Mauer: Geschichte in Bildern* (https://www.berlin-mauer.de/videos/sowjetischer-flugzeugabsturz-im-stoessensee-568/).

31 Gesine Dornblüth & Thomas Franke, 'Flugzeugabsturz über West-Berlin: Die vergessenen Helden vom Stößensee', *Deutschlandfunk Kultur*, 20 March 2019 (podcast at https://srv.deutschlandradio.de/themes/dradio/script/aod/index.html?audioMode=3&audioID=885649&state=).

32 Manificat, *Propousk!*, pp. 349–352.

33 Ibid.

34 'Beispiel eines Vorkommnisses mit Angehörigen der drei westlichen Militärverbindungsmissionen vom April 1969, aus dem zukünftig Gegenmaßnahmen abgeleitet werden müssen' (BStU MfS HA VIII, No. 1525).

35 Interview with Legendre in the film by Yves Jan, *Au Coeur de la Guerre Froide: Les Missions de Potsdam*, 2007.

36 Matthias Heisig, 'Gefährliche Begegnung: Autos, "Blockierung" und der Tod von Philippe Mariotti', in *Mission erfüllt: Die militärischen Verbindungsmissionen der Westmächte 1946–1990*, Berlin: AlliiertenMuseum, 2004, pp. 99–114.

37 See information labels about the mission vehicles in the special exhibition *Mission erfüllt* at the Allied Museum in Berlin in 2004.

38 'Operationsplan zur Durchführung eines operativen Einsatzes am Objekt der 11. MSD der NVA (Lettin) zur offensiven Abwehr der feindlichen Tätigkeit der westlichen MVM … in der Zeit vom 19.3.1984 bis 23.3 1984' (BStU MfS HA VIII, No. 7123).

39 'Vernehmungsprotokoll vom 22. März 1984', p. 3 (BStU MfS BV Halle, Abt. IX, No. 635).

40 A reconstruction of the events that led to the accident can also be found in Streckel, *Lizensierte Spionage*, pp. 138–139.

41 'Auszeichnung vom 27.3.1984 für die Beobachtergruppe von Paul Schmidt anlässlich der Blockierung der franz. MVM' (BStU MfS BV Halle KD Halle, XV 7481/75 vol. 2).

42 William E. Stacy, *The Nicholson Incident: A Case Study of US-Soviet Negotiations*, Heidelberg, 1988 (declassified October 2004), p. 6.

43 Helmut Trotnow, 'Schüsse in Techentin', in *Mission erfüllt: Die militärischen Verbindungsmissionen der Westmächte 1946–1990*, Berlin: AlliiertenMuseum, 2004, p.125.

44 For a description of the sequence of events see Stacy, *The Nicholson Incident*, pp. 7–11. See also Streckel, *Lizensierte Spionage*, pp. 146–147.

45 Trotnow, 'Schüsse in Techentin', pp. 130–131.

46 Stacy, *The Nicholson Incident*, pp. 34–35.

47 A detailed portrayal of Jessie Schatz is provided in Streckel, *Lizensierte Spionage*, pp. 156–164.

48 Ibid.

Chapter 5. Early confrontation

1 Wolfgang Leonhard, *Die Revolution entlässt ihre Kinder*, 22nd ed., Cologne: Kiepenheuer & Witsch, 2005, p. 440; cf. *Frankfurter Allgemeine Zeitung*, 14 May 2005.

2 *Die Zeit*, 7 May 1965.

3 'Wolfgang Leonhard', *Mein Kriegsende*, WDR Fernsehen, 2 May 2005.

4 *Die Zeit*, 7 May 1965.

5 Mario Frank, *Walter Ulbricht: Eine deutsche Biografie*, Berlin: Siedler, 2001, p. 190.

6 *Die Zeit*, 7 May 1965.

7 Peter Erler, *Polizeimajor Karl Heinrich: NS-Gegner und Antikommunist—Eine biographische Skizze*, Berlin: Jaron, 2007, p. 16.

8 Siegfried Heimann, *Karl Heinrich und die Berliner SPD, die sowjetische Militäradministration und die SED: Ein Fallbeispiel*, Bonn: Historisches Forschungszentrum, 2007, p. 28.

9 Cf. *Berliner Morgenpost*, 6 March 1992.

10 *Telegraf*, 31 March 1948.

11 Hans J. Reichhardt et al. (eds), *Berlin: Quellen und Dokumente 1945–1951—1. Halbband*, Berlin: Der Senat von Berlin, 1964, p. 262.

12 Cf. Arthur L. Smith, *Kidnap City: Cold War Berlin*, London: Greenwood Press, 2002, pp. 20–21. See also *Der Spiegel*, 20 June 1951.

13 Cf. BA Koblenz B141/11816, p. 127.

14 *Der Spiegel*, 20 June 1951.

15 Cf. BA Koblenz B141/11816, pp. 4–5.

16 *Illustrierte Berliner Zeitschrift*, 1951, no. 19.

17 *Stenografische Berichte des Deutschen Bundestages*, 1. Wahlperiode, p. 8424.

18 Smith, *Kidnap City*, p. 89.

19 Cf. *Telegraf*, 7 October 1948, and *Der Tagesspiegel*, 8 October 1946.

20 Cf. *Telegraf*, 3 January 1947, and *Der Tagesspiegel*, 3 January 1947.

21 BStU MfS ZA 1405, pp. 89–91.

22 *Telegraf*, 17 January 1947, and *Die Neue Zeitung*, 17 October 1946.

Chapter 6. Mielke's men

1 Cited in Wilfriede Otto, *Erich Mielke: Biographie*, Berlin: Dietz, 2000, pp. 111–112.

2 Cf. Torsten Diedrich & Hans Ehlert & Rüdiger Wenzke (eds), *Im Dienste der Partei: Handbuch der bewaffneten Organe der DDR*, Berlin: Ch. Links, 1998, p. 374.

3   Cited in Otto, *Erich Mielke*, p. 119. A list of the historical accounts produced by the Stasi can be found in Otto's book.

4   *Neues Deutschland*, 9 February 1950.

5   *Gesetzblatt der Deutschen Demokratischen Republik* 1950, p. 95.

6   *Gesetzblatt der Deutschen Demokratischen Republik* 1949, p. 11.

7   Otto, *Erich Mielke*, p. 130.

8   BStU MfS ZA AU 104/90, p. 24.

9   Dieter Dowe (ed.), *Kurt Müller (1903–1990) zum Gedenken*, Bonn: Friedrich-Ebert-Stiftung, 1991, pp. 57 and 82.

10   *Die Zeit*, 11 December 1952.

11   *Hamburger Abendblatt*, 13 May 1950.

12   *Hamburger Abendblatt*, 15 May 1950.

13   *Stenografische Berichte des Deutschen Bundestages*, 1. Wahlperiode, p. 2364.

14   Jens Gieseke, *Die hauptamtlichen Mitarbeiter der Staatssicherheit: Personalstruktur und Lebenswelt 1950–1989/90*, Berlin: Ch. Links, 2000, p. 202.

15   Cf. *Berliner Morgenpost*, 25 May 2003.

16   Cited in Bodo Wegmann, *Entstehung und Vorläufer des Staatssicherheitsdienstes der DDR: Strukturanalytische Aspekte*, Berlin: Helle Panke, 1997, p. 36.

17   Cited in Otto, *Erich Mielke*, p. 199.

18   *Der Spiegel*, 18 November 1953.

19   Cited in Wegmann, *Entstehung und Vorläufer*, p. 36.

20   Cited in Jens Gieseke, *Der Mielke-Konzern: Die Geschichte der Stasi 1945–1990*, Munich: Deutsche Verlags-Anstalt, 2006, p. 65.

21   Cf. Karl-Wilhelm Fricke & Roger Engelmann, *Konzentrierte Schläge: Staatssicherheitsaktionen und politische Prozesse in der DDR 1953–1956*, Berlin: Ch. Links, 1998, pp. 42–60.

22   *Neues Deutschland*, 1 November 1953.

23   Cf. SAPMO BA Berlin, DY 30 IV 2/1/132, pp. 147–148.

24   *Die Welt*, 25 February 2006.

25   SAPMO BA Berlin, DY 30 IV 2/12/102, pp. 315–316.

26   Cf. *Hamburger Abendblatt*, 1 and 9 November 1957; *Berliner Morgenpost*, 1 November 1957; *Neue Zürcher Zeitung*, 4 November 1957; *Bild*, 2 November 1957.

27   *Die Zeit*, 7 November 1957.

28   Cf. Klaus Bästlein, *Der Fall Mielke: Die Ermittlungen gegen den Minister für Staatssicherheit der DDR*, Baden-Baden: Nomos Verlagsgesellschaft, 2002, pp. 20–22; Otto, *Erich Mielke*, pp. 490–498.

29   Gieseke, *Der Mielke-Konzern*, p. 134.

30   Cited in Uwe Thaysen (ed.), *Der zentrale Runde Tisch der DDR—Wortprotokoll und Dokumente, Bd. 2: Umbruch*, Opladen: Westdeutscher Verlag, 2000, p. 502.

31   All the details of the Stasi payroll are in accordance with the copy of the file to be found in the archive of the authors.

32   Cited in *Die Welt*, 28 February 2007.

33   Cf. Klaus Behling & Jan Eik, *Vertuschte Verbrechen: Kriminalität in der Stasi*, Leipzig: Militzke, 2007; ibid., *Transit in den Tod: Kriminalität in der Stasi*, Leipzig: Militzke, 2008; ibid, *Lautloser Terror: Kriminalität in der Stasi*, Leipzig: Militzke, 2009.

34   Hans-Dieter Schütt, *Markus Wolf: Letzte Gespräche*, Berlin: Das Neue Berlin, 2007, p. 29.

35   Cf. Dieter Krüger & Armin Wagner (eds), *Konspiration als Beruf: Deutsche Geheimdienstchefs im Kalten Krieg*, Berlin: Ch. Links, 2003, p. 286; Schütt, *Markus Wolf*, p. 139.

36   Cf. Jochen Staadt & Tobias Voigt & Stefan Wolle, *Operation Fernsehen: Die Stasi und die Medien in Ost und West*, Göttingen: Vandenhoeck & Ruprecht, 2008, pp. 90–161; *Die Welt*, 25 November

2006; *Welt am Sonntag*, 4 May 1997, *Der Spiegel*, 29 August 1994; Hubertus Knabe, *Der diskrete Charme der DDR: Stasi und Westmedien*, Berlin: Propyläen, 2001, pp. 166–232.

37   *Der Spiegel*, 27 November 2000.

38   Cited in Deutscher Bundestag, Drucksache 13/10900, 28 May 1998.

39   Cf. Otto, *Erich Mielke*, p. 94.

40   Christian Halbrock, *Stasi-Stadt: Die MfS-Zentrale in Berlin-Lichtenberg*, Berlin: Ch. Links, 2009, p. 27.

41   Ibid., p. 50.

42   See the website of the Stasi Museum (https://www.stasimuseum.de/en/enindex.htm).

43   Cited in *Prenzlauer, Ecke Fröbelstraße: Hospital der Reichshauptstadt, Haftort der Geheimdienste, Bezirksamt Prenzlauer Berg—1889–1989*, ed. Berlin-Brandenburgische Geschichtswerkstatt, Berlin: Lukas Verlag, 2006, pp. 110–111.

44   Cited in Rainer Eppelmann, *Fremd im eigenen Haus: Mein Leben im anderen Deutschland*, Cologne: Kiepenheuer und Witsch, 1993, p. 188.

45   Cited in Hubertus Knabe, *Die Täter sind unter uns: Über das Schönreden der SED-Diktatur*, Berlin: Propyläen, 2007, p. 114.

46   Cf. Peter Norden, *Salon Kitty: Ein Report*, Munich: Südwest Verlag, 1970; *Berliner Zeitung*, 18 January 2006; *Bild*, 23 July 2004; *Die Welt*, 26 March 2004; *Der Spiegel*, 29 March 1976; *Berliner Kurier*, 25 October 2008.

47   Markus Wolf, *Spionagechef im geheimen Krieg: Erinnerungen*, Munich: List, 1997, pp. 94–96.

48   Cited in Uta Falck, *VEB Bordell: Geschichte der Prostitution in der DDR*, Berlin: Ch. Links, 1998, p. 110.

49   Cf. *Der Spiegel*, 4 September 1989.

50   *Der Spiegel*, 25 February 1991.

Chapter 7. In the 'jungle of espionage'

1   Cited in *Die Welt*, 27 November 2008. It is not entirely clear what Khrushchev meant by the 'the change of the situation in Berlin'.

2   *Spionage-Dschungel Westberlin: Eine Dokumentation über die westdeutschen und Westberliner Sabotage- und Spionageorganisationen und über die Geheimagenturen der imperialistischen Westmächte*, East Berlin: Ausschuss für Deutsche Einheit, 1959, p. 3.

3   DDR-Hörfunk, 18 June 1953 (copy in the archive of Sven Felix Kellerhoff).

4   DDR-Fernsehen, 13 August 1961 (copy in the archive of Sven Felix Kellerhoff).

5   *Der Schwarze Kanal*, 25 September 1989.

6   Cf. Kai-Uwe Merz, *Kalter Krieg als antikommunistischer Widerstand: Die Kampfgruppe gegen Unmenschlichkeit 1948–1959*, Munich: Oldenbourg, 1987; Gerhard Finn, *Nichtstun ist Mord: Die Kampfgruppe gegen Unmenschlichkeit—KgU*, Bad Münstereifel: Westkreuz-Verlag, 2000; Hanfried Hiecke, *Deckname Walter: Enthüllungen des ehemaligen Mitarbeiters der sogenannten 'Kampfgruppe gegen Unmenschlichkeit' Hanfried Hiecke*, East Berlin: Kongress-Verlag, 1953, pp. 8–17; Enrico Heitzer, *Affäre Walter: Die vergessene Verhaftungswelle*, Berlin: Metropol, 2008.

7   Open letter from Jochen Staadt to Enrico Heitzer, 9 September 2008 (copy in the archive of Sven Felix Kellerhoff).

8   *Hamburger Abendblatt*, 22 August 1949.

9   Cf. Arsenij Roginskij & Frank Drauschke & Anna Kaminsky, *Erschossen in Moskau: Die deutschen Opfer des Stalinismus auf dem Moskauer Friedhof Donskoje 1950–1953*, Berlin: Metropol, 2005, pp. 188, 256.

10   Cf. Falco Werkentin, *Politische Strafjustiz in der Ära Ulbricht*, Berlin: Ch. Links, 1995, p. 366.

11 Reinhard Grimmer et al. (eds), *Die Sicherheit: Zur Abwehrarbeit des MfS, Bd. 1*, Berlin: Edition Ost, 2003, pp. 502–503.

12 Cf. Armin Wagner & Matthias Uhl, *BND contra Sowjetarmee: Westdeutsche Militärspionage in der DDR*, Berlin: Ch. Links, 2007, pp. 38, 69, 93.

13 Cf. Reinhard Gehlen, *Der Dienst: Erinnerungen 1942–1971*, Mainz: v. Hase & Koehler, 1971, p. 201.

14 Cited in Fricke & Engelmann, *Konzentrierte Schläge*, p. 192.

15 *Spionage-Dschungel Westberlin*, ed. Ausschuss für Deutsche Einheit, p. 16.

16 Cf. Lars-Broder Keil & Sven Felix Kellerhoff, *Gerüchte machen Geschichte: Folgenreiche Falschmeldungen im 20. Jahrhundert*, Berlin: Ch. Links, 2006, pp. 135–158.

17 Mary Ellen Reese, *Organisation Gehlen: Der kalte Krieg und der Aufbau des deutschen Geheimdienstes*, Berlin: Rowohlt, 1992, p. 192.

18 Cf. *Der Spiegel*, 24 May 1971.

19 Cited in Fricke & Engelmann, *Konzentrierte Schläge*, p. 142.

20 Franz Josef Strauß, *Die Erinnerungen*, Munich: Pantheon, 2015, p. 389.

21 Wagner & Uhl, *BND contra Sowjetarmee*, pp. 119–120.

22 *Spionage-Dschungel Westberlin*, ed. Ausschuss für Deutsche Einheit, pp. 23–24.

23 Cited in Thomas Flemming, *Kein Tag der deutschen Einheit: 17. Juni 1953*, Berlin: bre.bra verlag, 2003, p. 51.

24 *Märkische Allgemeine Zeitung*, 12 June 2003. There were in fact four points rather than five as in Bahr's recollection.

25 Egon Bahr, 'Tag der gesamtdeutschen Geschichte', *Aus Politik und Zeitgeschichte*, no. 23, 2003, pp. 3–4, p. 3.

26 *Spionage-Dschungel Westberlin*, ed. Ausschuss für Deutsche Einheit, p. 5.

27 *... im Dienste der Unterwelt: Dokumentarbericht über den 'Untersuchungsauschuss freiheitlicher Juristen,'* East Berlin: Kongress-Verlag, 1959, blurb.

28 Walther Rosenthal (ed.), *Untersuchungsausschuss Freiheitlicher Juristen: Zielsetzung und Arbeitsweise*, Berlin: Untersuchungsausschuss Freiheitlicher Juristen, 1959, pp. 3–4.

29 *... im Dienste der Unterwelt*, pp. 63–64.

30 Siegfried Mampel, *Der Untergrundkampf des Ministeriums für Staatssicherheit gegen den Untersuchungsausschuß Freiheitlicher Juristen in West-Berlin*, 4th edition, Berlin: Landesbeauftragten für die Unterlagen des Staatssicherheitsdienstes der ehemaligen DDR, 1999, p. 10.

31 Friedrich Heller & Hans-Joachim Maurer, *Unrecht als System, Teil 3: 1954–1958*, Bonn: Bundesministerium für gesamtdeutsche Fragen, 1958, p. 221.

32 Mampel, *Der Untergrundkampf*, p. 13.

33 Bettina Effner & Helge Heidemeyer (eds), *Flucht im geteilten Deutschland: Erinnerungsstätte Notaufnahmelager Marienfelde*, Berlin: be.bra verlag, 2005, p. 130.

34 Cited in Mampel, *Der Untergrundkampf*, pp. 62–65.

35 Cited in ibid., p. 60.

36 Eberhard Heinrich & Klaus Ullrich, *Befehdet seit dem ersten Tag: Über drei Jahrzehnte Attentate gegen die DDR*, East Berlin: Dietz, 1981, e.g., pp. 131–141.

37 Cf. Dietmar Arnold & Sven Felix Kellerhoff, *Die Fluchttunnel von Berlin*, Berlin: Propyläen, 2008, pp. 94–104.

38 Cf. Marion Detjen, *Ein Loch in der Mauer: Die Geschichte der Fluchthilfe im geteilten Deutschland 1961–1989*, Munich: Siedler, 2005, passim.

39 Cf. Constantin Hoffmann, *Ich musste raus: 13 Wege aus der DDR*, Halle (Saale): Mitteldeutscher Verlag, 2009, pp. 85–196.

40 Claus Wolf, *Bosse, Gangster, Kopfgeldjäger: Flüchtlingskampagnen und Menschenhandel—Motive und Methoden*, East Berlin: Verlag Neues Leben, 1982, p. 22.

41 Cited in Karl-Wilhelm Fricke & Silke Klewin, *Bautzen II: Sonderhaftanstalt unter MfS-Kontrolle 1956 bis 1989—Bericht und Dokumentation*, Leipzig: Kiepenheuer, 2001, p. 233.

42 Wolf, *Bosse, Gangster, Kopfgeldjäger*, p. 127.

43 *Der Spiegel*, 27 February 1978 and 27 March 1978.

44 Cf. Detjen, *Ein Loch in der Mauer*, pp. 307–308.

45 *Berliner Zeitung*, 16 October 2012.

46 *Die Welt*, 7 June 2007.

47 Sven Felix Kellerhoff, 'Mit drei Mädchen im nassen 145-Meter-Tunnel', *Die Welt*, 3 January 2014, at https://www.welt.de/geschichte/article123492048/Mit-drei-Maedchen-im-nassen-145-Meter-Tunnel.html.

48 Wolfgang Welsch, *Der verklärte Diktatur: Der verdrängte Widerstand gegen den SED-Staat*, Aachen: Helios, 2009, pp. 32–136.

Chapter 8. The execution of espionage operations in Cold War Berlin

1 Cf. Siegfried Mampel, *Entführungsfall Dr. Walter Linse: Menschenraub und Justizmord als Mittel des Staatsterrors*, 3rd edition, Berlin: Landesbeauftragten für die Unterlagen des Staatssicherheitsdienstes der ehemaligen DDR, 2006, pp. 10–18; Mampel, *Der Untergrundkampf*, pp. 43–47; Benno Kirsch, *Walter Linse 1903–1953–1996*, Dresden: Stiftung Sächsische Gedenkstätten zur Erinnerung an die Opfer Politischer Gewaltherrschaft, 2007, pp. 61–85; Klaus Bästlein, *Vom NS-Täter zum Opfer des Stalinismus: Dr. Walter Linse—ein deutscher Jurist im 20. Jahrhundert*, Berlin: Landesbeauftragten für die Unterlagen des Staatssicherheitsdienstes der ehemaligen DDR, 2008, pp. 89–96.

2 Cf. *Berliner Morgenpost*, 8 October 2008.

3 BStU MfS GH 105/57, vol. 5, p. 41.

4 Bailey et al., *Die unsichtbare Front*, p. 162.

5 BStU MfS GH 105/57, vol. 5, pp. 192–193.

6 *Der Spiegel*, 16 July 1952.

7 *Neues Deutschland*, 11 July 1952 and 13 July 1952.

8 Mampel, *Entführungsfall Dr. Walter Linse*, p. 22.

9 *Telegraf*, 14 August 1952.

10 BStU MfS GH 105/57, vol. 5, p. 197.

11 *Telegraf*, 30 July 1952.

12 *Der Spiegel*, 22 October 1952.

13 Roginskij et al., *Erschossen in Moskau*, p. 250.

14 *Der Spiegel*, 28 July 1954.

15 Cf. Deutscher Bundestag, Drucksache 2/3728 (Bericht des Untersuchungsausschusses); Bailey et al., *Die unsichtbare Front*, pp. 233–255; Bernd Stöver, 'Der Fall Otto John', *Vierteljahrshefte für Zeitgeschichte*, vol. 47 (1999), no. 1, pp. 103–136.

16 *Der Spiegel*, 28 July 1954.

17 Ibid.

18 *Die Welt*, 26 July 1954.

19 *Der Spiegel*, 28 July 1954.

20 Cited in Stöver, 'Der Fall Otto John', pp. 103, 107–108.

21 Theodor Heuss & Konrad Adenauer, *Unserem Vaterland zugute: Der Briefwechsel 1948–1963*, Munich: Siedler, 1989, pp. 160–161.

22 Otto John, *Ich wählte Deutschland*, East Berlin: Ausschuss für Deutsche Einheit, 1954, pp. 7–8.

23 *Neues Deutschland*, 12 August 1954.

24 *Bulletin des Presse- und Informationsamtes der Bundesregierung*, 13 August 1954.

25 Ibid., 17 September 1954.

26 Stöver, 'Der Fall Otto John', p. 104.

27 Konrad Adenauer & Theodor Heuss, *Unter vier Augen: Gespräche aus den Gründerjahren 1949–1959*, Berlin: Siedler, 1999, p. 143.

28 *Neues Deutschland*, 14 December 1955.

29 Heuss & Adenauer, *Unserem Vaterland zugute*, p. 259.

30 Bailey et al., *Die unsichtbare Front*, pp. 242–243.

31 Cf. Karl-Wilhelm Fricke, *Menschenraub in Berlin: Karl-Wilhelm Fricke über seine Erlebnisse*, Bonn: Rheinischer Merkur, 1960, pp. 5–32; ibid., *Akten-Einsicht: Rekonstruktion einer politischen Verfolgung*, 3rd edition, Berlin: Ch. Links, 1996, pp. 23–181; *Berliner Morgenpost*, 25 March 2007.

32 Fricke, *Akten-Einsicht*, p. 67.

33 Facsimile in Fricke, *Menschenraub in Berlin*, p. 10.

34 Fricke, *Akten-Einsicht*, p. 165.

35 Fricke, *Menschenraub in Berlin*, p. 32.

36 Thomas R. Johnson, *American Cryptology during the Cold War, 1945–1989— Book II: Centralization Wins, 1960–1972*, National Security Agency Centre for Cryptologic History, 1995, p. 320, at https://nsarchive2.gwu.edu//NSAEBB/NSAEBB441/docs/doc%201%202008-021%20Burr%20 Release%20Document%201%20-%20Part%20A1.pdf.

37 Cf. *Welt am Sonntag*, 9 August 2011.

38 Bodo Hechelhammer (ed.), *Berlinkrise 1958 und Schließung der Sektorengrenzen in Berlin am 13. August 1961 in den Akten des Bundesnachrichtendienstes*, Berlin: Bundesnachrichtendienst Mitteilung der Forschungs- und Arbeitsgruppe Geschichte des BND, 2011, document 2.

39 Ibid., document 3.

40 *Berliner Morgenpost*, 11 August 1961.

41 BStU MfS GH 2/70, vol. 9, pp. 393–394.

42 BStU MfS GH 2/70, vol. 17, p. 126.

43 *Der Spiegel*, 1 June 2009.

44 BStU MfS GH 2/70, vol. 2, p. 34.

45 Cf. *Berliner Morgenpost*, 23 May 2009.

46 BStU MfS GH 2/70, vol. 2, p. 150.

47 Cf. *Berliner Morgenpost*, 5 June 2009.

48 Helmut Müller-Enbergs & Cornelia Jabs, 'Der 2. Juni 1967 und die Staatssicherheit', *Deutschland Archiv*, vol. 42 (2009), no. 3, pp. 395–400, p. 399. Translator's note: 'Stumm's Police' was a term often used by East German authorities for the West Berlin Police and was a reference to Johannes Stumm, who from 1948 to 1962 was the chief of police in West Berlin.

49 BStU MfS GH 2/70, vol. 1, p. 13.

50 BStU MfS GH 2/70, vol. 1, p. 117.

51 Cf. *Berliner Morgenpost*, 30 May 2007; *Die Welt*, 2 June 2009.

52 BStU MfS GH 2/70, vol. 17, pp. 97–99.

53 BStU MfS BV Berlin, KD Lichtenberg, 13088, pp. 1–5.

54 Sven Felix Kellerhoff, 'West-Berliner Polizei im Visier der Stasi', *Die Welt*, 4 June 2014, at https://www.welt.de/geschichte/article128727404/West-Berliner-Polizei-im-Visier-der-Stasi.html.

55 *Die Zeit*, 13 August 1993.

56 Cited in Mampel, *Der Untergrundkampf*, pp. 90–91.

57 *Die Zeit*, 13 August 1993.

58 *Bild*, 9 August 1993.

59 Mampel, *Der Untergrundkampf*, p. 96.

60 Cited in ibid., pp. 100–101.

61 *SuperIllu*, 1993, no. 8.

62 *Die Zeit*, 13 August 1993.

63 BStU MfS AIM, no. 9229/87, part II, vol. 1, pp. 179–184.

64 BStU MfS AIM, no. A 593/79, part II, vol. 1, pp. 3–4.

65 BStU MfS AIM, no. A 593/79, part II, vol. 7, pp. 160–167.

66 BStU MfS XV/2704/72; BStU MfS Teilablage A, no. 156/85.

67 BStU MfS AIM, no. A 593/79, part II, vol. 5, pp. 8–18.

68 BStU MfS AIM, no. 4902/88, part II, vol. 1, pp. 34–48.

69 BStU MfS AIM, no. 4902/88, part I, vol. 1, pp. 66–74.

70 BStU MfS AIM, no. 9229/87, part I, vol. 1, pp. 15–16.

71 BStU MfS AIM, no. 9229/87, part II, vol. 1, pp. 14–15.

72 BStU MfS AIM, no. A 593/79, part III, vols 1–3.

73 Inge Viett, *Nie war ich furchtloser: Autobiographie*, Hamburg: Nautilus, 1997, p. 179.

74 Cf. Michael Müller & Andreas Kanonenberg, *Die RAF-Stasi-Connection*, Berlin: Rowohlt, 1992, passim; Butz Peters, *Tödlicher Irrtum: Die Geschichte der RAF*, Frankfurt am Main: Fischer, 2007, pp. 532–591; Martin Jander, 'Differenzen im antiimperialistischen Kampf', in Wolfgang Kraushaar (ed.), *Die RAF und der linke Terrorismus, Band 1*, Hamburg: Hamburger Edition, 2006, pp. 696–713; quotations from Viett, *Nie war ich furchtloser*, pp. 179–180.

75 Viett, *Nie war ich furchtloser*, p. 196.

76 Cf. Stefan Aust, *Der Baader-Meinhof-Komplex*, Hamburg: Hoffmann und Campe, 2008, pp. 183–186.

77 Cf. Jander, 'Differenzen im antiimperialistischen Kampf', p. 699.

78 Klaus Schroeder & Jochen Staadt (eds), *Feindwärts der Mauer: Das Ministerium für Staatssicherheit und die West-Berliner Polizei*, Frankfurt am Main: Peter Lang Edition, 2014, pp. 432–439.

79 Robert Allertz, *Die RAF und das MfS: Fakten und Fiktionen*, Berlin: Edition Ost, 2008, p. 187.

80 For what follows, cf. Werner Stiller, *Im Zentrum der Spionage*, 5th edition, Mainz: v. Hase und Köhler, 1986, pp. 362–366; Helmut Roewer, *Im Visier der Geheimdienste: Deutschland und Russland im Kalten Krieg*, Bergisch Gladbach: Lübbe, 2008, pp. 442–448; *Der Spiegel*, 23 March 1992, 30 March 1992, and 6 April 1992.

81 Wolf, *Spionagechef im geheimen Krieg*, pp. 299–300.

82 Stiller, *Im Zentrum der Spionage*, p. 33.

83 Gieseke, *Die hauptamtlichen Mitarbeiter der Staatssicherheit*, p. 384.

84 *Der Spiegel*, 28 September 1992.

85 Gieseke, *Die hauptamtlichen Mitarbeiter der Staatssicherheit*, p. 385.

Finale

1 *The Washington Post*, 22 November 1998.

2 Cf. *Die Welt*, 14 April 2007.

3 *Der Spiegel*, 18 January 1999.

4 Klaus Eichner & Andreas Dobbert, *Headquarters Germany: Die US-Geheimdienste in Deutschland*, 3rd edition, Berlin: Edition Ost, 2008, p. 285.

5 *Der Spiegel*, 18 April 2005.

6 Helmut Müller-Enbergs, *Rosenholz: Eine Quellenkritik*, Berlin: Landesbeauftragten für die Unterlagen des Staatssicherheitsdienstes der ehemaligen DDR, 2007, p. 28.

Index